VATICAN
SECRET ARCHIVES

GRZEGORZ GÓRNY
JANUSZ ROSIKOŃ

ignatius press

VATICAN
SECRET ARCHIVES

Unknown Pages of Church History

PROLOGUE

There is no escape from history. It has shaped our reality, and in time, we become a part of it ourselves. We live in a civilization that arose on three hills: the Acropolis, the Capitoline, and Golgotha. Its foundation is a synthesis of Greek philosophy, Roman law, and the Christian religion. The latter factor in particular exerted a decisive influence on our civilization.

Jesus of Nazareth initiated a new era in human history, which is reflected in, for example, the calculation of time, adopted throughout the world. He also initiated the only institution on the globe that has maintained an unbroken continuity for two thousand years. Hence Church history is alive, still evoking emotions, generating discussions, and arousing controversies. Today, no one asks about the accountability of medieval officials and judges. No one cares about the guilt and mistakes of Renaissance university professors. It is otherwise with regard to the Church. The Crusades, the Inquisition, and the conquistadores are still invoked in contemporary debates, when important life choices of many are at stake. In that sense, Cardinal Giacomo Biffi was correct when he wrote that the Church, with her unchanging identity, is virtually regarded as a person, ever responsible for the world's transgressions.

In such debates, there are often myths and falsifications. In order to assess the past justly, one must first thoroughly and accurately ascertain the facts. Our visits to the Vatican Secret Archives were meant to serve that very purpose, as were our visits to other Roman archives and meetings with numerous historians, outstanding specialists in their fields. With them, we delved into the histories of the Crusades, the Templars, the Inquisition, the conquistadores, the Galileo trial, the French Revolution, the Spanish Civil War, and Pius XII and the Holocaust—issues that belong not only to the past, but also to the present, due to their ceaseless presence in public debates.

In going through numerous documents and talking to various scholars, who revealed to us the meanderings of the past, a question came to mind, one that Christian theologians have often posed themselves: What is God's preferred political system? Monarchy, that is, the rule of a single sovereign? Aristocracy, the rule of an elite minority? Or perhaps democracy, the rule of the majority?

The only answer we found was encompassed in the question: Who killed Jesus? It turned out that representatives of all three political systems were behind his death: Monarchy (Pontius Pilate, the emperor's governor); aristocracy (the Sanhedrin); and democracy (the crowd, demanding the crucifixion of the Nazarene in a "direct referendum"). No system in itself guarantees a just rule. It is a certain form, which can be filled out with specific content. It all depends on what is in a person's heart. Hence politics in particular needs people with upright consciences. Delving into archives, and studying history, teaches one humility. It shows us that we are not a community of angels and that we shall never build paradise on earth. However, all of us shall be put to the test, and it is most important to end up on the right side.

CONTENTS

VATICAN SECRET ARCHIVES OVER THE CENTURIES

Archive
in **Domus Aurea**

Martyrdom
of **St. Lawrence**,
papal archivist

Reorganization of the papal
archive on the imperial
pattern by **Julius I**

Vandal invasion
– archives
devastated

| 42 | 90--110 | 200--250 | 258 | 313 | 325--337 | 410 | 445 |

St. Peter arrived
in Rome

St. Mark is the pope's
first archivist. Archive
concealed in the Trastevere
quarter of Rome

Archive on the site
of the **Apostolic Chancery**

Archive
in **Lateran Palace**

Part of the archives
destroyed during
a **Visigoth invasion**

Some archival
collections moved
to Anagni and Perugia

Main headquarters
of the archive
in the Vatican

Part of the papal
archive housed
in Castel Sant'Angelo

Gregorian Calendar
worked out in the Tower
of the Winds

| 1245--1281 | 1180--1320 | 1309--1377 | 1390--1410 | 1471--1484 | 1480--1550 | 1527 | 1582 | 1612 |

Several popes kept
some archives in **Lyon**
and **Viterbo**.

Papal archive **in Avignon,
France** (parts ended up
in Carpentras and Assisi)

Library and archival
collections separated;
Vatican Library established

Archives destroyed
during the **Sack
of Rome**

Paul V established
Vatican Secret Archives

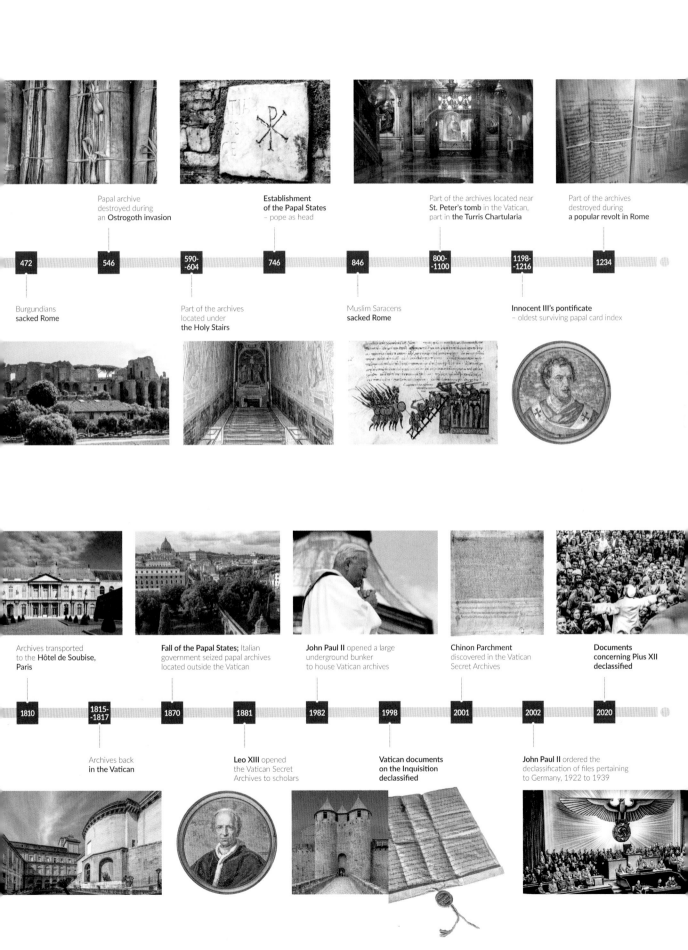

472
Burgundians
sacked Rome

Papal archive
destroyed during
an **Ostrogoth invasion**

546

**590-
-604**
Part of the archives
located under
the Holy Stairs

**Establishment
of the Papal States**
– pope as head

746

846
Muslim Saracens
sacked Rome

Part of the archives located near
St. Peter's tomb in the Vatican,
part in **the Turris Chartularia**

**800-
-1100**

**1198-
-1216**
Innocent III's pontificate
– oldest surviving papal card index

Part of the archives
destroyed during
a popular revolt in Rome

1234

Archives transported
to the **Hôtel de Soubise,
Paris**

1810

**1815-
-1817**
Archives back
in the Vatican

Fall of the Papal States; Italian
government seized papal archives
located outside the Vatican

1870

1881
Leo XIII opened
the Vatican Secret
Archives to scholars

John Paul II opened a large
underground bunker
to house Vatican archives

1982

1998
**Vatican documents
on the Inquisition
declassified**

Chinon Parchment
discovered in the Vatican
Secret Archives

2001

2002
John Paul II ordered the
declassification of files pertaining
to Germany, 1922 to 1939

**Documents
concerning Pius XII
declassified**

2020

CASTEL SANT'ANGELO

THIS ANCIENT BUILDING arose on the bank of the Tiber at the beginning of the 2nd century as the Mausoleum of Hadrian. Three hundred years later, it was converted into a fortress. Gregory the Great (590–604) gave it its present name. Towards the end of the 16th century, the papal archive was housed in the rotund premises, at the top of the castle, under the statue of an angel.

PASSETTO DI BORGO

A SECRET PASSAGE between the Apostolic Palace in the Vatican and Castel Sant'Angelo, which runs above the streets along the Roman wall. It saved the lives of two popes (Alexander VI and Clement VII), who managed to escape from their residence via this passage. The photo shows the beginning of the passage at a side door to the palace.

ST. PETER'S BASILICA AND SQUARE

AT THE CENTER OF THE SQUARE, there is an Egyptian obelisk from the Circus of Nero, where St. Peter was martyred. The square is surrounded by Bernini's colonnades, the construction of which was completed in 1663. The basilica, in its present form, took over one hundred years to build (1505–1626). It arose on the site of a basilica from the time of Constantine, which was located over St. Peter's tomb.

VATICAN SECRET ARCHIVES

PART OF BELVEDERE PALACE, where Paul V established a centralized papal archive (1612). The complex's highest building is the Tower of the Winds, where the Sundial Room is located. It was there that astronomers worked out the Gregorian Calendar in 1582. The view of the Vatican Secret Archives is from the Vatican Gardens.

TRADITION

TRUTH

Classified, Secret, Confidential

CHAPTER 1

Classified, Secret, Confidential

Two thousand years of the papal archives:
from St. Peter to the present time

Rome

ITALY

For anyone with a passion for history, the very mention of the Vatican Secret Archives brings a thrill of excitement. Containing unique collections of documents, countless confidential reports, and an inexhaustible quantity of sources on world history, all compiled by the world's finest diplomatic services, the Archives are a bottomless mine of knowledge. This has given rise to the conviction that the solution to many unsolved historical riddles could be found there. Let us try to draw back the curtain of secrecy that has shrouded this extraordinary institution for centuries and delve into its innermost corners.

MANY SHELVES
line the Vatican Secret Archives, which end-to-end are 53 miles long.

PAVLVS V PONTIFEX MAXIMVS ANNO XIIII

PREFECT OF THE VATICAN SECRET ARCHIVES, Bp. Sergio Pagano.

BRONZE DOOR, one of three main entrances to the Vatican Apostolic Palace.

But first, one has to get behind the Vatican walls, obtain a special permit, and pass through three checkpoints before finding oneself in the Belvedere Courtyard (or Belvedere Palace), where Bishop Sergio Pagano officiates as prefect of these extraordinary archives. He received us in his first-story apartment with Italian courtesy and warmth, though he was precise and economical with his words at the same time. He has been an archivist for over forty years and

15

BISHOP PAGANO, prefect of the Vatican Apostolic Archives, talks with Grzegorz Górny.

PREFECT OF THE VATICAN APOSTOLIC ARCHIVES

SERGIO PAGANO was born in Liguria, Italy, in 1948. He entered the Barnabite order at the age of eighteen and completed his studies in philosophy and theology in Rome, where he was ordained a priest in 1977. A year later, as a graduate of the Vatican School of Paleography, Diplomatics, and Archives Administration, he was employed by the Vatican Secret Archives, where he has worked for over forty years, coming to know it inside and out, advancing to positions of greater and greater responsibility.

In 1997, he was appointed prefect of the Vatican Secret Archives by Pope John Paul II, and a few days later he became director of the Vatican School of Paleography, Diplomatics, and Archives Administration. In 2007, he was consecrated titular bishop of Celene by Pope Benedict XVI. That same year, Pagano also became a member of the Pontifical Commission for the Cultural Heritage of the Church. He is an active member of numerous international historical committees and Church institutions and author of numerous scholarly publications.

DOCUMENTS are divided into 650 archival collections.

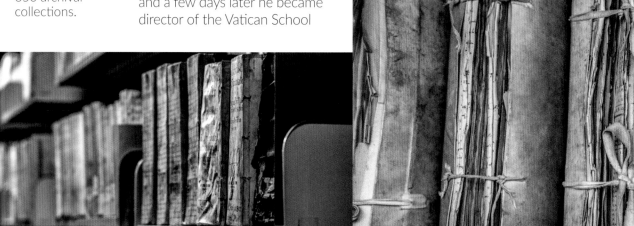

seems to embody the ethos of an archivist, whose mission is to serve as a custodian of memory.

There is no community without history, memory—for memory is the bearer of identity, the mother of society. Hence it is essential that every community have its own archives. These serve to store memory, preserve it, and pass it on to subsequent generations, so that it might continuously renew the bond between them. Even such small community organisms like the family typically have their own archives, to say nothing of states, authorities, and institutions.

At the same time, archives are treasuries of past knowledge and irreplaceable historical sources, thanks to which we might better come to know the details of past events as well as the dilemmas and

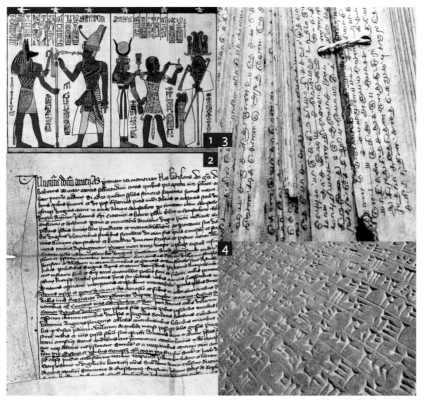

WRITING MEDIUMS:
1. papyrus,
2. parchment,
3. palm leaves,
4. clay.

CLAY TABLET
with cuneiform writing.

challenges that faced our ancestors. At times, they hold the keys to great mysteries.

The archives of ancient Eastern lands contained documents written on clay tablets. In India, scribes wrote on palm leaves, while in Egypt, Greece, and Rome, they initially wrote on papyrus, then on parchment. It is to the Greeks that we owe the word "archive", which derives from *archeion*, meaning a building wherein the seat of government was located, as such buildings housed collections of

THE TEMPLE in Jerusalem was not only a place of worship, but also the main community archive.

documents useful in administrative work. The authorities changed, but the documents remained.

The ancient Jewish people also had archives. For example, the genealogical scrolls of all the generations of Israel were kept in the temple in Jerusalem. These were to be useful in identifying the awaited Messiah, who, as foretold by the prophets, was to come from the Tribe of Judah, the Tree of Jesse, and the House of David. The destruction of Jerusalem, and the razing of the temple by the Roman legions in AD 70, meant that henceforth it would be impossible to carry out a "genealogical test" as to the authenticity of the Messiah.

LEGIONARIES carrying spoils after taking Jerusalem— from the Arch of Titus in Rome.

To the first generation of Judeo-Christians, this was conclusive proof that the Messiah must have appeared before that date; otherwise, the Old Testament prophecy had shown itself false.

Among the writings that foretold the coming of the Messianic Era, there were also scrolls discovered in the Qumran caves near the Dead

ONE OF THE SCROLLS that were discovered in caves near the Dead Sea from 1947 to 1956.

Sea, in the archives of the Jewish sect of the Essenes. Thanks to the scrolls, it became possible to solve many of the mysteries concerning Jewish religious life during the times that preceded the birth of Jesus.

The Catholic Church has kept archives from the very beginning. Like all growing communities, it needed ever more documentation,

19

ST. PETER,
whom Jesus
chose to lead
the apostles.

without which it would be impossible to administer any large institution. One could not rely solely on human memory, which is fallible and, after all, comes to an end.

St. Peter, the first pope, must have had his own archive. On arriving in Rome, he most probably stayed in Trastevere (beyond the Tiber), a Jewish district. We know that St. Mark the Evangelist was his secretary and translator, and perhaps the first papal archivist.

One might risk stating that the pope's archive was the oldest and, for a certain time, the only Church documentation. It contained lists of members, birth certificates, and a register of those who received aid from deacons. The first

ROME'S FIRST BISHOP,
St. Peter, suffered
a martyr's death
by being crucified
upside down.

ST. MARK, the first
papal archivist.

Christian communities accumulated their own documentation, for example, testimonies concerning martyrs.

The first great persecution of Christians broke out during Nero's reign in 44. Nero, wanting to allay suspicion that he had Rome set on fire, blamed the Christians. This launched a wave of bloody repressions, to which St. Peter fell victim, crucified upside down on Vatican Hill. Undoubtedly, the papal archives were then destroyed for the first time.

Russian theologian Mikhail Bulgakov once wrote that "manuscripts were not burned", which is untrue. Throughout history persecutions affected not only people, but documents, destroyed not only

by persecutors, but also by the persecuted. If certain writings had fallen into the wrong hands, they could well have exposed Christians in hiding.

Such was the case in subsequent years of the Roman Empire, with varied intensity, as waves of repression rose up and then subsided again. The persecuted Church, working underground, had to take all measures for security, hence the closely guarded secret as to the whereabouts of the Roman bishops' archives. In times of peace, they may well have been kept in a particular place for a longer time. When arrests began, they had to be moved from place to place. According to extant testimonies, it appears that many popes lived in the Trastevere district during the first centuries, so there is a strong probability that their archives were kept there.

One hypothesis states that during the pontificate of the fourth pope, St. Clement I—that is, towards the end of the 1st century—the archives may well have been stored in a so-called church house (*domus ecclesiae*) on the grounds of Nero's former elaborate villa, the Domus Aurea (Golden House), where Flavius Clemens and Flavia Domitilla, the emperor's cousins, lived. The couple converted to Christianity and secretly hosted a successor of St. Peter in their home. But they

DOMUS AUREA, Emperor Nero's Roman palace, now in ruins, where historians say the papal archive was once housed.

ST. CLEMENT I, pope, martyr, and first-known early Christian writer.

AGAPE FEAST, the meal that the first Christians would share after the Eucharist—mural in the Catacomb of St. Callixtus.

CATACOMB OF ST. CALLIXTUS, Rome, which occupies 86 acres and contains the remains of over 500,000 people, including 9 popes.

ST. CORNELIUS was the first pope to write letters in Latin.

were arrested. Flavius was sentenced to death, while Flavia was exiled. Today, one can visit the ruins of this *domus ecclesiae* underneath the Basilica of St. Clement.

Three centuries of persecutions, and the later barbarian invasions, can be blamed for our lack of knowledge as to what exactly was to be found in the papal library and archive. They most probably housed the oldest Gospel scrolls, apostolic letters, Bible commentaries, and administrative documents, which played a practical role in the daily functioning of the Church. How do we know? Pope Cornelius, whose pontificate lasted from 251 to 253, wrote in one of his letters that there were forty-six priests, seven deacons, seven subdeacons, and forty-two acolytes, as well as fifty-two exorcists, readers, and porters (*ostiarii*) ministering in Rome.[1] He could not have given such precise data without appropriate records.

Christians adopted methods of archive administration from the Romans. Some popes, prior to being elected, were officials familiar with systems of storing financial and administrative documents, and even adopted official names for Church institutions. For example, the

Roman word for "archive" was *scrinium*, and the Christians named their archives Scrinium Sanctae Romanae Ecclesiae.

According to an ancient Christian tradition, the 3rd-century administrative center of the Roman Church, including its archives, was found near the Pompey Theater, where the Apostolic Chancery was, next to the Basilica of St. Lawrence, whose patron was one of the best-known martyrs of the first few centuries. St. Lawrence was a close associate of Pope Sixtus II, who appointed him deacon and

EMPEROR VALERIAN
being defeated and taken captive in AD 260 by King Shapur I of Persia—bas-relief in Naqsh-e Rostam.

treasurer of the Church. St. Lawrence was also given charge of the papal library and archives.

In 258, Emperor Valerian issued an edict against Christianity, which unleashed a new wave of persecutions. As the state treasury was empty, the emperor decided to eliminate the leaders of the Church and seize her assets, about which improbable stories had been circulating. Pope Sixtus II and six deacons were arrested and beheaded.

ST. SIXTUS I
entrusting to St. Lawrence the chalice used by Christ during the Last Supper—fresco by Fra Angelico in the Vatican.

Lawrence, one of the deacons who had escaped death, became responsible for the Church's property.

Before he was arrested, he managed to distribute the gold and silver to the Roman poor. He also managed to hide some relics that belonged to the pope, for example, the chalice that was believed to have been used during the Last Supper. According to St. Donatus, this precious vessel turned up in Spain, the homeland of Lawrence's parents. All evidence indicates that the foresighted treasurer also managed to find a safe place for the Church's archive, which contained lists of names of

HOLY GRAIL, the chalice used by Christ during the Last Supper, is believed to be in Valencia Cathedral.

25

Christ's followers. Had the lists fallen into the hands of the imperial officials, the lives of many Christians would have been in serious danger.

Lawrence was arrested and found himself before Decius, the Roman prefect. When asked where the Church's treasures were to be found, he replied that they were in the souls of the sick and the poor. His attitude was seen as exceptionally impertinent, so his punishment

ST. LAWRENCE being interrogated, imprisoned, and executed—fresco by Fra Angelico in the Vatican.

had to be particularly severe. On August 10, 258, he was grilled alive on a gridiron. Though he was tortured, he did not reveal where he had hidden the Church's archive.

The last great wave of persecutions came at the beginning of the 5ᵗʰ century, during the reign of Emperor Diocletian. Christians were murdered, and objects sacred to them were destroyed. Eusebius, a Church chronicler and an eyewitness of these events, wrote: "I saw with my own eyes houses where Masses had been said get searched from top to bottom, to the very foundations, and inspired

COLOSSEUM in Rome, where Christians were killed.

DIOCLETIAN persecuted Christians.

Holy Scriptures get thrown onto fires in town squares." It was then that the papal library and archive were destroyed. It was not possible to replicate the burned books, letters, and documents.

The situation changed after 313, when Emperor Constantine the Great issued a decree of tolerance, the Edict of Milan, which allowed Christians to worship publicly. This ended the persecution of the Church in the Roman Empire, apart from the repressions during the reign of Julian the Apostate. Constantine turned out to be a great benefactor to the hitherto clandestine Christian community. The Orthodox

DONATION OF CONSTANTINE, by which the emperor gave the Lateran Palace to the Church—13th-century fresco.

ST. SYLVESTER I astride a horse led by Emperor Constantine—fresco in the Basilica of the Santi Quattro Coronati in Rome.

ST. PETER'S BASILICA
is where the first pope was buried.

ST. PAUL OUTSIDE THE WALLS
was built over the grave of the Apostle to the Gentiles.

Church venerates him as a saint to this day and has granted him, together with his mother, St. Helena, the title "Equal to the Apostles".

In Rome alone, he donated three basilicas to the Church, dedicated to three of the apostles: St. Peter's on Vatican Hill, the Basilica of St. Paul outside the Walls, and the Basilica of St. John Lateran, the last of which came with a magnificent palace that was inhabited by Pope Sylvester I, wherein the ecclesiastical seat of the papacy was situated for almost one thousand years. Conclaves and councils took place on Lateran Hill, where the most important decisions concerning the

ST. JOHN LATERAN, whose dedication is celebrated throughout the Catholic Church on Nov. 9.

POPE'S SEAT

THE BASILICA of St. John Lateran is the mother and head of all the Catholic churches throughout the world. The beginnings of the basilica go back to 313, when Constantine the Great donated a building, the former barracks of the Praetorian Guard (on Lateran Hill, Rome), to Pope Miltiades. Over the following thousand years, this site became the official seat of the heads of the Church. An architectonic complex arose, of which the most important buildings were: the Lateran Palace (papal residence), the Papal Chapel and the Holy Stairs (Scala Sancta), the baptistery, and most importantly the magnificent church, dedicated to the Most Holy Savior. The year 314 saw the beginning of the construction of the first five-naved basilica, which was consecrated by Pope Sylvester I ten years later. It was seriously damaged during an earthquake in 896 and rebuilt during the pontificate of Pope Sergio III (904–911). In 1144, it was dedicated to St. John the Baptist and St. John the Evangelist.

In 1308 came a turning point in the basilica's history, when it was seriously damaged by a huge fire. A year later, Clement V and the papal court moved to Avignon in France. His successors stayed there for seventy years, during which time the Lateran declined in importance. On returning to Rome in 1377, the royal court, however, did not return to the Lateran, as the basilica had been badly damaged in another fire (1360). Hence the Vatican became the main papal center. The basilica was not rebuilt until the 15th century. Its present classical facade is of the 18th century.

ST. JULIUS I,
the pope who
established
the Church's
chancery.

**ST. MARY
MAJOR,**
the basilica
where St. Jerome
is buried.

ST. DAMASUS,
the pope who
introduced Latin.

Church's fate were made. It was to this spacious palace that the central archive of the Vicar of Christ was eventually transferred.

The Apostolic Chancery arose during the pontificate of Julius I (337–352), modeled on the similar Imperial Chancery. Also organized in an analogous way was the Scrinium Sanctum, wherein archival and library collections were accumulated until the 15th century.

Papal collections expanded. Administrative and financial documents piled up: Acts of the Martyrs, biblical manuscripts, literary and theological texts, synodal resolutions, Church court verdicts, title transfers, deeds of sale, testaments and legacies, property rights, and documents freeing slaves. Material on theological disputes was collected to help popes to settle doctrinal issues. Correspondence with bishops throughout the world took up more and more space. Before sending letters, papal scribes copied them and placed them in

wooden cabinets made of a special kind of wood called *lignum scrinarium*.

Pope Damasus I changed the face of the Western Church by Latinizing her. Previously, even in Rome, the Greek liturgy dominated. He introduced Latin on a wide scale, commissioning his own secretary, St. Jerome, to translate the Bible into Latin. Thus came the

Vulgate, which was obligatory in the Catholic Church until the Reformation. It is highly probable that St. Jerome worked near the papal archive, where he would have had access to various versions of the Bible.

The pontificate of St. Damasus (366 –384) left a great mark on the form of the Roman Church. He initiated the centuries-old tradition of Catholic patronage of the arts. He was the first of a long line of Roman bishops who served as patrons to numerous architects, sculptors, and painters.

ST. JEROME, a Doctor of the Church, is most famous for his translation of the Bible into Latin, but also authored numerous biblical commentaries and theological works. In the 15th century, Antonello da Messina depicted him at work in his study.

**TOMB OF
ST. DAMASUS**
in the Crypt
of the Popes
in the Catacomb
of Callixtus
in Rome.

Thanks to St. Damasus, there is evidence allowing one to locate the former central repository of the archive close to the historic location of the Apostolic Chancery. He was not only a clergyman, but also a writer of epigrams and epitaphs in honor of the deceased, including many martyrs. He also commissioned a headstone for his father, Antonius, who came to Italy most probably from the Iberian Peninsula, worked many years in the Church archive, and as a widower, was ordained a priest. St. Damasus had the following epigram, which he composed himself, inscribed on his father's headstone:

Here lies my father, archivist, lector, deacon, and priest,
Benefactor and a man of merit.
Here Christ honored me with supreme authority
Over the Holy See.
I erected a new roof over the archive building,
And added columns on both its sides,
That the name of Damasus might live for evermore.[2]

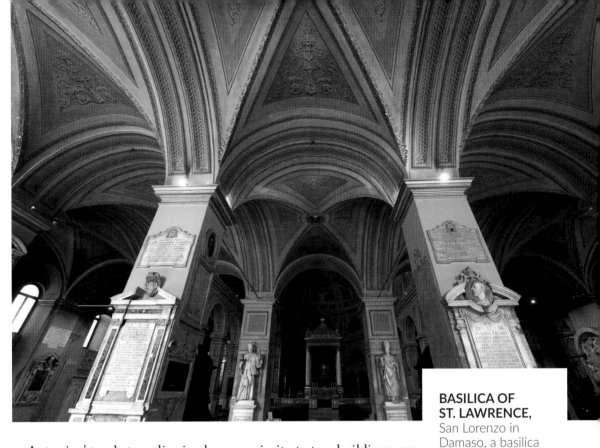

Antonius' tombstone lies in close proximity to two buildings connected with the papal archive: St. Jerome's Church, built on the site of the former palace—belonging to a Roman patrician, Paula—wherein the pious translator worked on the translation of the Bible into Latin; and the Basilica of St. Lawrence, built by Damasus, who particularly venerated the martyr. Today, it is part of the old Apostolic Chancery complex and thus is easy to miss even when one is close to it. This close proximity lends credence to the theory that the Church's archives were once to be found in this area.

Unfortunately, papal documents from the 4th century did not survive to our times, as they were destroyed during barbaric invasions. The Visigoths, led by Alaric, were the first to capture the Eternal City (in 410), plundering it for three days. Admittedly, its inhabitants were spared, but they were forced to give up their wealth. Many buildings were burned down, while the Lateran Palace, which housed the main part of the archive, was seriously damaged. Later, Rome was sacked by the Vandals (445), the Burgundians (472), the Ostrogoths (546), and the Saracens (846). Some 5th-century papal documents survived, as they were transferred to other cities and stored in the archives of local bishops. Thus, for example, a large collection of letters of Pope St. Leo the Great was saved.

ST. LEO I, one of two popes in Church history called "the Great".

Why were archives destroyed? In order to deprive a community of its history, its memory, its spirit, and its identity. Hence, whenever the Eternal City became restless, the popes transferred the more precious documents elsewhere, for example, to Monte Cassino, a Benedictine abbey.

There was a chancery in the Lateran Palace, as in the courts of secular rulers, run by an official, the *primicerius*. There, papal documents

MONTE CASSINO was established by St. Benedict of Nursia in 529. Papal archives were once stored in this Benedictine abbey.

were drawn up and, among other things, copies were made of correspondence with missionaries who had been sent to distant countries. The chancery employees even developed their own style of calligraphy: *curiale romana, curiale nova,* or *minuscula cancellaresca.*

The chancery became the most important source of archival material. Thanks to papal rulings and verdicts, successive popes could maintain the continuity of the Holy See's stance in relation to specific matters. Such matters were countless, since the great and powerful of that world often had recourse to the papacy as the final resort in definitively resolving disputes.

During the pontificate of St. Gregory the Great (590–604), the papal archive at the Lateran was located under the Sancta Sanctorum (chapel), dedicated to St. Lawrence, and the Scala Sancta, or Holy Stairs, which St. Helena brought from Jerusalem in 326. (According to tradition, Jesus climbed these marble steps in Pontius Pilate's palace.)

A part of the papal archives was also located on Vatican Hill, for there was a custom of laying signed documents on St. Peter's tomb, signifying a most solemn vow. Only important personages like kings

SCALA SANCTA, the Holy Stairs in the Lateran Palace, which were reputedly brought from Jerusalem by St. Helena. At one time, the papal archives were located underneath.

ST. GREGORY I, the second of the two popes called "the Great".

35

ST. PETER'S TOMB, in St. Peter's Basilica, became an important place in the history of the papal archives.

and bishops were permitted to do this, typically only in matters of the greatest import. The documents were stored near the tomb, at the feet of the apostle, so to speak. When there was no room for new documents, the old ones were transferred to the Lateran.

A third place where, starting in the 9th century, another part of the papal archives was to be found was the Turris Chartularia (Tower of the Papers) on Palatine Hill. High and difficult to conquer, the stone tower seemed to be a safer place than the Lateran or the Vatican for

precious documents. But even this did not save the papal archives. Frequent struggles between powerful Roman families meant that the tower kept changing hands, the defenders ending up in graves and the archival documents in flames. The valuable archives that were saved from the barbarians were, in great measure, destroyed in the 10th century by the inhabitants of Rome themselves.

Emperor Henry IV demolished the Turris Chartularia in 1083. He decided to set an antipope, Clement III, on the throne of Peter, capturing the Eternal City and expelling the lawful pope, Gregory VII. But the latter called upon the Normans for help. They came to the rescue, but after taking over Rome, they completely devastated it, putting it to the torch and wiping out the inhabitants. Hence the Church archives were lost without a trace, and today, the oldest surviving file of papal documents is dated as late as the pontificate of Innocent III (1198–1216).

CHURCH OF ST. JUSTUS, Lyon, where Innocent IV and his court stayed during the First Council of Lyon in 1245 – the papal archives were then transported to the church.

The majority of papyrus manuscripts from the first thousand years of Christianity did not survive to our times, not even those preserved from invaders, as papyrus conservation methods were unknown; it became brittle and decayed with age. Such was the case until the 11th century, when parchment came into common use. There were

several practical reasons for this. Firstly, as already mentioned, it was much more durable. Secondly, papyrus documents were scrolls, while parchment documents were codices (books), and it was easier to navigate a codex text. Thirdly, the frequent unrolling of scrolls brought about their rapid deterioration, whereas leafing through codices entailed much less wear. Fourthly, codices were more convenient to transport and store.

Between the 11th and 14th centuries, popes frequently went on long journeys around Italy and France, taking chancery clerks and archival documents along with them. They usually took copies of documents, thinking that it would be safer to leave the originals in Rome. However, it often turned out to be the reverse: the documents in Rome were lost, but their contents were saved thanks to the copies taken on journeys. This happened, for example, in 1234, when a popular revolt broke out in Rome. Many palaces were plundered, including the Lateran. As unrest continued, in 1257 Pope Alexander IV moved to Viterbo, where popes lived with some of their archives until 1281.

The years 1309 to 1377 saw a new chapter in the history of the papal archives, the so-called Babylonian Captivity of the Papacy. It was a time when all the popes were French and preferred to reside in Avignon, an enclave of the Papal States in Provence. Hence the bishops

TURRIS CHARTULARIA, a tower on Palatine Hill, where papal archives were housed—view from the 17th century, when the building was already a ruin.

OLDEST BOOK

THE *LIBER DIURNUS ROMANORUM PONTIFICUM* is the Vatican Secret Archives' oldest book (8th century).
It contains a collection of about one hundred blank forms compiled by the Apostolic Chancery

A PAPAL PARCHMENT that disappeared in the 11th century and was not rediscovered until 1641.

pertaining to such events as the death of a pope, the election of a successor, the papal inauguration, the consecration of a bishop, the granting of privileges and dispensations, the founding of monasteries, the authorization to have a private chapel, and so on.
Part of the book consists of copies of documents from as early as the end of the 5th century, going back to the pontificates of Gelasius I (492–496) and Gregory the Great (590–604). *Liber Diurnus*

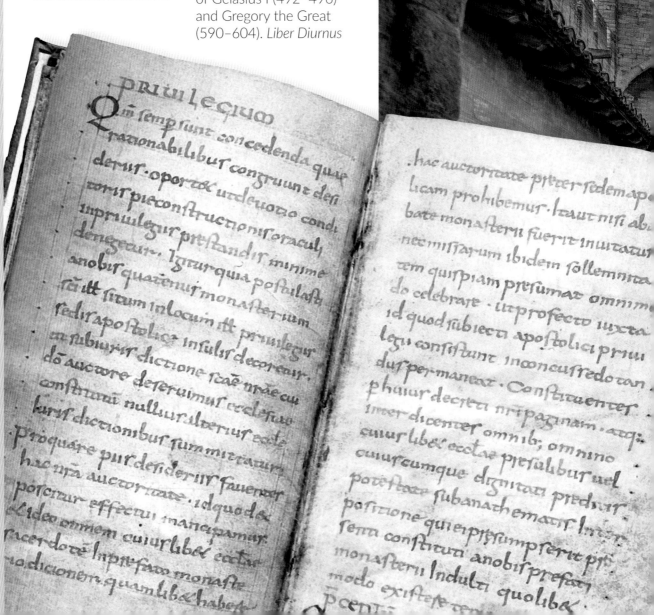

Romanorum Pontificum was used by papal officials up to the 11th century, but in time, it was replaced, not meeting the requirements of Church administration.

PALACE OF THE POPES,
Palais des Papes, in Avignon, France, the seat of the Catholic Church for decades.

AVIGNON POPES lived here in the Palais des Papes from 1309 to 1376. With 18,000 square yards of floor space, it is the largest Gothic palace in Europe.

of Rome resided outside the city for almost seven decades, keeping the most important Church documents under their care.

The Western Schism (1387–1417) began shortly after the return of the papacy to the Eternal City. During this period, there were two claimants to the Holy See (even a third for a certain time). This was due to the lack of agreement among the cardinals, largely because of

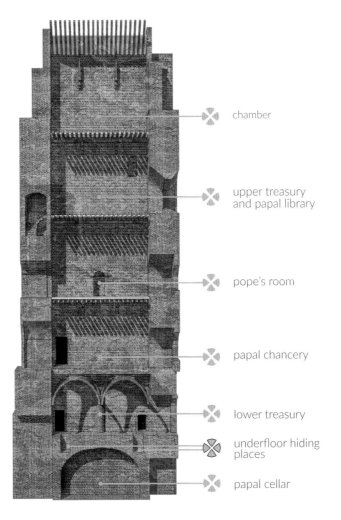

chamber

upper treasury
and papal library

pope's room

papal chancery

lower treasury

underfloor hiding
places

papal cellar

ROOMS OF THE PALACE:

1. great hall, where conclaves were held (bottom left on opposite page),

2. lower treasury, with a hiding place for the most valuable items and documents,

3. hiding place beneath the floor of the lower treasury.

THE LOWER TREASURY

in the tower of the papal palace contained the most valuable objects and documents, transported to Avignon by Clement V and his successors. It had four large hiding places under the floor of stone slabs, which were raised with a hoist. There, the documents were kept in locked iron chests and labelled alphabetically.

3

ST. CATHERINE OF SIENA persuaded Gregory XI to move the Holy See from Avignon back to Rome.

TOMB OF ST. CATHERINE in Santa Maria sopra Minerva, Rome.

PAPAL PALACE in Viterbo – the papal residence from 1257 to 1281, was home to six popes during unrest in Rome.

political reasons. One claimant was in Rome, the other in Avignon. Hence two separate papal archives were functioning at that time— and even a third, in Pisa (from 1409 to 1417).

The schism was ended by the Council of Constance. Martin V was elected pope, and the Holy See was transferred to Rome again. However, he decided to have the ecclesiastical seat in the Vatican, not the Lateran, and so did his successors. The fragmented archive began to be consolidated in one place—where the head of the Church resided. Many of the scattered documents, however, did not return to the Eternal City, ending up, for example, in Paris.

Peace reigned in Rome during the following decades. The Renaissance dawned. Many distinguished humanists worked at the papal court, sometimes as secretaries. Some of the Church leaders were famous, sophisticated intellectuals, such as Pius II and Nicholas V.

231

A PARDON granted on May 24, 1441, to Johannes Smyth, a Glasgow diocesan priest who travelled to Rome from Scotland to seek absolution. During a game of soccer on the Feast of St. Catherine, he had collided with an opponent, who was then stretchered off the field and died shortly afterward. According to canon law, a person with blood on his hands could not exercise his priestly office. Hence Johannes Smyth made his way to Rome to obtain a dispensation. The document is housed in the Apostolic Penitentiary Archive in Rome (Reg. Matrim. et Divers. 2bis, c. 231r.).

Thanks to them, the Vatican Library, which housed the Church archive, became ever more impressive.

As more collections were accumulated, new facilities were necessary. A building arose during the pontificate of Sixtus V (1585–1590) on the grounds of the Apostolic Palace. But in time, even this turned out to be too small. Hence the pope had the most valuable documents transferred to Castel Sant'Angelo. This ancient building emerged

43

at the beginning of the 2ⁿᵈ century, then serving as the Mausoleum of Hadrian. Three hundred years later, it was converted into a fortress, to which Pope Gregory the Great (pontificate: 590–604) gave its present name. The Church's archive was located in the rotund premises, at the top of the castle, under the statue of an angel.

The fortress turned out to be a safe place, not only for documents but also for the bishops of Rome, as it was connected to the papal palace at the Vatican by a secret passage (the Passetto di Borgo). This passage saved the life of Alexander VI in 1494 and Clement VII in 1527.

POPE SIXTUS V
had part of the Vatican archive enlarged toward the end of the 16ᵗʰ century.

IRON CHESTS
held precious objects, including documents, in the Castel Sant'Angelo.

PASSETTO DI BORGO
is a passage between the Vatican Palace and Castel Sant'Angelo that saved two popes from death.

The second of these dates is connected with an event that has gone down in history as the Sack of Rome (Sacco di Roma). Emperor Charles V, infuriated by the pope's alliance with Francis, the king of France, dispatched his army against Rome. On May 6, 1527, this army of 20,000 Italians, Spaniards, and Germans captured the capital of Christendom. Their commander allowed them to pillage the city. Eight days of rape, murder, and plunder ensued. There were a large number of German Lutheran mercenaries in the army, who murdered priests, raped nuns, desecrated churches, and profaned and destroyed relics. The occupation lasted until October 17, when the army withdrew, leaving Rome completely devastated.

Castel Sant'Angelo was the only place that was not taken, and Clement VII observed the Sack of Rome from its walls. Had it not been for the Swiss Guards, he would not have escaped. Not one of the Guards survived.

Most of the archives were saved, part of them because they were in the castle, another part, because one of the emperor's commanders had his quarters in the Vatican Library. Nonetheless, some of the archival material was used as tinder for fires, bedding in stables, and insoles for shoes.

ALEXANDER VI,
a pope infamous for numerous scandals.

CLEMENT VII,
pope who survived the last sack of Rome in 1527.

CASTEL SANT'ANGELO,
or Castle of the Holy Angel, long home to the papal archive.

SACCO DI ROMA

IT IS A HISTORICAL PARADOX that the most terrible plunder of Rome in modern times was not the work of pagan barbarians, but ordered by an ultra-Catholic Habsburg, Holy Roman Emperor Charles V. In 1527, the invaders, mainly Spaniards and Germans, murdered thousands of inhabitants, looted the city, and destroyed many precious works of art.

Protestant lansquenets in particular manifested their destructive fury. For them, the capture of Rome was equivalent to the fall of godless Babylon. They organized blasphemous processions in front of Castel Sant'Angelo, shouting to Pope Clement VII (sheltered within), *"Vivat Lutherus pontifex!"* ("Long live Pope Luther!"). Someone, using his sword, inscribed Luther's name on Raphael's *Disputation of the Holy Sacrament* fresco.

Due to the great number of unburied bodies, an epidemic broke out in the city. As a consequence, the population of Rome— fifty-five thousand before the attack—fell to barely ten thousand. Historians see these events as a symbolic end to the Renaissance period in the Eternal City. After the destruction, the city was rebuilt in the Baroque style.

The city rose again like a phoenix from the ashes, this time in a yet more impressive form. A new basilica was built on the site of the former St. Peter's, which dated from the times of Constantine. It took over one hundred years to build (1505–1626), while Bernini's colonnades, surrounding St. Peter's Square, were completed in 1663.

The Council of Trent (1545–1563) commissioned the pope to reform the calendar. It was clear to all that the Julian Calendar was inexact, the March equinox falling earlier and earlier with the years. Gregory XIII (pontificate: 1572–1585) had an astronomical observatory built in the Belvedere grounds, the Tower of the Winds, which later became part of the Vatican Secret Archives. There, in the Zodiac Room, scientists observed the motions of the stars. They discovered

TOMB OF GREGORY XIII depicts scholars presenting the new calendar to the pontiff.

that the prior calculation of the length of the year entailed a one-day delay every 126 years. Hence they worked out the Gregorian Calendar, named after the pope, which was much more accurate, entailing a one-day delay every 3,322 days. The pope brought it into general use in his 1582 bull, *Inter Gravissimas*.

The archive, as we know it today, came in 1612, when Pope Paul V, who descended from a distinguished Roman family (Borghese), had all the Church documents, which were scattered around various parts of Rome, stored in one place in the Vatican. In time, material from various corners of the Papal States, and from throughout the world, began to pour in.

The name Vatican Secret (Apostolic) Archive (Archivum Secretum Apostolicum Vaticanum) appeared in the 17th century. The word

GREGORY XIII, the pope responsible for the Gregorian Calendar.

OBSERVATORY floor in the Tower of the Winds, part of the Vatican Secret Archives.

LUNARIO NOVO (NEW ALMANAC)

TEN DAYS, October 5 to 14, 1582, have disappeared from the history of Western civilization. They were removed due to a change in the calculation of time upon the replacement of the Julian Calendar, introduced in 45 BC during the reign of Julius Caesar, by the Gregorian Calendar, introduced by Pope Gregory XIII. Thus the difference in time that had grown for over seventeen centuries— which saw the March equinox fall earlier and earlier—was eliminated, as 16th-century scholars were capable of calculating the length of time it took the earth to orbit the sun more precisely than their predecessors from the days of the Roman Empire.

The initiator of the Julian Calendar reform was a Calabrian doctor, Luigi Giglio, who unfortunately died in 1576, not seeing the realization of his project. Cristoforo Calvio, a German Jesuit, a mathematician, an astronomer, and a professor at the Roman College, led a team of scholars in completing the work. The team included Giuseppe Scala, an astronomer from Sicily, and Ignazio Dante, a mathematician from Perugia. In their work they utilized Nicolaus Copernicus' discoveries, contained in his *On the Revolutions of the Celestial Spheres*.

The Gregorian Calendar was introduced immediately (October 15, 1582) in Poland, Lithuania, Italy, Portugal, Spain, and the Netherlands. In time, other Catholic countries adopted it, while Protestant countries adopted it even later; Anglican Britain did not do so until 1752. Countries from other cultures accepted it, too, including Japan (1873), Egypt (1875), China (1912), and Turkey (1927). Among Christian countries, the last to accept it were those where the Orthodox Church dominated, for example, Greece (1923).

secretum signified not only secret but also private, and it was meant to emphasize that this was the pope's own private archive.

Rome was spared any historical upheavals for almost three hundred years. The archive expanded, as did the book collections in the neighboring Vatican Library. But new dangers loomed large towards the end of the 18th century. Napoleon Bonaparte ordered the kidnapping of eighty-one-year-old Pope Pius VI in 1798. A year later, the aged pontiff died, imprisoned in the citadel in Valence.

His successor, Pius VII, tried to compromise with Bonaparte, the most powerful man in Europe, agreeing to serious concessions, but the excessive demands were ultimately rejected by the Church.

As emperor of France and king of Italy Napoleon occupied Rome in May 1808, and a year later the pope was arrested and taken to Savona. The occupying forces seized many valuable sculptures and paintings, as well as priceless jewels.

In 1810, Bonaparte ordered the seizure of the Vatican Secret Archives. He dreamt of establishing the world's largest and richest library in Paris. Hence he had the court archives of the various capitals he had occupied—for example, Vienna, Madrid, and Rome—brought to the French city. The papal collections were packed into three thousand crates and loaded onto wagons drawn by mules and oxen. Like other important documents from across Europe, they ended up at the Hôtel de Soubise in Paris, located in the former Knights Templar palace. The empire's head archivist, Pierre Claude François Daunou, had the documents closely scrutinized in order to find material that compromised the papacy. But the search proved to be fruitless.

After the defeat of Napoleon, the French were ordered to return stolen parchments, books, documents, sacred objects, and works of art, but not all were returned. Amid the confusion, almost two thousand papal *regesta*—handwritten copies of official papal letters—were lost, many ending up as waste paper.

In 1881, Pope Leo XIII took an unprecedented step, opening the Vatican Secret Archives to scholars doing historical research because, in the pontiff's words, the "Church needs the truth." Initially, only documents from before AD 815 were made available, but in time more recent ones became accessible as well.

Such discretion is not unusual. State archives throughout the world are also partly classified. (In many countries, documents remain inaccessible for varying periods of time depending on

POPE PAUL V,
who in 1612 established the Vatican Secret Archives as we know it today.

POPE PIUS VII
and his papal archives were transported to France by order of Napoleon.

PIERRE CLAUDE FRANÇOIS DAUNOU,
Napoleon's head archivist.

49

CODED SECRETS

OVER THE CENTURIES, the papacy kept up a voluminous correspondence that traveled the whole world, some of which was of a highly confidential nature, for example, the Holy See's letters to and from nunciatures in various countries. Such correspondence was coded. There was even a special Secretariat of Codes in the Vatican, the head of which was appointed personally by the pope. There was a time when only a certain papal official had access to code keys, which were changed periodically. Roman cryptography was not a unique phenomenon. Coded correspondence was universally used by emperors, kings, and princes throughout Europe. However, Vatican diplomacy was the best thought-out, its cryptography regarded as the world's best. In the 14th century, the papacy introduced a polygrammatic code system, which integrated clever traps to counteract decoders.

the contents: thirty, fifty, seventy, or even one hundred years.) The collections of the Congregation for Bishops, concerning episcopal appointments, are unavailable to scholars, as are the Roman Rota's declarations of marital nullity, which include intimate details about the personal lives of specific individuals. Documents concerning post-1939 events are not available to researchers either.

The Vatican Secret Archives are a real gold mine for historians, as they contain documents concerning the Papal States, the Roman Rota, the Apostolic Nunciature, ancient Roman families, consistory protocols, conclave sessions, diplomacy. They house correspondence with emperors, kings, princes, presidents, and prime ministers; petitions from national assemblies, senators, lords, and councilors; indulgence registers; court statements; Inquisition reports; imperial diplomas; and much more. Some documents—reports from nuncios, legates, or papal envoys, for example—are coded and can be deciphered only by using a special code book.

Many states, episcopates, and colleges have their own history centers in Rome, whose employees and scholarship holders carry out research in the Vatican Archives on the histories of their own countries, perhaps investigating hitherto unknown documents. Some even engage private individuals to this end, such as the Polish countess Karolina Lanckorońska, who established

LEO XIII
was the first pope to develop the foundations of Catholic social teaching.

COURTYARD
of the Apostolic Palace, one of whose wings houses the Vatican Secret Archives.

a foundation in 1967 to seek documents concerning diplomatic relations between the Holy See and Poland.

Once again, new facilities were needed, because the collections continued to expand. As there was no longer room in the Vatican complex, it was decided to go below ground. In 1982, John Paul II officially opened an underground bunker whose construction had begun during the pontificate of Paul VI. Located under the Vatican Museums, it has two air-conditioned rooms where the most precious parchments are kept.

The last major change occurred on October 28, 2019, when Pope Francis issued, motu poprio, an apostolic letter, wherein he decreed a change of name from Vatican Secret Archives to Vatican Apostolic Archive, while maintaining its hitherto mission. According to the pope, the institution's name (from the 17th century) is misleading, as it suggests that it houses information which is reserved for

SCHOLARS have access to the Vatican Secret Archives, where materials are available only in the reading room and photographing texts is prohibited.

a privileged few. The Latin term *secretum* signified not so much "secret" but "private" or "personal" and so intended for the exclusive use of the pope. Today, it is not applicable, as the archives have been accessible to historians for a long time. Hence, the pope decided to adapt the name to contemporary circumstances.

Over the centuries, the papal archive shared the Roman Church's ups and downs—destroyed and ransacked, then continually revived after successive wars, fires, and raids. Its oldest document is from the 8th century, but documents from the first thousand years of Christianity are rare. Virtually all the oldest collections date from the pontificate of Innocent III (1198–1216), when brittle papyrus was supplanted by significantly more durable parchment. In total, all the materials stored in the 650 collections take up about fifty miles of shelving.

Sergio Pagano, prefect of the Vatican Secret Archives, could talk about this institution for hours. He has worked there for over forty years, fulfilled numerous functions, and had the opportunity to

familiarize himself with many extraordinary documents, the most fascinating of which, he says, concern the trial of Galileo Galilei, which we shall deal with in a later chapter.

During laborious preliminary archival research, Pagano's employees managed to find dozens of unknown documents, which sometimes threw new light on past events. One such discovery was the Chinon Parchment, that is, the original protocol concerning the interrogation of the Knights Templar leaders on August 20, 1308, in the Château de Chinon, a castle in the Loire Valley (on the banks of the Vienne River). For seven centuries, the parchment was regarded as lost. Barbara Frale, an Italian historian and employee of the Vatican Secret Archives, came across it on September 13, 2001. Hence we can become more familiar with the circumstances of one of the most controversial trials in history, which involved the treasure of the Knights Templar, charges of heresy, secret rituals and initiations, and two knights—Geoffroi de Charney, master of Normandy, and Jacques de Molay, the grand master—who summoned the pope and the king to the tribunal of Heaven. Within a year, both the pope and the king were dead. The knights were burned alive at the stake in Paris, on an island in the Seine.

So let us delve now into the Vatican Archives, going back to the Middle Ages to fathom out the mystery of the Knights Templar order.

UNDERGOUND BUNKER beneath the Vatican Museums contains most of the Vatican Secret Archives' documents.

53

FUNERAL IN VIETNAM
- an 1840 rice paper painting by Fr. Giuseppe Maria de Morrone, a French missionary.

TIBETAN FREEDOM of conscience privilege issued on rice paper in 1741 by the Dalai Lama.

LETTER IN ARABIC
(1627) to Pope Urban VIII from Matthew the Coptic Orthodox Patriarch of Alexandria (47¼"x11").

FIRST MAP OF AUSTRALIA
– drawn up in 1676 by Fr. Vittorio Riccio, a Dominican missionary.

THE PROPAGANDA FIDE HISTORICAL ARCHIVES

MORE ARCHIVES developed in the Vatican as papal institutions emerged and grew. All the Holy See's dicasteries had archives. The Sacred Congregation for the Propagation of the Faith (or Sacra Congregatio de Propaganda Fide), established in 1622 (now the Congregation for the Evangelization of Peoples, but still commonly known as Propaganda Fide), was particularly distinguished in this respect. Its first secretary, Msgr. Francesco Ingoli, in office from 1622 to 1649, began to accumulate documents that were needed for missionary pastoral work. Thus arose an enormous collection of unique documents: reports, letters, petitions, protocols, instructions, circulars, and decrees. To this day it remains a priceless mine of knowledge, not only regarding evangelization, but

also regarding the history, geography, culture, customs, and beliefs of people from Africa, Asia, Oceania, and other regions of the world. Initially, the archive was located in the Vatican Palace. Later, it was moved for a short time to the Apostolic Chancery. It eventually ended up in the Palazzo di Propaganda Fide at the southern end of Piazza di Spagna in Rome. During Napoleonic times, it shared the fate of the Vatican Secret Archives, as it too was transported to Paris. After the fall of Napoleon, it was returned to Rome, though incomplete. The last documents did not reach Rome until 1925, sent from Vienna. Presently, the Propaganda Fide Historical Archives are located in a modern building, made available in 2002, at the Pontifical Urban University.

DIRECTOR
of the historical archives for Propagation of the Faith, Fr. Luis Manuel Cuña Ramos.

FABRIC OF ST. PETER (FABBRICA DI SAN PIETRO)

The Fabric of St. Peter is a Vatican institution responsible for the administration, maintenance, conservation, and decor of St. Peter's Basilica. It was established in 1523 by Pope Clement VII, who set up a commission of sixty members to supervise and administer the construction of the world's largest church; work started in 1506 and ended in 1626.

Pope Clement VIII (pontificate: 1592–1605) elevated the aforementioned commission to the status of a congregation, and it remained one of the Vatican's most important dicasteries for over 360 years. Pope Paul VI lowered its status in the 20th century. Over several centuries, the institution accumulated a wealth of documentation pertaining to everything connected with St. Peter's history, architecture, and works of art. Today, their archive is located behind one of the basilica's pilasters.

BEAUTY AND UTILITY are the trademarks of Fabric of St. Peter employees.

A "DREAM ARCHIVE" that many architects, conservators, and art historians long to visit.

Trial of the Knights Templar

CHAPTER 2

Trial of the Knights Templar

Dissolution of one of medieval Europe's most powerful orders and the execution of its leaders

Rome

ITALY

It was September 13, 2001. People throughout the world were still living the events that had occurred two days earlier, when Islamic terrorists attacked the World Trade Center in New York City. Barbara Frale, however, an Italian medievalist, had other matters on her mind, as she was carrying out an investigative search at the Vatican Secret Archives. She was poring over registers of Avignon documents from the time of Benedict XII, whose pontificate was from 1334 to 1342. She came across a parchment that was catalogued as a protocol of one of the many French Inquisition investigations in the diocese of Tours. She would probably not have paid much attention to it had she not noticed a name that was familiar to her: Bérenger Fredoli.

THREE SEALS representing the signatures of three cardinals on the Chinon Parchment.

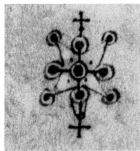

Frale was very familiar with this man's biography. She immediately realized that she had no ordinary document before her. Bérenger Fredoli was one of the most influential Catholic hierarchs of the early 14th century: a French cardinal, the most outstanding canonist of his time, and a trusted associate—even nephew—of Pope Clement V, who sent him to various corners of the world on particularly delicate missions. What could such a person have possibly done during interrogations carried out by some provincial inquisitor in the diocese of Tours?

LANDOLFO BRANCACCIO
was a papal legate
in England and the Kingdom
of Naples.

ÉTIENNE DE SUISY
was, among other things,
camerlengo of the College
of Cardinals

BÉRENGER FREDOLI
was, among other things,
a papal legate in France.

Frale looked at the bottom of the document. There were three seals on the parchment: one from Fredoli and two from other cardinals, Étienne de Suisy and Landolfo Brancaccio. Frale could not believe her eyes. She realized that she had found a seven-hundred-year-old document that historians had regarded as irretrievably lost, since it had been mistakenly catalogued in 1628 and again in 1912. It shed new light on the most notorious trial of the Middle Ages, particularly on the attitude of Pope Clement V, who, together with King Philip the Fair of France, was generally regarded as the main culprit in the dissolution of the Knights Templar and the execution of its leaders.

French historians certainly did not encounter this parchment at the beginning of the 19th century, when Napoleon had the Vatican Secret Archives transported to Paris. Enlightenment anticlerical officials were particularly interested in the catalogues pertaining to the Knights Templar trial and the trial of Galileo Galilei. They expected to find confirmation of facts that would set the Holy See in an unfavorable light. The French kept the files on the Knights Templar trial even after the fall of Napoleon, the restoration of the monarchy, and a decree to return all documents to the Vatican, as they still hoped to find material compromising the papacy. Fr. Marino Marini, the chamberlain of the prefect of the Vatican Secret Archives, persuaded them to return the files, telling them that the publication of the complete dossier would tarnish not Pope Clement's image, but King Philip's.

CATALOGUES
of documents
in the Vatican
Secret Archives.

Was Fr. Marino Marini bluffing in order to regain the files? The answer became evident when Bishop Sergio Pagano, the prefect of the Vatican Secret Archives, presented an over three-hundred-page publication, *Processus Contra Templarios*, at the Vatican Palace's Aula Vecchia del Sinodo on October 25, 2007. The publication contained the most important material concerning the Templars' trial, including the Chinon Parchment, discovered by Barbara Frale.

The parchment takes its name from a castle in the Loire Valley where five leaders of the order were imprisoned. They were incarcerated

BARBARA FRALE

BARBARA FRALE loves working in archives. As a twenty-five year old, she published a highly praised work concerning 15th-century Italy, based on an analysis of seven thousand documents. Thanks to her postgraduate studies at the Vatican School of Paleography, Diplomatics, and Archives Administration, she was able to pore over papal documents pertaining to the Avignon Papacy. Later, this experience was of use during her work in the Vatican Secret Archives, which she undertook in 2001. She became an expert on the Knights Templar, publishing several books that have been translated into numerous languages. Her discovery of the Chinon Parchment consolidated her position as a leading scholar in the world of medievalists.

CHINON PARCHMENT

THE CHINON PARCHMENT contains the protocol of the interrogation of five Templars: Grand Master Jacques de Molay; Hugues de Pairaud, visitor of the Temple; Raimbaut de Caron, preceptor of Cyprus; Geoffroi de Gonneville, preceptor of Aquitania; and Geoffroi de Charney, preceptor of Normandy. They were interrogated between August 17 and 20, 1308, at Chinon Castle in the diocese of Tours by three emissaries of Clement V—Cardinal Bérenger Fredoli, Cardinal Étienne de Suisy, and Cardinal Landolfo Brancaccio—in the presence of public notaries and witnesses. The accused did not admit to the charges of heresy and sodomy. They explained that the ostensible renunciation of their faith, and spitting upon the cross, were elements of a rite which was to prepare them in the event they fell into the hands of the Saracens. Obscene words and gestures were also part of the initiation.

In the document is this account:

"As they humbly asked for the Church's forgiveness for those offenses, begging for the blessing of exoneration, we decree that they might be exonerated by the Church, rehabilitated in communion with the Catholic Church, and that they might receive the Christian sacraments."[2]

As noted in the document, after interrogating the monks, the pope's plenipotentiaries deemed the charge of heresy to be groundless, and in the name of Clement V, they granted the prisoners absolution.

CHINON CASTLE, in the Loire Valley, is more than 400 yards long and 70 yards wide.

GRAFFITI by imprisoned Templars, carved on a cell wall.

in the dungeons of Coudray Tower, in the eastern part of the castle. Graffiti on the dungeon walls has survived to this day. According to Raymond Mauny, a French historian, the graffiti was the work of monks or nuns, while Louis Charbonneau-Lassay, an archeologist, believes the graffiti bears witness to the deep faith of the prisoners themselves. It depicts motifs of Christ's Passion: crosses on a hill, figures with haloes around their heads, and angels. They make a profound impression, particularly on those who are familiar with the fate of the prisoners: five years later, two of them were burned at the stake as heretics.

Today, people climb the same tower stairs that the Templars took to face three cardinals who had been sent to Chinon by Pope Clement V. The interrogations lasted from August 17 to 20, 1308. The course of the interrogations remained unknown for seven centuries, though it was scrupulously recorded. The Chinon Parchment allows us to dispel some of the doubts connected with the dissolution of the order.

 Chinon

FRANCE

COUDRAY TOWER
in Chinon Castle, where the Templar leaders were imprisoned.

STAIRCASE
used by Jacques de Molay and companions to attend interrogations by Clement V.

65

According to Marion Melville, a Scottish medievalist, the seven-year trial cast a shadow on the two-hundred-year history of the order. Without being familiar with its history, it would be difficult to understand why one of the most powerful institutions of the Middle Ages met with such a tragic fate.

Let us go back over nine centuries, to 1099, when the Crusaders captured Jerusalem and established their own kingdom in the Holy Land. Pilgrims and settlers from throughout Europe began to arrive in this land regained from the Muslims. However, en route, many of them became victims of armed bands that robbed and even murdered defenseless travelers.

CRUSADERS
as custodians of the Holy Sepulchre and other holy places in Jerusalem.

HOLY LAND

Jerusalem

In 1118, Hugues de Payens, a knight from Champagne (eastern France), and eight companions decided to devote themselves to protecting pilgrims from attacks. They took vows of poverty, chastity, and obedience and undertook to protect pilgrims from brigands and kidnappers. In 1120, King Baldwin II of Jerusalem offered them the Al-Aqsa Mosque, built by the Muslims between 660–691, as their central headquarters. After the capture of the Holy Land, the Christians had converted it into a church. The building was located on the Temple Mount, exactly where the Temple of Solomon once stood. Hence the name of the new order: Poor Knights of Christ and of the Temple of Solomon, popularly known as the Templars, from the Latin *templum*, that is, temple.

According to canon law, the order was founded on January 13, 1129. That day, during the Council of Troyes, the Templars adopted their

BALDWIN II, king of Jerusalem, entrusting the Temple Mount to Hugues de Payens, the Templars' first grand knight.

religious rule. The deliberations were presided over by the papal legate Mateusz d'Albano and St. Bernard of Clairvaux, reviver of the Cistercian Order and one of the greatest theologians and mystics in the history of Christianity. His presence was due to the fact that two people close to him were among the Templars, his uncle André de Montbard (later grand master of the order) and a close friend, Hugh, Count of Champagne. A maxim of the new organization was *Memento finis* (Remember thy end).

The Templars' baptism of fire took place not in the Holy Land but in the Iberian Peninsula, where they fought the Moors. It was a time

COAT OF ARMS of St. Bernard of Clairvaux.

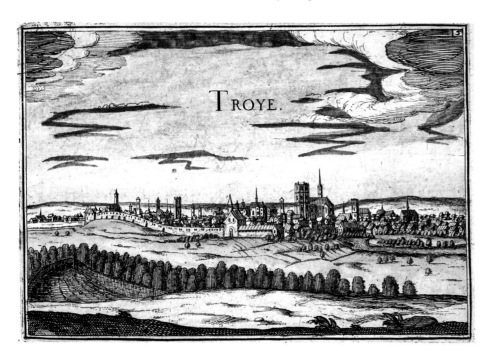

PANORAMA OF TROYES showing the cathedral as the highest building in the city, where a synod approved the rule of the Knights Templar in 1129.

67

when most of the Iberian Peninsula was ruled by Muslims, who were outflanking Europe and so posed a threat not only from the East, but also from the West.

Patrolling pilgrim and trade routes, the Templars quickly gained the gratitude of pilgrims, merchants, and travelers. They assumed a

BATTLE OF MURET, when French Crusaders defeated the Cathars in 1213.

TEMPLAR SEAL has two Crusaders on one horse, symbolizing the order's poverty.

policing role, combating predatory gangs, as well as a military role, fighting the Muslims. Their ranks included not only those of noble birth, but also the noble-minded who desired to serve others. They were recruited from all over Europe, but most were Franks.

The Christian world was aware of the threat of Islam. Hence the Templars enjoyed great authority in society, both among simple people and ruling elites, as attested to by numerous donations and gifts from European rulers. The first donation was from Queen Teresa of Portugal, who gifted the Castle of Soure, situated on the Mondego River, a borderland fortress built to defend the southern boundary of the kingdom against Moor invasions.

The order was also granted privileges by popes. The most important was granted by Innocent II in his bull *Omne Datum Optimum* of 1139,

wherein he exempted the Templars from the jurisdiction of bishops, directly subordinating the Templars to the Holy See. He also authorized them to build chapels and churches that would be exempt from episcopal jurisdiction, as well as from tithes.

In 1147, Pope Eugene III personally attended the order's general chapter deliberations in Paris. He was accompanied by King Louis VII

Constantinople

Edessa

Jerusalem

NEAR EAST

of France. It was then that the Vicar of Christ conferred a new emblem upon the Templars: a red cross on a white background.

From 1147 to 1148, the Templars participated in the Second Crusade, which was to recapture the County of Edessa. The crusade ended in failure, but the scale of the defeat could well have been greater, had it not been for the Templars, who distinguished themselves by their great fortitude.

Over the following decades, the knights with red crosses on white cloaks participated in campaigns in the Near East with mixed success,

HELMET worn by a Templar.

KING BALDWIN I entering Edessa during the First Crusade.

BATTLE OF HATTIN, when Muslims defeated the Crusaders in 1187.

SWORD of a Templar.

establishing a whole system of fortresses. The year 1187 proved a turning point in the order's history, when the Muslims, led by Saladin, sultan of Egypt, first defeated the Crusaders in a pitched battle at Hattin and then captured a series of Christian strongholds, including Jerusalem. The Muslim leader offered favorable conditions of surrender: he spared their lives and set them free—apart from the Templars and Hospitallers, whom he had beheaded. The Latins lost the Holy Land, and the Templars lost their central headquarters, which Saladin reconverted into the Al-Aqsa Mosque.

In response, European rulers organized the Third Crusade. From 1189 to 1192, they only managed to recapture a part of the Palestine coast. The Templars' headquarters was moved to Acre. The eventual

71

Acre

Jerusalem

HOLY LAND

loss of this port, one hundred years later (1281), signified the definitive expulsion of the Crusaders from the Holy Land. The Templars then moved their central headquarters to Cyprus.

With the loss of the Holy Sepulchre and the cessation of pilgrimages to the Levant, the Templars had to change their modus operandi. The most urgent need became the organization of another crusade to recapture

ACRE fell to the Muslims in 1291 (right).

CRUSADERS' LAST STRONGHOLD in the Holy Land was Acre.

Jerusalem. But funds were needed to raise a sizeable army capable of defeating the Muslims. The Templars took on the task of gathering the appropriate means for a crusade, receiving donations from all over Europe. People spared no expense, as they wanted the places connected with Christ to be retaken. However, the campaign was delayed. The Templars, with greater and greater funds at their disposal, began to act as bankers. They themselves did not take advantage of the accumulated wealth, but they prudently amassed a fortune.

They already had some experience in financial matters. Pilgrims on their way to the Holy Land would deposit their money with the Templars in Europe in exchange for letters of credit that could be redeemed in Jerusalem. That way, pilgrims could travel without carrying large sums of money. Thus the Templars developed a secure deposit-credit system that was universally trusted. They became masters in sound investments and lent money–even to kings and popes. Importantly, they granted loans from their own funds, maintaining a 100 percent reserve for deposits on demand.

Under these new circumstances, the Templars seldom reached for the sword, but more frequently for the purse; they began to be more involved in finance than in military campaigns. However, soldiers who do not fight for years, but deal instead with money, start to function differently. Discipline slackens; the original charism

FINANCE became the Templars' main activity at the turn of the 14th century.

TEMPLAR BANKERS worked as pawnbrokers and moneylenders.

73

is gradually forgotten. Thus arose the greatest controversy in the order's history. Only this time, the foe was not an infidel.

Philip the Fair of the House of Capet became King Philip IV of France in 1285, at the age of seventeen. Athletically built, stone-faced, and ice-cold in contacts with people, he lived an ascetic lifestyle at his gloomy, somber court. To many of his contemporaries, he was like the mythical Sphinx, an unsolved riddle. Bishop Bernard Saisset compared him

THE INVESTITURE CONTROVERSY

KING VS. POPE
Henry IV and Gregory VII were antagonists in the Investiture Controversy.

DICTATUS PAPAE
(1075) is one of the most important documents in papal history.

GREGORY VII defended the independence of the spiritual powers against the temporal powers.

THE DISPUTE between Philip IV of France and Boniface VIII was not Europe's first dispute between the monarchy and the papacy. That of greatest consequence was the conflict between Holy Roman Emperor Henry IV and Pope Gregory VII in the 11th century. For most of that century, the Catholic Church went through a great spiritual and moral crisis, which also affected Rome. Numerous European magnates took advantage of this, deciding to appoint their own people to Church offices, such as bishoprics and abbacies, often for money. There were even cases where emperors decided who was to be pope.

Hildebrand, a monk who became Pope Gregory VII in 1073, decided to cease this infamous practice and reform the Church (Gregorian Reforms). He condemned secular investitures—that is, the right of rulers to fill Church offices—which became punishable by excommunication. His stance was contained in a twenty-seven-point document, *Dictatus Papae*, wherein he presented the doctrine of the supremacy of papal authority over the imperial authority. Gregory VII even provided for the possibility of a pope to release a person from an oath (e.g., feudal) made to an unworthy ruler. This outraged Emperor Henry IV, who announced the dethronement of the pope at a synod in Worms in 1076. In response, Gregory VII excommunicated him, while the German princes took the pope's side. The emperor was forced to humble himself. In January 1077, he appeared within the walls of Canossa Castle and, dressed in sackcloth, spent three days asking Gregory VII to forgive him and revoke the excommunication.

The emperor was reconciled with the Church according to the Holy See's conditions. Henry IV, however, did not give up the fight. In 1084, he occupied Rome, dethroned Gregory VII, and saw to it that an antipope, Clement III, was elected. But the Normans came to Pope

Canossa

ITALY

HENRY IV arriving in Canossa— 14th-century miniature.

Gregory's aid, driving out the emperor's soldiers, though they themselves plundered Rome. Gregory VII died in exile in Salerno, having defended the independence of the papacy. The dispute did not end until 1122, when Pope Callixtus II and Emperor Henry V signed the Concordat of Worms. Eventually, the right of investiture remained the Church's prerogative.

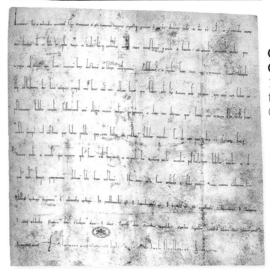

CONCORDAT OF WORMS, 1122, ended the Investiture Controversy.

CANOSSA CASTLE, where Henry IV humbled himself before Pope Gregory VII.

to an owl, which can stare motionlessly at one spot for a great length of time.

From the very beginning of his reign, his eyes were fixed on Aquitaine and Flanders, over which he waged a bitter war against the English. Constant wars swallowed up a great deal of money, depleting the kingdom's treasury. King Philip levied higher and higher taxes on his subjects, but funds were always short. So he had silver coins debased, cutting their real silver content but maintaining the same value. This was effective, but only for a short time, as it ultimately brought about inflation, the impoverishment of the population, social unrest, and revolts. A folk saying went: Philip the Fair was as false as the coins he minted.

The growing financial crisis saw the Crown reaching for Church funds, levying a new tax on the clergy. That displeased Pope Boniface VIII, who condemned it in his bull *Clericis Laicos* of 1296. In response, King Philip prohibited any exportation of gold and other valuables

PHILIP IV,
"the Fair", despot on the throne of France.

BONIFACE VIII,
first pope to organize a Jubilee Year, in 1300.

from France. This was undoubtedly a blow to the papacy, which could not thenceforth collect Peter's Pence. So Rome was forced to compromise and acknowledged that the king had the right to tax the clergy.

However, the financial conflict turned out to have less-far-reaching consequences than the dispute over power. Pope Boniface was aware that the present kings of France and England, Philip IV and Edward I, were manifesting ever more absolutist aspirations. They were not as great a threat as the Holy Roman emperors Henry IV and Frederick II had once been, but, nonetheless, the pope decided to restrain their impulses.

In 1301, Boniface VIII promulgated a bull, *Ausculta Fili,* aimed at Philip the Fair. It started with the following words: "Listen, my son, to your father's words and the teaching of your lord, the representative of the one God and Lord on earth." King Philip, who did not recognize

AUSCULTA FILI,
Boniface VIII's
1301 bull, directly
addressed Philip IV,
who saw
it as a challenge
to his authority.

BONIFACE VIII,
advocate of the
primacy of papal
authority over
royal power.

any authority over his own, including Rome, saw the wording of the bull as condescending and offensive. He had the document burned, and his first minister, Pierre Flotte fabricated a sham bull, *Scire Te Volumus*, attributed to Boniface VIII, according to which the pope arrogated to himself, among other things, temporal power over France and condemned those who objected as heretics.

Philip IV was the first European ruler to utilize propaganda on a very large scale. He did not recognize chivalric rules of combat; he was a pragmatist who favored practical results over high ideals. He was Machiavellian, before the world had even heard of Machiavelli.

Heinrich Graetz, a Jewish historian, wrote that he was "one of those monarchs who made arrogant and unprincipled despotism familiar to Europe".[1]

Philip the Fair was surrounded by people without any inhibitions whatsoever, such as Guillaumede Plaisian, who was responsible for forming public opinion and published political works slandering and deriding the pope. Boniface VIII was accused of hating the French nation, of wanting to destroy it, and of calling all Frenchmen dogs. Anti-Roman leaflets, written in simple and pointed language, reached everyone: knights, townsmen, parish priests, and peasants. In the dispute with Rome, the majority of the nation was with the king, including professors from Sorbonne University, the most famous Catholic university in Europe.

Philip IV was the first ruler to summon the Estates General (1302), which several centuries later became the National Assembly and heralded the beginning of the French Revolution, as well as parliamentarism in that country. The king called together the assembly of clergy,

KING PHILIP IV of France reigned for 21 years.

BONIFACE VIII in the company of cardinals and scholars from the papal chancery.

nobility, and commoners under the pretext of settling his dispute with the pope. But in actual fact, it was a political platform aimed to gain societal support for his policy, invoking slogans about endangered French sovereignty. Thus he could claim that the whole nation was behind him.

In 1302, Boniface VIII promulgated a bull, *Unam Sanctam*, wherein he underlined the absolute primacy of spiritual papal power over temporal royal power. He wrote that if the temporal power erred, it ought to be judged by the spiritual power, whereas if the supreme spiritual power erred, then God alone could be the judge.

Pope Boniface was energetic and resolute, but his Achilles' heel, his sharp tongue, needlessly made him many enemies. *Unam Sanctam* was replete with categorical stipulations, but what really maddened Philip IV was something the pope said at a public consistory. Boniface recalled

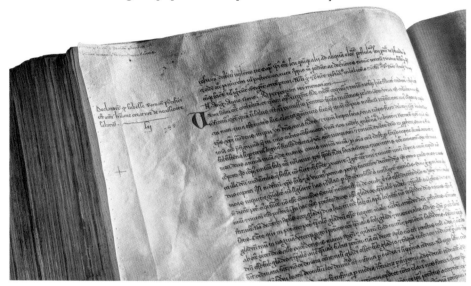

UNAM SANCTAM, Boniface VIII's 1302 bull, confirmed the supremacy of spiritual power (papal) over secular power (royal).

that his predecessors had deposed three kings of France and that he himself could reduce the present king to the role of an ordinary servant.

King Philip took that as a personal insult, one he could not overlook. For the showdown with the pope, he chose his most trusted associate, Guillaume de Nogaret, whom Yves de Loudéac, a contemporary, saw as "a man without a soul". Nogaret addressed an assembly of French bishops and peers in the Louvre on March 12, 1303. He called Pope Boniface a "false prophet", "a master of lies", and an "evident heretic". The pope was accused of sexual abuse—bisexuality and pedophilia—as well as of blasphemy, contact with the devil, murder of his predecessor Celestine V, nepotism, simony, and other evil deeds. Such an event was unheard of in medieval Europe: an ordinary government official daring to accuse the Vicar of Christ publicly of the worst possible transgressions while the bishops present, though aware that the charges were false, remained silent and even supported the slanderer.

However, this was but a prelude to the events to come. On September 8, 1303, Pope Boniface was to have promulgated a bull against King Philip. He did not manage to do it. A day earlier, September 7, Guillaume de Nogaret and an army thirteen-hundred strong attacked Anagni, a town thirty-seven miles from Rome, where the pope was residing in a palace. The papal stronghold was penetrated and the pope captured. Some of the soldiers were intent on killing the pope, but Nogaret restrained

WILHELM DE NOGARET
was Philip IV's trusted associate, a man for special tasks.

DEATH OF BONIFACE VIII
in Rome, October 11, 1303.

ARREST
of Boniface VIII in Anagni Castle.

them. He knew that the murder of the pope would evoke a great outrage throughout Europe. He did not want to kill the pope, just to force him into making concessions. But the pope remained inflexible and was even prepared to be martyred.

So a problem arose. What was to be done with the prisoner? His transportation to France was out of the question, as such a scanty escort would not have been able to fight its way through the Papal States. The next morning, the inhabitants of Anagni began to storm the papal palace. The French withdrew without resisting. The pope was released,

but physically and mentally exhausted, he died in Rome a month later. Dante, in his Divine Comedy published in 1320, located Boniface VIII in the eighth circle of Hell, which was reserved for simonists.

In October 1303, a conclave elected the next pope, Cardinal Nicola Boccasini, who took the regnal name Benedict XI. He aspired to mitigate the dispute with Philip IV. Hence he revoked the excommunication of the king, though he had not shown any signs of remorse, while excommunicating Guillaume de Nogaret and all those who participated in the attack on Boniface VIII. However, Benedict's pontificate was unexpectedly interrupted, when he died of dysentery on July 7, 1304, apparently after eating fresh figs.

The next conclave was held that same month in Perugia. A French legation turned up, headed by Guillaume de Nogaret, which exerted pressure on the participants to elect Cardinal Bertrand de Got from Bordeaux, France, which they did.

The newly elected bishop of Rome, Clement V, wanting to appease Philip IV, had himself crowned in the king's presence in Lyon, not in the Eternal City. According to chronicles, a high wall, under the pressure of a dense crowd, collapsed onto the solemn procession making its way along the city streets. That was seen as a bad omen. John II, the Duke of Brittany, was killed, while the king's brother Charles, the Count of Valois, was seriously injured. The pope himself fell off his horse and was also badly hurt. A large ruby fell off his tiara, and it was never recovered.

BENEDICT XI, whose pontificate lasted just eight months.

Clement V tried to avoid conflicts with Philip IV, as he knew that things could end badly, not just for him, but also for the papacy. Unlike Boniface VIII, he was not a resolute man with a strong character, which explains his policy of appeasement with regard to the king. An indication of this was the revocation of his predecessor's bulls *Clericos Laicos* and *Unam Sanctam*. Despite his submissiveness, however, he did not want to be completely subordinated to the king, but to maintain as much independence as possible. Yet that was increasingly difficult in view of the king's political aspirations.

CLEMENT V, a Frenchman on St. Peter's throne, sought reconciliation with the Paris court.

Subjection to Paris increased for another reason. Rome was then steeped in ongoing conflicts between rich patrician families, particularly the Orsinis and the Colonnas, whose descendants included numerous cardinals and even some popes. Such families arrogated to themselves the right to influence conclave decisions and Holy See policies. At times, disturbances broke out, creating dangerous situations. Hence, Clement V preferred to reside in France. Seeking independence from the Roman aristocracy, the pope ended up dependent on Paris.

Meanwhile, Philip the Fair was seeking funds for the empty state treasury. This time his eyes fell upon the Jews, whose wealth was legendary. On January 21, 1306, he sent a secret order to government officials throughout the country to arrest all Jews—on the same day, and at the same hour, and without exception, including the elderly, women, and children. This occurred on July 22. The imprisoned Jews were informed that all their property was being confiscated, that they had but one month to leave France, and that whoever did not comply would be executed. In effect, about one hundred thousand Jews were banished from France.

They were not allowed to take with them their gold, silver, or valuables, which the king appropriated. Their property was auctioned or given to people as gifts. King Philip, for example, gave his favorite coachman a synagogue in Paris. In order to justify the banishment and plunder of wealth, he had trumped-up charges pressed against the Jews. The king's propagandists, with a successful antipapal campaign under their belts, effectively generated a mass anti-Semitic hysteria.

The robbing of the Jews improved the Crown's financial situation for only a limited time. The financial crisis deepened. There was galloping inflation, which impoverished the population. Riots broke out throughout the country as discontent with the government spread.

So in 1309, the king found new victims. He robbed Italian bankers who were resiliently active in France and had substantial monetary means at their disposal. These people were commonly called Lombards. They too were banished from France, and their wealth confiscated. The expulsion and robbery of the Jews and Italians found favor with some

JEWS WERE EXPELLED

47 times from various countries across Europe. They often found refuge in Poland, where they were never expelled. This painting shows Jews being welcomed into Poland by King Casimir the Great in the 14th century.

of the nobility, who were heavily indebted to them; from day to day, more and more of their financial obligations disappeared.

However, before the crackdown on the Lombard bankers, the king's eye fell upon the Templars, the most powerful and wealthy Church organization in the world, which had amassed huge funds over the years to finance the next crusade. Its wealth was kept in the order's central treasury, located in a tower within the grounds of the the Temple, a fortress in Paris. The king turned to Grand Master Jacques de Molay for a loan, but he refused, knowing that the king, heavily in debt, would never repay the loan.

Barbara Frale relates that the grand master had incurred the king's displeasure for yet another reason. At that time, another crusade was being planned, and Jacques de Molay did not want Philip IV to be its

PLAN OF PARIS
showing
the Temple,
the Templars'
main
headquarters,
where the order's
treasury was
located.

LE TEMPLE

leader, proposing King James II of Aragon instead. Molay was also aware that the organization of a crusade was but a cover for another plan the ambitious Capetian monarch had in mind; for he insidiously intended to attack the Eastern Christians, not the Muslims. He wanted to conquer the Armenian Kingdom of Cilicia and turn it into a French colony. The idea never came to fruition, since Molay revealed the king's true intentions. From that moment, the fate of the Templars was sealed. On September 14, 1307, the king sent a secret order to all his commanders in France instructing them to arrest Templars.

JACQUES DE MOLAY,
the Templars'
last grand
master.

83

The operation was to be coordinated and carried out at the same time in various places. On October 13, at dawn, soldiers appeared at all the order's commanderies in France and arrested the knights. Guillaume de Nogaret led the operation.

Those arrested were immediately interrogated and tortured. The king's officials very rapidly accumulated documentation and sent it to the pope. According to the documents, the Templars were heretics. In reality, though, the documentary evidence had already been prepared some time earlier, and the confessions were but to confirm it. Several years earlier, Philip IV had the knightly order infiltrated in order to collect information on anything that could be used to compromise the Templars.

Frale draws attention to how incredibly quickly, for those times, the indictment against the Templars was drawn up. King Philip wanted to tie the pope's hands by not giving him enough time to respond. The pope was the only person in Catholic Europe who could publicly pronounce

GRAND MASTER
Jacques de Molay during his imprisonment.

binding judgment on a matter pertaining to heresy, especially when it concerned an order that was directly subject to the Holy See.

However, before Clement V managed to respond, the propaganda machine in France had again moved into action, directed by Guillaume de Plaisian. On October 14, the day after the Templars were arrested, Guillaume de Nogaret, then chancellor of France, summoned professors from Sorbonne University to the Cathedral of Notre Dame and declared that the Templars were guilty of denying Christ, profaning the cross, worshipping a deity with a human head, desecrating the Mass, and practicing homosexuality. Public assemblies were organized throughout the country, where the Templars' heresy was presented as an indisputable fact. The king's officials supplied material to Dominican and Franciscan preachers incriminating the order; these preachers then roved about the country publicly repeating the charges. Thus a public judgment was made before the pope announced his own verdict.

ARREST
of Templars accused of heresy.

NOTRE DAME
Cathedral, Paris, where lecturers from the Sorbonne were assembled to be informed of the guilt of the Templars.

The charges against the order began to circulate all over Europe. Its leaders could not defend themselves publicly, while the disoriented Clement V did not have enough information to speak out competently on the matter. The Templars' good name was completely in tatters.

Initially, there were only seven charges against them, but as the investigation proceeded, the number rose to over seventy. The charges seemed to be credible, as they contained a grain of truth. According to Barbara Frale:

> The Templars had a certain secret rite, a custom passed on to new members in utmost secrecy, subjecting recruits to a certain trial in order to prepare them for what often occurred in the Holy Land; the Saracens, when they took Christian prisoners, forced them to

85

✣

renounce their faith, so the Templars recreated situations to inure the participants to the hardships that they might have to face during a crusade. During the rite, the new members had to spit upon the cross and deny Christ. In time, new elements were added to this strange rite, which were characteristic of army practices: humiliating jokes and gestures, and suggestions concerning homosexual acts. However, that which was but a trial was presented by Guillaume de Nogaret as apostasy and perversion.

As to the charge of worshipping a secret deity with a human face, sometimes called Baphomet, many researchers support the theory that the Templars were then in possession of the Shroud of Turin, which they secretly venerated. We know that the relic was stolen in Constantinople during the Fourth Crusade (1204), its whereabouts unknown for a long time. Pope Innocent III condemned the plunder of the capital of the Byzantine Empire and excommunicated the thieves. Hence, admitting to possessing stolen relics would have been tantamount to excommunication. For this reason, the locations of most of the objects that had been looted in Constantinople were unknown for many years. The Shroud of Turin itself was not found until 1357, in Lirey, not far from Troyes in Champagne. It was in the possession of the family of Geoffroi de Charney, a member of the Knights Templar.

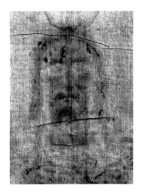

FACE OF JESUS on the Shroud of Turin could well have been mistaken for Baphomet.

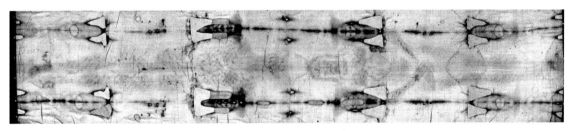

SHROUD OF TURIN was probably in the hands of the Templars after the sack of Constantinople in 1204.

Geoffroi de Charney was one of the four highest-ranked Templars whom King Philip had arrested in 1307. The others were Grand Master Jacques de Molay, Hugues de Pairaud, and Godefroi de Gonneville. In all, 140 monks were detained in France, of whom as many as 136 admitted to blasphemy and sacrilege.

On November 22, 1307, Clement V promulgated a bull, *Pastoralis Praeeminentiae*, wherein he called for the arrest of the Templars and the requisition of their property in favor of the Church. The pope thus wanted to take control of the investigation started by Philip IV and so take the initiative in the matter. He guaranteed that the trial would be held in public and jointly presided over by papal legates and the king's lawyers.

It was not until February 1308 that the papal emissaries were allowed to see the Templars, who were imprisoned in Paris, including Grand Master Jacques de Molay. Most of them had withdrawn their earlier confessions, claiming that they had been exacted under torture. On hearing of this, Clement V suspended the activities of the French Inquisition, which had turned out to be an obedient instrument in the king's hands. So the trial was adjourned.

King Philip, however, wanted the Templars sentenced as quickly as possible, for he had already appropriated their property and required a tribunal decision to legalize his actions. He was counting on proving heresy, as it was a crime that entailed the requisition of goods. Hence he again summoned the Estates General (March 1308), where all supported the movement to suppress the order. The king also saw to it that an antipapal mood was fomented among those assembled. At his instigation, the anonymous pamphlet *Remontrance au peuple de France* (Admonition to the People of France) was circulated. It accused Clement V of inexplicable leniency and deference toward the vile Templars. Another pamphlet, probably written by royal lawyer Pierre Dubois, called on Philip IV to fight the antichrist who supported the corrupt order.

The pope, however, did not want to condemn the order until he was absolutely certain that

87

REPORT OF INTERROGATION
of 13 Templars in 1307,
Caen, France.

FRANCE

ESTATES GENERAL were summoned by Philip IV to meet in this building in Tours.

the charges were true. So he demanded a personal hearing for the accused. King Philip agreed, and the prisoners made their way under escort from Paris to Poitiers, where Clement V officiated. Between March 28 and July 2, 1308, he personally presided over the investigation.

According to Frale, the pope became convinced that the Templars were not heretics, but he found the order guilty of tolerating a vulgar army tradition, unworthy of people who had made religious vows. He did not formally censure them for blasphemy, sacrilege, or apostasy but prescribed penance as a condition of absolution.

The Chinon Parchment, discovered by Barbara Frale in 2001, pertains to the proceedings at the castle. It contains the protocol

concerning the interrogation of the four highest-ranked dignitaries of the Knights Templar. The document reveals facts that were not widely known before. The interrogators did not find the accused guilty of heresy, and they absolved them of other offenses on behalf of the pope. The cardinals saw the initiation rite as the worst offense.

A mitigating circumstance was the fact that the new members had to deny Christ solely in word, not in the heart (*ore non corde*), and then confess to that sin after the rite. So the parchment is proof that the Catholic Church dismissed the worst charges against the Templars and granted them absolution.

However, the further course of events did not end in favor of the Templars. Philip IV decided to attack the papacy directly. He had Bishop Guichard of Troyes accused of sorcery and sentenced to be burned at the stake. Ultimately, the bishop was not executed, but still the matter became another source of pressure on Pope Clement. Yet the king was not satisfied, returning to the old charges of heresy and blasphemy against the deceased Boniface VIII. He demanded

CHINON CASTLE
cell where the Templar leaders were imprisoned.

a posthumous trial, the exhumation of his remains from his tomb in St. Peter's Basilica, the burning of them at the stake, and the scattering of his ashes to the four winds. The king also reached for his most powerful weapon: he threatened to separate the Church in France from the Holy See. The pope was faced with the spectre of a schism.

It was not an idle threat. King Philip decided on a show of strength to convince Pope Clement that the French bishops were on his side. On May 12, 1310, fifty-four Templars, who had withdrawn their earlier confessions, exacted under torture, were burned alive at the stake on a bank of the Seine, singing the Te Deum. They perished, against

Paris ✛

FRANCE

the pope's will, as a consequence of a decision taken by a French provincial council held in Sens.

Clement V yielded and agreed to three of the four conditions laid down by Philip IV: the summoning of a general council on French territory, the condemnation and dissolution of the Knights Templar order, and the establishment of the papal headquarters in France. The pope did not agree to the fourth demand, the condemnation of Boniface VIII and the burning of his remains, since he was aware that to charge his predecessor with heresy would have been tantamount to contradicting the Magisterium of the Church, as well as severing the continuity of St. Peter's throne. It was here that Clement V said: "*Non possumus.*"

90

TEMPLARS
burned
at the stake.

✛

The matter of the Knights Templar order was addressed at the Council of Vienne (1311–1312), not far from Lyon. The majority of the participants did not believe that the Templars were guilty and wanted to allow them the right to defend themselves. The pope, however, was afraid of such a turn of events, as Philip IV threatened to have

Boniface VIII condemned if the council fathers allowed the Templars to speak. In order to prevent this, the pope even imprisoned nine Templars who had turned up in Vienne to defend the good name of their order.

On March 20, 1312, Philip IV entered the town at the head of an armed detachment to keep an eye personally on the course of the council deliberations. Two weeks later, on April 3, in the Cathedral of St. Maurice, Clement V, with the king of France on his right and the king's son on his left, read the bull *Vox in Excelso*. It dissolved the order, but did not condemn it. The dissolution was of a purely administrative nature. The pope emphasized that he had taken the decision "not without bitterness or a sad heart". As if in a tone of self-justification, he added that the Church had dissolved even highly distinguished orders in the past for far less grievous transgressions.

Philip IV accomplished what he had set out to achieve in Vienne, and more: in exchange for not proceeding with the posthumous trial of Boniface VIII, the king received from Clement V the city of Lyon, which had hitherto been a bishop's fief.

Towards the end of the council, the pope promulgated several more bulls concerning the Knights Templar. One of the bulls vested the Templars' property—except for property on the Iberian Peninsula—in another military order, that is, the Order of Knights of the Hospital of Saint John of Jerusalem, later known as the Sovereign Order of Malta. However, the property that the king had seized seven years earlier was lost for good.

In another bull, the pope stated that the Templars who had reconciled themselves with the Church should return to the former commanderies of the order or to other monasteries, while dissenters ought to be punished in accord with canon law, adding that he

COUNCIL OF VIENNE, during which the Knights Templar order was disbanded.

VIENNE CATHEDRAL, where the Council of Vienne was held 1311–1312.

PORTAL St. Maurice Cathedral, Vienne.

91

THE AVIGNON PAPACY

FRANCE

Avignon

AVIGNON was the seat of popes from 1309 to 1377. Clement V was the first to reside in this French city in Provence. He was followed by six successors, all of whom were French: John XXII, Benedict XII, Clement VI, Innocent VI, Urban V, and Gregory XI. In fear for their lives, they preferred to stay far from Rome, which was an arena of populist revolts and constant struggles with and between local patricians. Safety, however, had its price: a state of subjection to the kings of France, who aspired to influence papal policies. The authority of St. Peter's successors suffered because of this, as they lost control of the life of the Church. Eventually, however, Gregory XI, yielding to the advice of St. Catherine of Siena, returned to Rome, ending the so-called Babylonian Captivity of the Papacy.

PALAIS DES PAPES, in Avignon, where seven popes resided.

CLEMENT V   JOHN XXII   BENEDICT XII   CLEMENT VI   INNOCENT VI   URBAN V   GREGORY XI

reserved to his own judgment the fate of the grand master and his closest associates.

On December 22, 1313, Clement V appointed three French cardinals to pass judgment on Jacques de Molay and his three companions. The Templars, in accord with the decision of the Council of Vienne, ought to have been released from prison, as they had been reconciled with the Church. However, the judges, who were of the king's faction, were aware that the grand master knew too much and could well be a threat to Philip IV. Hence they decided to change the decision.

TESTIMONIES of 231 French Templars written on a 65-yard parchment, housed in the Vatican Secret Archives.

On March 18, 1314, the four Templar leaders appeared on a specially built platform next to Notre Dame Cathedral in Paris before three seated Church dignitaries. A crowd gathered to hear the long-awaited verdict: life imprisonment.

Then something unexpected occurred. Jacques de Molay cried out that he was innocent and that the false confessions had been exacted under torture. After a short while, Geoffroi de Charney joined in. The dismayed cardinals adjourned the proceedings. They considered consulting the pope as to further decisions, but Philip IV, quickly informed about the incident, intervened. He had the rebellious prisoners taken to the Ile-des-Javiaux, an island in the Seine, where

93

they were burned alive at the stake that same day, together with thirty-seven other Templars who had withdrawn their confessions. The only Templars to survive were those who had confessed to offenses they had not committed, including Hugues de Pairaud and Godefroi de Gonneville, who died while serving their life imprisonment sentences.

The condemned perished while looking at Notre Dame Cathedral. According to chroniclers, both leaders died calmly, with dignity, reconciled with God. The grand master was said to have called out again that he was innocent and to have summoned the pope and the king of France to appear before the tribunal of God.

Later events caused the widespread belief that God punished those responsible for the Templars' horrible fate. Clement V died

ILE-DES-JAVIAUX, an island in the Seine River, where Templar leaders were executed.

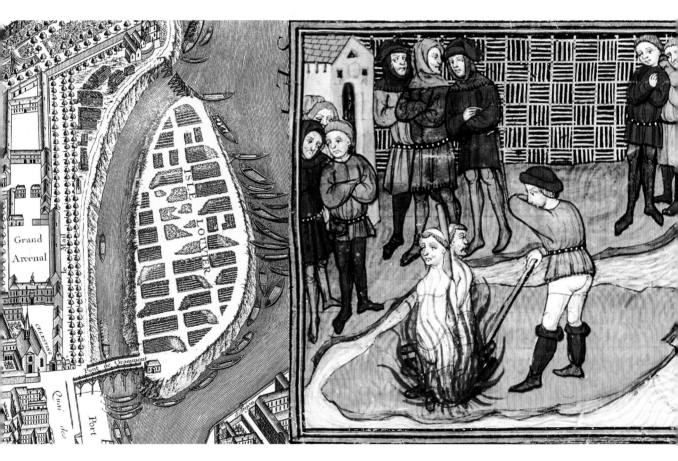

AT THE STAKE Jacques de Molay and Geoffroi de Charney.

of a bowel infection on April 20, 1314, one month after the death of Jacques de Molay. Medical treatment, in the form of powdered emeralds, had been ineffective. Philip IV did not live much longer. That same year, on November 4, he fell off his horse while hunting and suffered a stroke, after which he could not speak. He died as he had lived: morose, silent, and introverted. He passed away on November 29, 1314.

Within a dozen or so years, three of King Philip's sons died unexpectedly: twenty-six-year-old Louis X, "the Quarreler", twenty-eight-year-old Philip V, "the Tall", and thirty-three-year-old Charles IV, "the Fair". Thus the main line of the Capetian dynasty, which had ruled France from 987, died out in 1328, and the House of Valois succeeded to the throne. Philip IV himself contributed to the demise of the dynasty. He accused the wives of two of his sons of adultery and

PHILIP IV
died after falling off his horse while hunting.

had them sentenced to life imprisonment (the lovers of both princesses met a worse fate: tortured, maimed, and burned); his daughters-in-law did not leave male descendants.

As for the Templars, only those who lived in France were tried, imprisoned, and executed. They were not persecuted in other countries: the king of Cyprus took no notice of their condemnation, the Council of Tarragona exonerated the Templars in Catalonia and Aragon, the Council of Salamanca cleared them of all the charges against them in Castile, and the archbishop of Lisbon established their innocence in Portugal. So the campaign against the Knights Templar was solely an intrigue concocted by King Philip IV.

The rulers of the Iberian Peninsula highly valued the Templars' piety and knightly fortitude. After the dissolution of the order, they offered them new opportunities: King James II of Aragon founded the Order of Montesa specially for them, and King Denis I of Portugal also founded an order for them, the Military Order of Christ, with its headquarters in Tomar Castle. The defense of the southern

CORONATION
of King Philip V, "the Tall", who died at the age of 28 after drinking dirty water from a well.

95

Tomar

PORTUGAL

border of the kingdom against the Moors was a new mission for the monk-knights. Later, during the age of geographic discoveries, they evangelized other continents. The Templars' red cross fluttered on the white sails of Portuguese galleons, brigs, and frigates.

Barbara Frale, having scrutinized a great number of documents on the Templars' trial, has no doubts as to its glaring injustice. As a result of false charges, innocent people perished, and a large amount of wealth was misappropriated.

CLOISTER
of Tomar Castle, headquarters of the Military Order of Christ, Portugese branch of the Templars.

Asked if the onus of this crime committed against the Templars was on both the king of France and the pope, Frale replied that their levels of responsibility were incomparable: "Philip IV acted with premeditation from the very beginning in order to seize the Templars' wealth, stopping at nothing, whereas Clement V was blackmailed and put into situations where he had to choose the lesser evil. Of course, some responsibility rests with him too, but he never took the initiative in destroying the order. He even tried to salvage what was possible and minimize the losses."

Frale does not attempt to justify the pope, but she does try to understand his motives.

He found himself in a dramatic situation. He lived in France, practically at the mercy of the king, who had him and the Templars in his hands, threatening the Church with a schism. The pope had almost the whole of the episcopate against him. He was faced with a terrible alternative: to yield to the king and condemn the order, or else to save it and face the trial of Boniface VIII and the severing of France from the Church, which could occasion terrible results for the whole Catholic world, as France was the largest Christian country in Europe. Hence the pope sacrificed a part to save the whole, for which he was responsible. He sacrificed an institution numbering two thousand members for a France of twenty million. The order itself, after a seven-year investigation, was practically in ruins and surrounded by an aura of scandal.

There was nobody willing to join the order. It had lost its usefulness to the Church. Hence its dissolution seemed the only option for Clement. As a canon law expert, he used legal formulas that did not condemn the Templars but still dissolved their order on an administrative basis. He strived to save Jacques de Molay, but he proved helpless before the extremely strong-willed king.

Frale has no doubt that the main reason for the pope's deference to the king was the Church's subjection to the Crown. If Clement V had been beyond the reach of Philip IV, things would have certainly turned out otherwise. That scenario has recurred in history many a time.

Philip IV was something of a prototype for a new kind of European ruler: recognizing no spiritual power above his own, capable of any crime whatsoever, prepared to make false charges, to murder, and to seize his victims' wealth. Guillaume de Nogaret was a forerunner of future secret police and security service chiefs, who specialized in administering torture, exacting confessions, and organizing show trials. Guillaume de Plaisian foreshadowed ministers of propaganda who conducted campaigns of hate. As this book continues, we will come across such characters yet again.

CROSS
belonging to the Knights Templar.

MILITARY ORDER OF CHRIST

The Military Order of Christ, founded after the dissolution of the Knights Templar, played a significant role in Portugal's history. A new stage began in 1417, when Prince Henry the Naviga-

tor, regarded as the creator of Portugal's colonial empire, became the order's grand master. He was the founder of the University of Lisbon and the world's first nautical school in Sagres. He sponsored the development of the naval fleet and funded sea voyages that led to many geographical discoveries. The order participated in those undertakings. At the beginning of the 16th century, it had 454 commanderies on three continents.

In 1492, Pope Alexander VI dispensed the knights from their religious vows. So the order was reformed into a secular institution and as such was subordinated to the Portuguese Crown. Only the priests in Tomar continued to lead a monastic life. In time, it was transformed into a mere order of merit—Portuguese kings conferred membership in such orders for outstanding services to the Crown—while the office of grand master was assumed by the king himself. To this day, it is a high state commendation in that country.

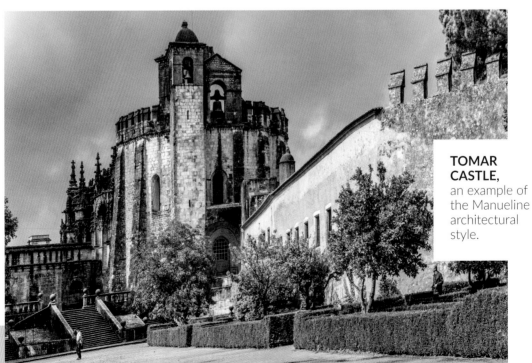

TOMAR CASTLE, an example of the Manueline architectural style.

CHAPEL,
Tomar Castle,
the spiritual
center of the
Military Order
of Christ.

TRADITION

The Crusades

CHAPTER 3

The Crusades

Dangerous links between the Cross
and the sword: from triumph to defeat

Vatican

ITALY

**TOMB OF
INNOCENT III**
Archbasilica
of St. John
Lateran.

The oldest complete file of papal documents in the Vatican Secret Archives pertains to the pontificate of Innocent III (1198–1216). Due to historical turmoil, there are few documents connected with preceding popes, while those on Innocent, one of the most influential popes in Church history, amount to over six thousand letters—including abundant correspondence with European rulers—not to mention encyclicals, bulls, and other writings, together constituting an all but inexhaustible source of historical knowledge.

In a letter to one of his legates, Innocent III wrote: "I put action above contemplation." And he did indeed act with extraordinary vigor.

Elected pope at the age of thirty-seven, he had boundless energy: he called for Crusades, excommunicated monarchs, interdicted states, and reconciled feuding rulers. He undoubtedly shaped European politics, as well as leaving a great mark on the religious life of his time—and of times to come. He convened the largest medieval Church gathering, the Fourth Lateran Council (1215), which saw 1,200 participants, and also initiated a reform that led to a spiritual renewal of the Church. Further, he approved two religious orders, those of Dominic and Francis, whose ideal of poverty was close to his heart – he had gold and silver tableware in his apartments replaced with wooden and glass tableware, and limited his meals to three courses. His dynamism would earn the Church's gratitude for centuries.

Innocent III was also a poet. Tradition attributes to him the hymns "Come, Holy Spirit" and "Stabat Mater". He also wrote *De Miseria*

ST. DOMINIC DE GUZMÁN founded the Dominicans (Order of Preachers), approved by Innocent III.

ST. FRANCIS of Assisi founded the Order of Friars Minor, approved by Innocent III.

RULE OF LIFE drawn up by St. Francis in 1223.

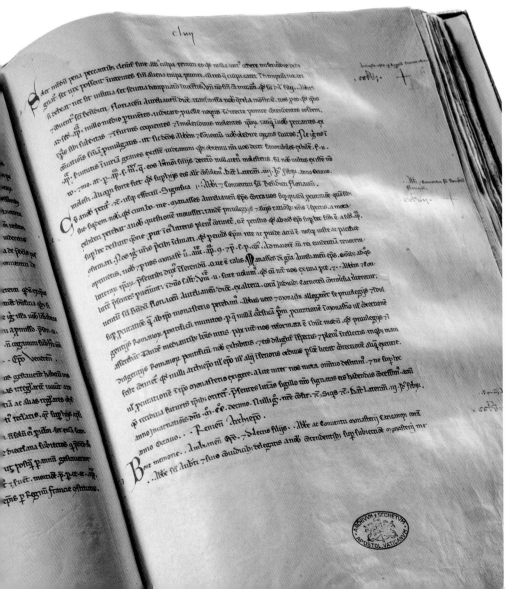

INNOCENT III'S DREAM

IN THE BASILICA of St. Francis of Assisi, there is a famous series of twenty-eight frescoes, known as the Legend of St. Francis, painted by Giotto di Bondone towards the end of the 13th century. The sixth fresco is a scene entitled *The Dream of Innocent III*, which depicts the pope asleep on a bed under a baldachin and a monk in a brown habit supporting a leaning church. The scene pertained to a dream that Innocent III was said to have had regarding the Lateran Basilica in Rome: the basilica was close to collapsing but then was saved at the last moment by an inconspicuous monk, namely, St. Francis of Assisi, who was in Rome seeking the pope's endorsement for the order he intended to found. The extraordinary dream persuaded the pope to approve it.

INNOCENT III is regarded as one of the greatest popes of the Middle Ages.

FRESCO BY GIOTTO in the basilica in Assisi, depicting Innocent III's dream.

Assisi

ITALY

Condicionis Humane (On the Wretchedness of the Human Condition), which states:

O my mother, why did you give birth to a son of sadness and bitterness? . . . O wicked humiliation of human existence! . . . Let us consider the plants and trees: they produce flowers, leaves, and fruits, and alas, you, O man, produce lice and tapeworms. They pour forth oil, wine, and balm, and you, spit, urine, and dung. They give off sweet fragrance, and you, you spread an abominable stench. . . . Man is conceived from blood corrupted by the heat of lust, and in the end, his body's only companions are worms in the grave. Living, he breeds lice and tapeworms; dead, he breeds worms and flies. Living, he produces dung and vomit; dead, he produces rot and stench. Alive, he only fattens himself; when he dies, a host of worms will fatten themselves. For what stinks worse than a human corpse? What is more terrible than a dead man? The sight of man whose embrace we cherished in life will become unbearable in death.[1]

An extraordinary work for a pope, a bitter testimony to his reflections on the sinful human condition and on the vanity of existence. He had no illusions about himself, fully aware of his own sinfulness. Yet he saw himself as a servant of God, and that self-abasement only pertained to him personally, as he saw the office that had been entrusted to him in a completely different light. He wrote a letter at the very beginning of his pontificate (1198) to the prefect Acerbius and the nobles of Tuscany, putting forth a bold vision of the papacy:

Just as the founder of the universe established two great lights in the firmament of heaven, the greater light to rule the day, and the lesser light to rule the night, so too He set two great dignities in the firmament of the universal church, . . . the greater one to rule the day, that is, souls, and

the lesser to rule the night, that is, bodies. These dignities are the papal authority and the royal power. Now just as the moon derives its light from the sun and is indeed lower than it in quantity and quality, in position and in power, so too the royal power derives the splendor of its dignity from the pontifical authority.[2]

He not only wrote of the vision, but also implemented it. His predecessors were constantly embroiled in disputes with successive emperors, who strove to subordinate the Church to themselves along the lines of Byzantine rulers. Providence turned out to be charitable to Innocent III. Three months before he became pope, Holy Roman Emperor Henry VI, who raised claims to supremacy over the pope, died of malaria at the age of thirty-two. Henry left behind a three-year-old heir, Frederick, who was too young to rule. It was an opportune moment for the pope, who diplomatically maximized the Church's independence from the state and even demonstrated the supremacy of the spiritual power over the temporal power. Historians see his pontificate as the zenith of the papacy's influence in Europe.

Innocent III called for three Crusades during his pontificate. One of them was a success and regarded as a decisive moment in Reconquista history. On July 12, 1212, the Castilian, Aragonese, Navarrese,

HENRY VI,
Holy Roman emperor and king of Sicily, one the greatest rulers in German history (left).

FREDERICK II,
Henry VI's son and heir to the imperial throne (right).

and Portuguese armies defeated the Moors at the Battle of Las Navas de Tolosa, thereby precipitating the expulsion of the Muslims from Western Europe. The Emirate of Granada soon became the last Islamic enclave, a vassal state of Castile, in the Iberian Peninsula.

The Albigensian Crusade (or Cathar Crusade), the second Crusade initiated by Innocent III, was against the Cathars in southern France and

lasted for twenty years, ending with a hard-won victory thirteen years after Innocent III's death. The Fourth Crusade, which he saw as the most important, vexed him most. Its stated intent had been to recapture the Muslim-controlled city of Jerusalem. However, it compromised Catholic soldiers and deepened the divisions in the Christian world.

Innocent III's bull of December 1202 excommunicated the participants in the Fourth Crusade. Why did he excommunicate Crusaders who were on their way to fight the Muslims? Well, en route the Catholic Crusaders plundered a Catholic city: Venetians and Franks attacked and plundered Zadar—including its churches—on November 24, 1202.

Innocent III learned of the Crusaders' plans before they attacked. His emissary Abbot Guy of Vaux-de-Cernay appeared before the leaders of the Crusade with a letter from the pope, wherein he threatened

LAS NAVAS DE TOLOSA, key victory for Christians led by Alphonso VIII in 1212.

107

to excommunicate anyone who attacked the Croatian city. The Crusaders ignored the papal ultimatum and stormed the town.

How did the pope, universally acknowledged as the highest spiritual and moral authority of the time, lose the respect of these knights who saw themselves as defenders of the Faith and the Church? Why did they ignore the Vicar of Christ, thus risking the ultimate punishment—eternal damnation?

GUY OF VAUX-DE-CERNAY, papal delegate.

CHURCH OF ST. DONATUS in Zadar.

In order to understand this, we have to go back several centuries, when, after the fall of the Roman Empire and the migrations of peoples, a new order emerged in Europe. One veritable curse of that era was the abundance of private, local wars between feudal lords, universally seen as the best way to redress wrongs. They mainly occurred in the world of the Franks, appealing to the old Germanic right

KNIGHTS in battle—bas-relief in the Château d'Angers.

of private vengeance, which obliged all the members of a family, including distant cousins, to participate in such conflicts, often initiated for spurious reasons. So the nobility were in a state of permanent conflict. No principles of honor were upheld, and robbery, violence, and murder were daily occurrences.

The Church tried to oppose this destructive nightmare, but she was too weak to be effective. It was not until the beginning of the 11th century that the *Treuga Dei* (Truce of God), one of the most important peace initiatives in European history, was introduced. It envisaged a ban on waging wars from Wednesday evening to Monday morning, and later throughout the whole of Advent and Lent. It was

CRUSADERS taking a city—illumination from 13th-century *Morgan Bible* (*Crusader Bible*), wherein Old Testament scenes are set in medieval Europe

ARMOR, medieval French knight's helmet and shield.

first propagated in 1027 at the initiative of Abbot Oliba, a Catalonian Benedictine, during a synod in Elne, France.

The Order of St. Benedict played a prominent role in civilizing the nobility and raising its moral level. In the 10th century, it launched a renewal of European Christianity. Cluny Abbey was its center, where the main ideas of the Gregorian Reforms were formulated. Under the influence of the Cluny movement, a new chivalric code developed between

Clermont

FRANCE

POPE URBAN II
initiated the First
Crusade.

**CLERMONT-
FERRAND
CATHEDRAL,**
where Urban II
proclaimed
the First Crusade.
A monument
stands in
the square.

1170 and 1220, with its own code of honor. Pope Gregory VII and Pope Urban II, regarded as two of the most outstanding popes in history, came from the ranks of the Cluny movement. The latter initiated the First Crusade in 1095 at the Council of Clermont in order to retake the Holy Land, especially the Holy Sepulchre, from the Seljuq Turks.

In Rome, we had a meeting with Massimo Viglione, an Italian historian, one of the foremost experts on the Crusades in the Apennine Peninsula. He maintains that it not possible to understand that episode in European history without going back to the 7th century, when Islam first arose. The Muslim religion expanded through conquest from the very outset. The Koran itself is full of exhortations and incentives to use force, which Muhammad frequently employed himself. Al-Tabari (d. 923), a Persian historian and theologian, lists as many as twenty-seven great armed incursions by the first generation of Muslims on the direct orders of the Muhammad.

The new religion began to conquer the Christian world by the sword. The Muslims first attacked places that were part of the Byzantine Empire, capturing Damascus in 635, Jerusalem and Antioch in 638, and Alexandria in 643. After mastering Syria and Egypt, some of the Muslims marched west and occupied North Africa, while some went east and subjugated Armenia and Persia (now Iran). In

711, the Moors invaded Spain and Portugal, and in a short time, they occupied almost the whole of the Iberian Peninsula, apart from the mountainous territory in the north. From 717 to 718, the Arabs besieged by land and sea Constantinople, though they failed to take it. In 732, they attacked the Franks. They got as far as the Loire, but were defeated at the Battle of Tours (or Battle of Poitiers) on October 10, by an army led by Charles Martel. That did not discourage them from further conquests. They harassed Italy throughout the 9th century, establishing the Emirate of Bari and the Emirate of Taranto and occupying Sicily and Sardinia. In 846, they even sacked Rome, plundering and profaning St. Peter's Basilica and the Basilica of St. Paul outside the Walls. Torn apart by internal conflicts, Europe was unable to resist those invasions.

In conquered territories, the Muslims treated Christians and Jews as second-class subjects. It is true that as "People of the Book",

Poitiers

FRANCE

BATTLE OF TOURS,
or Battle of Poitiers. In 732, the Franks were victorious.

THE SPIRITUAL CENTER OF THE MIDDLE AGES

THE BENEDICTINE abbey in Cluny, Burgundy, was founded in 910, the largest monastery ever built in Europe. It gave birth to the reform that renewed the face of Christianity in Europe between the 11th and 13th centuries. The Cluniac Reforms, based on St. Benedict's original rule, which focused on the spiritual and intellectual development of the faithful, imparted a new momentum to the spreading of Christ's teaching. Pope Gregory VII, a product of Cluny, was accustomed to saying that no abbey could compare with Cluny as there had not been a single abbot there who was not a saint.

The abbey created its own federated order, in which subsidiary houses (priories), all adhering to the same rule, answered directly to the abbot of Cluny. It is estimated that in its heyday the federation had over one thousand houses and twenty thousand monks. From the 13th century on, Cluny gradually became less significant, with other orders coming into prominence, such as the Cistercians, Franciscans, and Dominicans. In 1790, the abbey was closed during the French Revolution. Two decades later, the main church—the longest-lasting building of the Middle Ages, a real pearl of Romanesque architecture—was destroyed in 1811 on the orders of Napoleon Bonaparte, who had a stable built in its place. A side chapel, ending a transept arm, has survived, the size of which bears testimony to how large the church once was, its interior recalling the Roman Forum.

Cluny

FRANCE

BENEDICTINE ABBEY in Cluny once radiated spiritually throughout Europe.

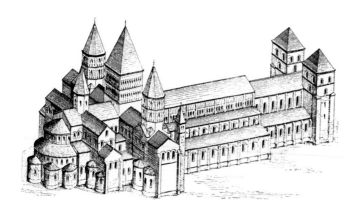

Christians and Jews were allowed to practice their religion, but they could not display their religious symbols and were forced to pay a high *jizya* tax. Christians could not build new churches, which limited the development of Christianity. Europeans were permitted to go on pilgrimages to the Holy Land, but they had to pay a tribute. In 800, caliphs from the Abbasid dynasty even returned sacred places in Palestine into the care of Charlemagne, but Islam gradually pushed Christian influences out of the Near East, where it is estimated that in the 7th century Muslims made up barely 10 percent of the population; by the 10th century they were 80 percent.

The situation of Christians in those lands worsened in the 11th century, as those who wanted to retain official positions had to give up the Faith and accept Islam. Caliph Al-Hakim bi-Amr Allah, of the Fatimid dynasty, unleashed a bloody persecution of Christians (1009–1014). A great number of churches were burnt down, and a large part of the Church of the Holy Sepulchre in Jerusalem was destroyed. A conflict-ridden, powerless Europe could only listen to the alarming news from the Levant. The situation did not improve until the death of the mad and despotic tyrant, who even claimed to be God.

CHARLEMAGNE
first emperor in Western Europe after the fall of the Roman Empire.

MAHMUD OF GHAZNI
created a vast Muslim empire in Asia in the 11th century.

In 1070, Palestine was conquered by a new Near East power, that is, the Seljuks, who also professed Islam. Compared to the Arab rulers from the Fatimid dynasty, who allowed free access to holy places, the new rulers were less tolerant. In 1076, the inhabitants of Jerusalem rose up against the invaders, but the Seljuqs crushed the revolt and slaughtered the population. Turkish detachments also massacred pilgrims and pilgrimages to the Holy Land all but ceased.

This time the Muslim aggression chanced on another historical moment. As Massimo Viglione says, Europe was then in the prime of its youth, bursting with energy. The economy developed dynamically, trade flourished, the population grew. Due to the Cluniac Reforms, the Church's authority also grew, particularly the papacy's, which during Pope Gregory VII's pontificate managed to stay independent of the

WALLS OF JERUSALEM, which were repeatedly besieged, stormed, destroyed, and rebuilt.

emperor. In such a favorable situation, Pope Urban II initiated the First Crusade in 1095.

To the pope, and to the Christians of that time, the First Crusade was a defensive war, a response to Muslim aggression. Its aim was not the occupation of Jerusalem, but the liberation of the Holy City. Summoning Catholic knights to make haste to aid eastern Catholics, the pope saw it as an act of mercy towards fellow believers. Apart from that, the emperors, threatened by the expansion of Islam, continually appealed for help from Constantinople.

The lack of access to the Holy Sepulchre caused the first great crisis of European consciousness. People began to ask themselves questions: Did God want the Holy Land to be in pagan hands and the followers of Christ denied access to it? Were Christians incapable of uniting to regain their Savior's homeland? What did God want them

COUNCIL OF CLERMONT organized the First Crusade in 1095.

to do? Those questions bothered not only scholars and theologians of the time, but also ordinary people.

Urban II realized that an extraordinary opportunity had arisen for the knights' energy—which had hitherto been expended in fratricidal wars, senselessly shedding Europe's blood—to be utilized for a more noble cause. On November 27, 1095, he gave a solemn speech during the Council of Clermont, mentioning the enslavement of Christians in the Holy Land and the destruction of churches by the Muslims.

According to Fulcher of Chartres, he said:

> Let those who, for a long time, have been robbers, now become knights. Let those who have been fighting against their brothers and relatives now fight in a proper way against the barbarians. Let those who have been serving as mercenaries for small pay now obtain the eternal reward. Let those who have been wearing themselves out in both body and soul now work for a double honor.[3]

In Baldric of Dol's version, the pope was even more vivid:

You, girt about with the badge of knighthood, are arrogant with great pride; you rage against your brothers and cut each other in pieces. . . . The Holy Church has reserved a soldiery for herself to help her people, but you debase her wickedly to her hurt. . . . You, the oppressors of children, plunderers of widows; you, guilty of homicide, of sacrilege, robbers of another's rights; you who await the pay of thieves for the shedding of Christian blood. . . . If, forsooth, you wish to be mindful of your souls, either lay down the girdle of such knighthood, or advance boldly, as knights of Christ, and rush as quickly as you can to the defence of the Eastern Church.[4]

In Robert the Monk's account, the pope added:

Jerusalem is the navel of the world; the land is fruitful above all others, like another paradise of delights. This the Redeemer of the human race has made illustrious by his advent, has beautified by residence, has consecrated by suffering, has redeemed by death, has glorified by burial. This royal city, therefore, situated at the centre of the world, is now held captive by His enemies and is in subjection to those who do not know God, to the worship of the heathens. She seeks therefore and desires to be liberated, and does not cease to implore you to come to her aid.[5]

The pope closed with the following admonition:

Whoever, therefore, shall determine upon this holy pilgrimage and shall make his vow to God to that effect and shall offer himself to Him as a living sacrifice, holy, acceptable unto God, shall wear the sign of the cross of the Lord on his forehead or on his breast. When, truly, having fulfilled his vow he wishes to return, let him place the cross on his back between his shoulders. Such, indeed, by the two-fold action will fulfill the precept of the Lord, as He commands in the Gospel, "He that taketh not his cross and followeth after me, is not worthy of me."[6]

When Urban II had finished his call to liberate Jerusalem, the assembled believers loudly cried out: "It is the will of God." The assembled were fired with enthusiasm, as were the masses throughout Western Europe. Someone was finally responding to the greatest challenge that had ever faced the Christian world. Multitudes throughout Europe were prepared to leave their land, homes, and families behind, endanger their health and lives to make their way to a distant, unknown land

POPE URBAN II
granted
all the participants
of the Crusade
a plenary
indulgence.

in order to do battle against one of the world's most powerful armies. Viglione stresses that it is not possible to understand such an attitude without a religious motive. Volunteers were inspired by the most worthy cause one could imagine, bereft of any political considerations or a desire to get rich. This Crusade ruined many a feudal lord who had to borrow money or sell his estate to maintain his retinue and soldiers.

RAYMOND OF TOULOUSE promising to liberate Jerusalem in the First Crusade.

Urban did not use the word "crusade". It did not appear until the 13th century. The first Crusaders talked of making a pilgrimage, of a journey overseas, or an expedition to the Holy Land. They saw their undertaking in a spiritual light rather than a military one.

A question arose at the very outset: Who was to lead the Crusade? Theoretically, the leader ought to have been the most important of the Catholic rulers, that is, the emperor. But Emperor Henry IV had been excommunicated by Urban II, hence he could not participate in the Crusade. King Philip I of France had also been excommunicated, as had King Eric I of Denmark. And King William II of England refused to recognize Urban II as pope. No other European ruler had sufficient authority to lead the Crusade. Hence Urban II appointed his legate Adhemar de Monteil, bishop of Le Puy, to lead

117

the Crusade. As he had no experience in warfare, he was rather the spiritual leader, while prominent feudal lords led the army. So the First Crusade turned out to be a collaborative affair between the papacy and the nobility.

However, before an army had been raised, the People's Crusade had already set off for the Near East. It was a spontanous grassroots movement that managed to gather tens of thousands in a short time, mainly from communes, including peasants, paupers, minor knights, and common criminals. The majority were unskilled in warfare. They set off from Germany, led by Peter the Hermit, a charismatic orator, and Walter Sans Avoir, a well-trained minor knight. The pope and the bishops tried to persuade the people, unfamiliar with war, to forgo the expedition, but their enthusiasm, fired by the preachers, was too intense. That great crowd, including a host of women and

PETER THE HERMIT,
Peter of Amiens, showing Crusaders the way to Jerusalem.

children, marched through Germany and Hungary towards Byzantium. En route, those undisciplined masses massacred Jews, led by some well-known rabble-rousers, namely, Count Emicho of Flonheim, a priest named Folkmar, and a monk named Gottschalk.

Massimo Viglione, who has thoroughly researched the matter, is of the opinion that the massacres were not of a religious nature, but of an economic and social one. At that time, Christians in Europe were forbidden to practice moneylending, so Jews, who were forbidden from practicing many other professions, became bankers and financiers. They enjoyed great favor among feudal lords, to whom they granted loans, whereas ordinary people had an aversion to them. The entire Jewish people was identified with usury, enriching itself—as the people saw it—at the cost of poor peasants. Participants in the People's Crusade, beyond any control, were finally able to vent their anger against them; hence the pogroms.

In Germany, local bishops defended the Jews in, for example, Speyer, Worms, and Mainz. In Hungary, King Coloman the Learned took steps to prevent attacks and murders. The most lawless of the Crusaders, led by Gottschalk, were surrounded near Székesfehérvár

KING COLOMAN
of Hungary fought against the People's Crusade.

118

and forced to lay down their arms, after which the Hungarian cavalry massacred them. Others, from Germany, besieged Moson Castle in Hungary, but after six weeks, they were defeated.

The People's Crusade was made up of two self-proclaimed armies: a German army led by Peter the Hermit and a French one led by Walter Sans Avoir, which turned out to be the better prepared. At first, it seemed that they would make their way through Hungary without any major incidents, but in Zemun, on the Byzantium border, they killed four thousand Hungarians. They then fled across the Sava to Belgrade. After taking Belgrade, they pillaged and burned the city. Inspired by that success, they reached Constantinople, attacking Christian villages

PEOPLE'S CRUSADE
disarmed and undressed by Hungarian soldiers.

and destroying churches along the way. The Byzantine emperor Alexios I Komnenos, wanting to get rid of the troublesome rabble as quickly as possible, equipped them and sent them off eastward.

They made their way toward Nicaea, occupied by Seljuk Turks. They initially had successes en route, until they came up against Sultan Kilij Arslan I's large army, which defeated them during the siege of the fortress in Xerigordos and then, on October 21, 1096, routed them at the Battle of

GODFREY OF BOUILLON, a leader of the First Crusade, "Defender of the Holy Sepulchre".

TROUBADOURS sang about the heroism of Crusader knights.

120

BATTLE OF DORYLAEUM, in which the Crusaders defeated the Seljuk Turks in 1097.

Civetot. Only a few survived. Thus ended the unfortunate People's Crusade, which did not have much in common with Urban II's ideals.

In the meantime, a true Christian army had been raised. Feudal lords headed four contingents, who had not, however, established a joint command. The names of some of the lords were to be lauded by bards and troubadours throughout Europe. The first contingent was led by Hugh, Count of Vermandois, the brother of King Philip I of France; Godfrey of Bouillon, Duke of Lower Lorraine; and his Godfrey's cousin Baldwin of Bourg. The second contingent was led by Prince Bohemond of Taranto, leader of the Normans from southern Italy, and Tancred of Hauteville, his nephew.

Count Robert of Flanders, Duke Robert Curthose of Normandy (William the Conqueror's son), and Count Stephen of Blois led the third contingent. The largest contingent was led by Count Raymond of Toulouse and included Adhemar de Monteil, the apostolic legate and bishop of Le Puy; all in this contingent were commonly called Franks.

The international army, initially of four thousand cavalry and twenty-five thousand infantry, arrived in Constantinople and was warmly welcomed by Emperor Alexios I. On June 19, 1097, it recaptured Nicaea, which was returned to the Byzantines. On July 1, it defeated the Seljuk Turks at the Battle of Dorylaeum. On June 2, 1098, after a seven-month siege, it captured well-fortified Antioch, just three days before the arrival of Muslim reinforcements. After the Crusaders had taken the city, the roles reversed, the Turks laying siege to Antioch. But the knights made a bold sally and defeated the enemy.

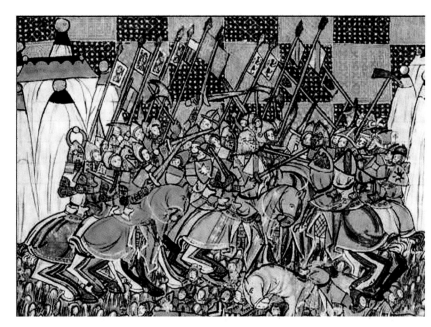

After that victory, there was a serious difference of opinion among the leaders of the Crusade, namely between Bohemond and Raymond of Toulouse. The former took control of Antioch and did not want to fight on. The latter insisted on marching to Jerusalem. Bishop Adhemar, who mediated at such times, had died of an illness in 1098. Lacking his intervention, neither strong-willed leader would back down. The majority of the Crusaders, however, wanted to continue the fight, and they issued an ultimatum: if no one would give them the order to march out, they would destroy the walls of Antioch. Bohemond then agreed to push on toward Jerusalem.

On June 7, 1099, after capturing Muslim strongholds on the way, the Franks saw Jerusalem on the horizon. Six days later, they launched the first attack, which ended with heavy losses. Shortly afterwards, they received news that a powerful Fatimid army had left Egypt to lift the siege and was but forty-seven miles away in Ashkelon. Hence the Crusaders had to capture Jerusalem before reinforcements arrived. So virtually the same situation as at Antioch arose again, except that there were fewer soldiers (1,500 cavalry and 25,000 infantry), while the Jerusalem walls were much more massive (almost fify feet high) and held a strong and rested garrison, recently arrived from the Nile delta. The Crusaders were in a difficult situation. They were short of water, as the Muslims had poisoned nearby water sources, and food supplies were low. It was the middle of summer, and the heat was intense, particularly for Europeans dressed in full armor. It was impossible to capture the city without siege engines. Yet they did not lose hope. Their main asset was extraordinary determination. They had covered thousands of miles over three years, fighting bloody battles en route, finally to reach their destination. Only one thing remained: the liberation of the cradle of Christianity, Jerusalem, the center of the earth,

LEADERS OF THE FIRST CRUSADE: **1.** Tancred of Hauteville, **2.** Bohemond I of Taranto, and **3.** Raymond IV, Count of Toulouse.

121

as Urban II had said. Despite the hopeless situation, they believed that they would succeed.

The arrival in Jaffa of a flotilla from Genoa on June 17 turned out to be a turning point. After taking the port, the Genoese, covering forty miles, provided the Crusaders with wood to build siege

JULY 15, 1099, Jerusalem was liberated from the Muslims.

engines. On July 15, the Crusaders launched an attack and captured the city.

What took place afterward casts a shadow on the Crusades to this day. The Crusaders carried out a bloody massacre. Contrary to what is sometimes said, the Crusaders did not murder Syrian, Armenian, or Greek Christians living in the city, or Jews, since the governor Iftikhar al-Dawla ordered them to leave before the arrival of the Franks, not wanting to risk mutiny within the city walls.

During the siege, Muslim civilians were permitted to leave the city, as there were not enough Crusaders to guard the forty-foot city wall; so they concentrated almost all their forces on selected parts of the fortifications. The lack of a tight blockade saw a large part of the inhabitants depart, attested to by contemporary accounts of the serious overcrowding in nearby Ashkelon.

Hence, when the city was attacked, there were mainly soldiers present, along with some inhabitants. They were concentrated at the Temple Mount, in the Al-Aqsa Mosque, and in the Dome of the Rock, which were the last resistance points. The Crusaders killed all of them, except those who had taken refuge in the Tower of David, to whom Count Raymond of Toulouse personally gave a guarantee

BATTLE SCENE between Crusaders and Muslims.

of safety. The governor Iftikhar al-Dawla, and his retinue were among those set free.

According to Massimo Viglione, there was no justification for the massacre, but one can attempt to explain why it came about. One must remember that in those days similar things happened very frequently. The rule was as follows: if a city surrendered voluntarily, it was shown mercy; if it resisted, it could be plundered. That was the practice of the Muslims. On August 10, 1096, the Turks slaughtered twelve thousand of the People's Crusade in Xerigordos. On June 4, 1098, they butchered the whole Pont de Fer fortress garrison. The same rule also applied to battles among Muslim believers. On August 26, 1098, one year before the arrival of the Crusaders, Jerusalem was recaptured from the Seljuqs by the Egyptians, who murdered all the defenders.

Running amok on the battlefield, the Crusaders, says Viglione, no doubt had in mind four centuries of Muslim conquests, when men were killed, women sold to harems, and children Islamized. But now they could finally take revenge for centuries of defeat and humiliation. They also probably did not want to take prisoners due to the approaching Fatimid army.

We know that the leaders of the Crusade did not participate in the massacres (with the exception of Tancred of Hauteville). Godfrey of Bouillon fasted for one month on his knees in the Church of the Holy Sepulchre to atone for the crimes committed by the Crusaders.

After capturing Jerusalem, a question arose as to who was to rule the city. Count Raymond of Toulouse was certainly the most deserving. Without his iron will and resolve, success would not have been possible. On being offered the throne, he said that he would not wear a gold crown in the place where his Savior, Jesus Christ, wore a crown of thorns. Godfrey of Bouillon, the first to break through the city walls, also refused, using a similar argument, but agreed to assume the title "Defender of the Holy Sepulchre".

BATTLE OF ASCALON, 1099, sealed the European knights' victory in the First Crusade.

The Franks did not rest on their laurels. On September 12, they surprised an Egyptian army, routing it near Ascalon. Count Raymond of Toulouse, who soon after left the Holy Land, distinguished himself in the battle. Most of the Crusaders also returned home, having fulfilled the vows they had made. Thanks to reinforcements from Europe, most of Judea and Galilee were occupied. Later, new Christian states were established: the Principality of Antioch, the County of Edessa, and the County of Tripoli.

In July 1100, Godfrey of Bouillon, barely forty years of age, suddenly fell ill and died. He was replaced by Baldwin of Boulogne, Count of Edessa, his brother, who had no scruples about taking the title of king. Thus arose the new Kingdom of Jerusalem, which lasted

CORONATION
of Baldwin II,
third ruler
of the Kingdom
of Jerusalem.

CHAPEL
of the Holy
Sepulchre,
in the Jerusalem
basilica.

**KINGS
RICHARD
AND PHILIP II**
receiving the keys
to Acre after
the city was
taken in 1191.

**FORTRESS
IN ACRE,**
the Crusaders'
main port in
the Holy Land.

JERUSALEM after it was liberated by the Crusaders — 12th-century painting.

ST. BERNARD OF CLAIRVAUX, initiator of the Second Crusade.

almost two centuries, until 1291, when Acre, the Crusaders' last stronghold in the Holy Land, was lost.

Over almost two centuries, several more Crusades were organized with but one aim, that is, to protect the Crusader states in the Levant against Islamic aggression. In 1144, the Muslims captured Edessa, the easternmost Christian outpost. In response, Bernard of Clairvaux initiated the Second Crusade, which set out in 1147, led by Emperor Conrad III of Germany and King Louis VII of France. The Crusaders

were defeated at the second Battle of Dorylaeum and later forced to withdraw from Damascus.

In 1187, Saladin, the new ruler of Egypt and founder of the Ayyubid dynasty, defeated the Crusaders at the Battle of Hattin and then captured Jerusalem. On hearing of this, Pope Gregory VIII initiated the Third Crusade, which set out for the Holy Land in 1189, led by Emperor Frederick Barbarossa, King Richard I of England, and King Philip II of France. The Crusaders defeated the Muslims several times, reaching Cilician Armenia. However, on June 10, 1190, Barbarossa fell off his horse and drowned when crossing the Saleph River. Richard I of England, "the Lionheart", took over command and conducted a number of brilliant campaigns, capturing Acre and defeating Saladin at the Battle of Arsuf and the Battle of Jaffa, but then he decided against a siege of Jerusalem. On September 2, 1192, he signed a three-year truce with Saladin, under which the Palestine coast remained in

Christian hands, while the interior of the country was to be ruled by the Muslims. Saladin, however, undertook to allow Christian pilgrims access to the Holy City.

In 1198, Lotario dei Conti di Segni became Pope Innocent III and at the very outset of his pontificate initiated the Fourth Crusade to liberate Jerusalem. As had been the case with the Third Crusade, there was no obvious leader, since the most important European rulers were either too young, excommunicated, or engaged in other wars. In April 1199, Richard the Lionheart, the most predisposed to lead the Crusade, died after having been wounded. Hence the feudal lords, mainly French and Flemish, took control. They chose Marquess Boniface of Montferrat as their leader and decided to reach the Holy Land by sea rather than by land. Thus they sought a fleet that would be capable of transporting an enormous number of Crusaders to the Holy Land. They turned for help to the Republic of Venice, at that time the mightiest sea power in Europe.

Venice was ruled by Enrico Dandolo, an aged and blind doge who enjoyed great authority and who, despite his advanced age, impressed

BONIFACE OF MONTFERRAT was chosen as the leader of the Fourth Crusade.

HISTORIC VENICE, with the cupola of the Basilica of St. Mark in the background.

people by his inexhaustible energy and iron will. The *Chronicle of Novgorod* mentions that he had been blinded in 1173 by order of the Byzantine emperor Manuel I Komnenos. The rulers of Constantinople mutilated their opponents in this way, including the Bulgarians and the Venetians, against whom they fought for mastery over the seas. Historians are of the opinion that a desire for revenge on the hated enemy was one of the motives behind the old doge's actions.

GREAT COUNCIL CHAMBER in the Doge's Palace, 59 yards long and 27 yards wide.

Enrico Dandolo came to an extremely favorable arrangement with the Crusaders, undertaking to transport the whole army to the Levant for eighty-five thousand silver marks, a tremendous amount of money at the time. The payment was to be made regardless of whether anyone actually boarded a ship. On top of that, the Venetians were to receive half the territory gained in the Near East.

ENRICO DANDOLO, the blind doge of Venice, addressing participants in the Fourth Crusade.

PORTRAIT of Doge Enrico Dandolo.

DOGE'S TOMB in the Hagia Sophia.

THE BLIND DOGE

THERE WERE no monarchs in the merchant Republic of Venice. The doge was the most important official, elected for life in two stages: (1) by an assembly of all the adult citizens; and (2) by an electoral college selected by the Great Council of Venice, composed of 480 representatives of rich patrician families.

In 1192, eighty-five-year-old Enrico Dandolo became the doge, and one of the creators of Venice's power. He harbored a grudge against Constantinople for two reasons: (1) because the Byzantine emperor had confiscated his property in the East in 1171; and (2) because the emperor had him blinded two years later. Hence the doge sought an opportunity to take revenge, which he did in 1204. A year later, at the age of ninety-eight, he died in Constantinople, which he had conquered, and he was buried in the Hagia Sophia.

The Crusaders expected four and a half thousand knights, nine thousand squires, and twenty thousand infantry to participate in the Crusade, and so arranged for an appropriate number of ships. But as it happened, only half that number of Crusaders turned up in Venice, and they were short thirty thousand marks to pay for the transport. The doge would not agree to a reduction in either the number of ships or their cost. He suggested that the Crusaders capture the Croatian port of Zadar for him in lieu of payment. Zadar had belonged to Venice, but the city had sought its independence by accepting the rule of neighboring kingdoms. Venice tried repeatedly to regain Zadar, but the city appealed to the pope and the king of Hungary for protection. The cunning doge saw in the Crusaders' problems an opportunity to win back the strategic port.

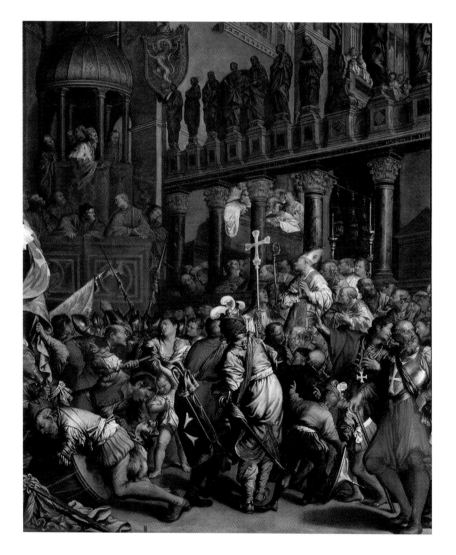

VENETIAN DOGE RECRUITING soldiers from the Fourth Crusade.

The majority of the Crusade leaders accepted the doge's proposition. Marquess Boniface of Montferrat and papal legate Peter of Capua, a cardinal, immediately set off to Rome to inform Pope Innocent III of what had transpired. Dismayed, the pope sent an emissary, the abbot Guy of Vaux-de-Cernay, to stop the Crusaders, threatening them with excommunication. The doge, however, appealed to the chivalric code and the promises the feudal lords had made. The majority put their honor before the pope's demand and decided to attack Zadar. Only Enguerrand de Boves and Simon de Montfort refused to comply with the shameful arrangement.

ZADAR CAPTURED in 1202 by the Crusaders.

Zadar was captured on November 24, 1202. Despite the fact that its inhabitants had hung crucifixes on the walls, the city was looted, the churches plundered and desecrated. On hearing of this, the pope excommunicated the Venetians, but that did not deter them. Worse was to come.

A Byzantine prince turned up in Zadar, a pretender to the imperial throne. He proposed that the Crusaders set off with him to take Constantinople. In return, he would pay them two hundred thousand marks, provide them with ten thousand soldiers, maintain five hundred knights in the Holy Land for life, end the Great Schism, and subordinate the Eastern Church to the pope. He was not in a position to fulfill these promises, but the feudal lords accepted the proposal, persuaded by the doge and Boniface of Montferrat, who saw it as the only chance for the Crusade to succeed. And again, only Enguerrand de Boves and Simon de Montfort protested. The pair decided to leave their companies, and together with their soldiers, they crossed the sea to Syria, where they successfully fought against the Muslims.

INNOCENT III'S BULL
excommunicating participants in the Fourth Crusade.

133

At the beginning of April 1203, the Crusaders' fleet set sail. One week later, the Venetians who had remained in Zadar completely destroyed the city, thus punishing the rebellious inhabitants for years of revolt and resistance. Meanwhile, the fleet captured and plundered the island of Corfu, which was part of Byzantium.

On July 17, 1203, the Crusaders captured Constantinople—regarded as the richest city in the Christian world, though its days of glory were over—and placed Alexios IV Angelos on the throne, expecting payment from him. Just as he had promised, the new emperor recognized the pope's sovereignty, but he only paid his allies one hundred thousand marks, half of what was due to them, the proceeds from the melting of precious liturgical vessels from Orthodox churches. Aware that his power was fragile, he persuaded the Crusade leaders to stay until March the following year, while he went about finding the rest of the money that was due them. The Byzantines, however, became increasingly dissatisfied with his rule, as he burdened them financially in order to pay the Crusaders. Eventually, Alexios was overthrown and replaced by Alexios V Doukas, who prohibited the Crusaders from entering the city. The French and the Venetians decided to take what was owed them—with interest.

CONSTANTI-NOPLE CAPTURED, a painting by Domenico Tintoretto in the Doge's Palace, Venice.

Hence Constantinople was taken on May 12, 1204. Three days of slaughter, robbery, and rape ensued. Even holy places were not spared: churches were profaned, and relics looted, including the Shroud of Turin, which was not found until the mid-14th century in Champagne, France.

The chronicles do not mention whether the blind doge felt any satisfaction in taking revenge on his hated enemy. But Venice, it is certain, benefitted most from the rogue expedition, for it broke the power of its most dangerous rival in the battle over the seas and seized most of the spoils during the sack of Constantinople. To this day, one can see treasures from Constantinople in Venice, including the famous Bronze Horses on the balcony above the portal of St. Mark's Basilica.

The Crusaders did not stop at conquering the city but introduced a new order. On May 16, 1204, Count Baldwin of Flanders and Hainaut, one of the leaders of the Crusade, was proclaimed the first emperor of the Latin Empire of Constantinople. Shortly afterward, an ordinary Venetian subdeacon, Thomas Morosini, became the first Latin Patriarch of Constantinople. The end of the schism was also announced, but the Byzantines never came to terms with the loss of their capital, though they retained power in several small countries in Asia Minor. They eventually recaptured Constantinople in 1261.

BRONZE HORSES plundered from Constantinople, above the portal of St. Mark's Basilica in Venice.

135

PRICELESS RELICS in the St. Mark's Basilica treasury, looted from Constantinople during the Fourth Crusade.

ALEXIOS IV ANGELOS was the Byzantine emperor for under six months.

Thanks to the documents housed in the Vatican Secret Archives, we know that Pope Innocent III bent over backward at critical moments to prevent a catastrophe. He sent letters throughout the world, pleaded, threatened, imposed excommunications and interdicts. Even before the Crusaders had set out from Venice, he—as if sensing something—warned that they could not be used to fight Christians, particularly those subject to the king of Hungary. After the enthronement of Alexios IV, he ordered them to set out for the Holy Land rather than stay in Constantinople. But all his requests were ignored.

News from the East reached him somewhat late. The leaders of the Crusade presented a version of events in their letters that significantly differed from reality. The pope did not learn the truth about the sack of Constantinople until the beginning of 1205, whereupon he excommunicated those who took part in it. In a letter to Baldwin of Flanders, he wrote:

The Latins [have given] nothing except an example of affliction and the works of Hell, so that now [the Greek Church] rightly detests them more than dogs. . . .You rashly turned away from the purity of your vow when you took up arms not against Saracens but Christians, not aiming to recover Jerusalem but to occupy Constantinople, preferring earthly wealth to celestial treasures. . . . For they, who we believed to be seeking things not for themselves but for Jesus Christ, showed no mercy for reasons of religion, age, or sex. . . . [They ripped] away silver tablets from altars

CAPTURE AND SACK of Constantinople, 1204, opened up centuries of hostility between the Orthodox Church and the Roman Catholic Church.

and br[oke] them into pieces among themselves, violating sacristies and crosses, and carrying away relics.[7]

The outcome of the Fourth Crusade was tragic. The Crusaders, not meeting a single Muslim along the way, turned their destructive forces against their fellow believers. They plundered Catholic Zadar and Orthodox Constantinople, committing the worst kinds of crimes. They contributed to the fall of the Byzantine Empire, humiliating the Greeks, and deepened the rift between the Eastern and Western Churches, which has lasted to this day. In the eyes of many, they ultimately compromised the idea of a Crusade altogether. Jerusalem was not liberated.

VENETIAN MANUSCRIPT depicting Crusaders attacking Constantinople.

THE CRUSADERS' LAST STRONGHOLD

ACRE WAS ONE of the most important settlements of the Phoenicians, a people that boasted the greatest sailors and merchants of antiquity. Its heyday, however, was in the 12th and 13th centuries, when it served as the capital and the main port of the Kingdom of Jerusalem. In 1291, Acre, the last Crusader stronghold in the Levant, fell to Muslim forces. In later centuries, it became a stopover for pilgrims on their way to the Holy Land. Its importance decreased in the 19th century due to the dynamic development of nearby Haifa.

Today, one can still admire the underground city of the Crusaders in Acre and the city built by the Ottoman Turks on top of it. In the lower part, one can see defense walls, foundations of buildings, residential and commercial areas, streets and passages, as well as underground corridors. Later, on the ruins of the medieval capital, high-density housing appeared in the Near East style.

UNDER-GROUND CITY of Crusaders in Acre, a major tourist attraction.

CITADEL built atop the foundations of a Crusaders' fortress in the 18th century.

FREDERICK II AND AL-KAMIL AYYUBID met and signed an agreement on the control of Jerusalem.

Later, further attempts were made to liberate the Holy Land, but they ended in failure. There was a Fifth Crusade against Egypt (1217–1221), which even saw the Crusaders take Damietta, a port on the Nile, but after two years, they were forced to withdraw.

The Crusade (1228–1229) headed by Emperor Frederick II led to the most bizarre course of events. As the emperor had been excommunicated, this expedition could not receive official sanction from the pope. Rather than engaging the Muslims in battle, he entered into negotiations with the sultan of Egypt Al-Kamil Ayyubid, signing an agreement on February 18, 1229, under which Jerusalem (excepting the Temple Mount, the Dome of the Rock, and the Al-Aqsa Mosque) was to be under Christian control for ten years. In return, the emperor undertook not to support any military action against the Muslims. Frederick II crowned himself king of Jerusalem, declaring that he generously forgave Pope Gregory IX for

POPE GREGORY IX excommunicating Frederick II.

139

**KING
OF FRANCE**
Louis IX in
a painting
by El Greco.

ST. LOUIS
receiving
Communion on
his knees in a
Franciscan habit.

**BLANCHE
OF CASTILE**
with her son
St. Louis.

excommunicating him. Many saw this as impertinence, but it was in line with the monarch's character, as well as the battle for primacy between the papacy and the empire.

When Jerusalem was captured by the Khwarezmian Tatars in 1244, another Crusade was organized, which set off four years later, led by St. Louis IX, king of France. The Crusaders took Damietta, but were later defeated at Cairo. The king was taken prisoner but was ransomed for a huge sum. He, however, did not give up the idea of another Crusade, which set out in 1270. But during the siege of Tunis, bubonic plague broke out. The king and a great number of Crusaders

died, while the rest quickly returned to Europe. Thus the Seventh Crusade, and the last, ended in defeat.

During the following years, the pressure of Islam increased. 1291 saw the fall of the port city of Acre, the Crusaders' last stronghold in the Holy Land. The news caused a stir in Europe. Money was raised for another crusade, but King Philip IV of France got his hands on all the funds, having had the Knights Templar order disbanded and their treasury seized. Despite this, Catholics did not forget about the liberation of Jerusalem. Even several dozen years later, St. Catherine of Siena wrote that the aim of every Christian ought to be the regaining of the Holy Sepulchre. The situation changed radically towards the end of the 14th century, when the Ottoman Turks, dominant in the Balkans, began to advance on the rest of Europe. The Hungarians and the Poles took the main brunt of the attack. From then on, people

ST. CATHERINE OF SIENA, born 56 years after the expulsion of the Crusaders from the Holy Land, held that the task of Christians was to regain the Holy Sepulchre.

did not think about retaking the Holy Land but rather about defending Europe.

In Massimo Viglione's opinion, it is necessary to separate two elements in Crusade history: the idea of a just war, which is justifiable in certain cases, and the sinfulness of people, who even in a just war manage to commit unjust deeds. The Crusades did not tame the wild instincts of Crusaders. What began with noble goals eventually suffered a moral collapse. Pope Innocent III's correspondence shows that if the Crusaders had listened to him, history would have turned out completely different.

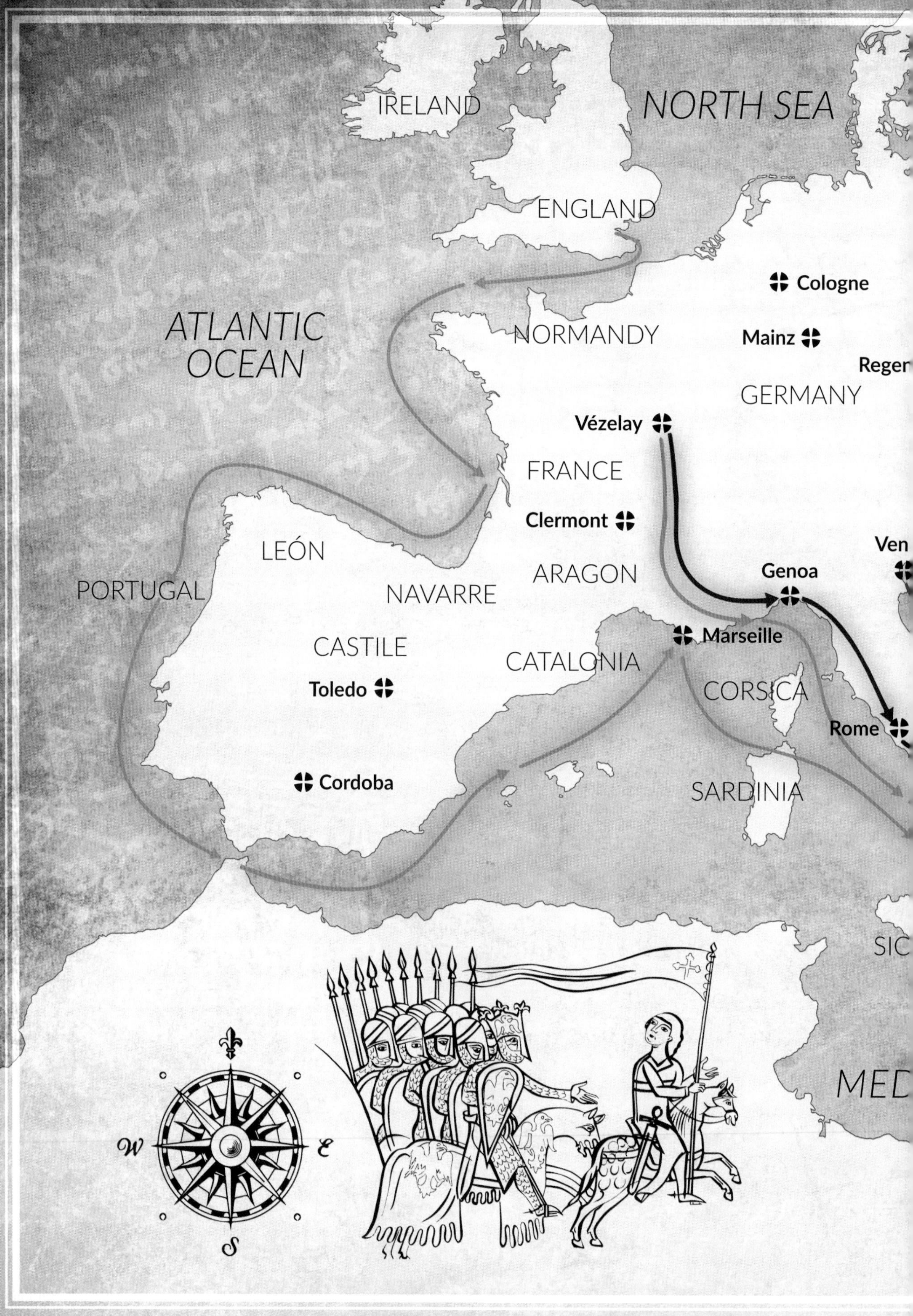

IRELAND

NORTH SEA

ENGLAND

Cologne

Mainz

Reger

GERMANY

ATLANTIC
OCEAN

NORMANDY

Vézelay

FRANCE

Clermont

LEÓN

ARAGON

Ven

PORTUGAL

NAVARRE

Genoa

CASTILE

CATALONIA

Marseille

Toledo

CORSICA

Rome

Cordoba

SARDINIA

SIC

MED

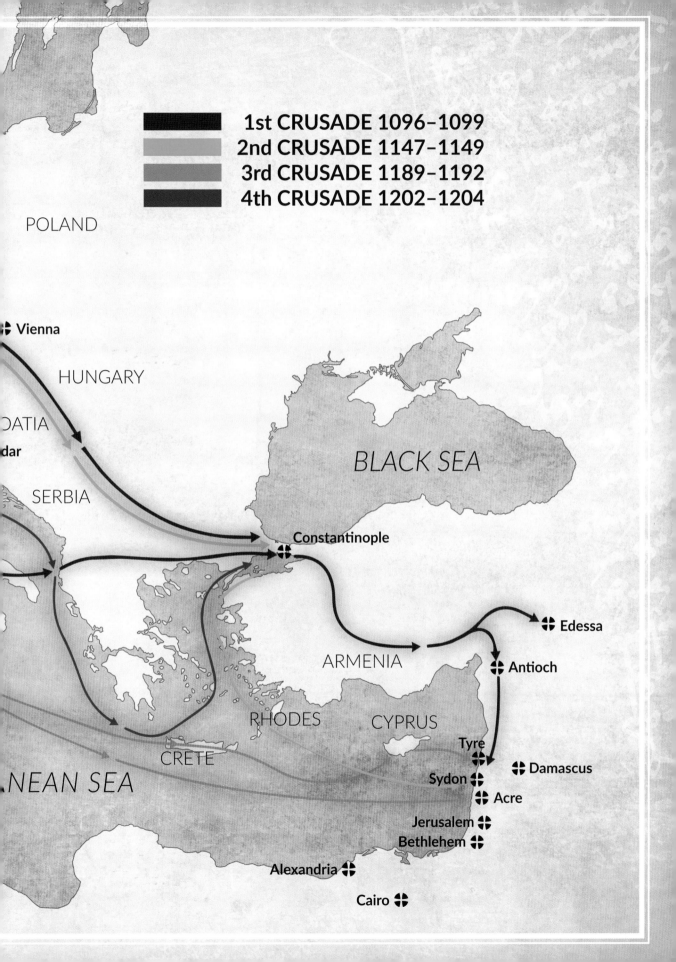

1st CRUSADE 1096–1099
2nd CRUSADE 1147–1149
3rd CRUSADE 1189–1192
4th CRUSADE 1202–1204

POLAND

Vienna

HUNGARY

OATIA

dar

SERBIA

BLACK SEA

Constantinople

ARMENIA

Edessa

Antioch

RHODES

CYPRUS

Tyre

Damascus

Sydon

Acre

CRETE

Jerusalem

Bethlehem

NEAN SEA

Alexandria

Cairo

HISTORY

DISCOVERY

TRADITION

Paradoxes
of the Inquisition

CHAPTER 4

Paradoxes of the Inquisition

✙

Harbingers of totalitarianism and the rule of an "amoral superhuman elite"

In 1998, Pope John Paul II decided to declassify all the Vatican Secret Archives' files (4,500 documents) pertaining to the Inquisition. An international research commission was set up under the leadership of Prof. Agostino Borromeo from the Sapienza University of Rome. An eight-hundred-page volume, the fruit of six years of toil—containing the conclusions of sixty historians from across the world—completely rejects the Black Legend associated with the infamous Spanish Inquisition.

Vatican ✙

ITALY

AGOSTINO BORROMEO, history professor, expert on the history of the Inquisition.

JOHN PAUL II maintained that the Church had nothing to hide regarding the Inquisition.

It is not possible to understand the Inquisition without understanding the nature of heresy, a religious opinion that arises from Christianity but is contrary to the official teaching of the Church. From the very beginning, the Church has opposed erroneous teaching, because by falsifying salvific truths, it could prevent believers from attaining eternal life. Already in the first century, Christians were constantly confronted with various sects that advocated different understandings of Christ and his teaching. In early medieval Europe, debates with the sects were based on theological arguments, very often at a high level of abstraction, while punishments were usually of a canonical nature. The situation was somewhat different in Byzantium, where in consequence of the alliance between the emperor and the Eastern bishops, religious disputes automatically

DISPUTE
between two adversaries—11ᵗʰ century bas-relief.

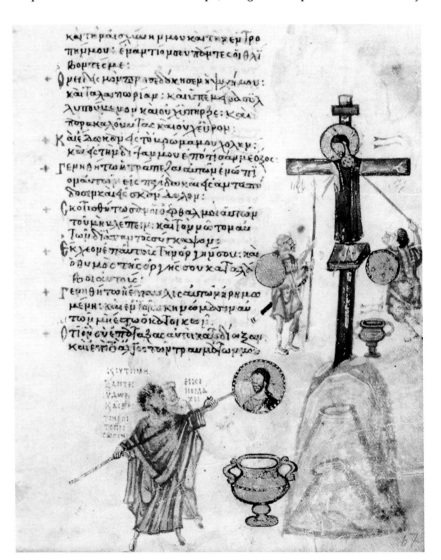

HERESY
has always caused problems in the Church. At the bottom of this Russian illumination, an Iconoclast pierces an image of Jesus. The Inquisition was established to combat such heresy in a peaceful and orderly manner.

147

took on a political character, which sometimes took a very brutal course.

The situation began to change in the 10th century, when mass heretical movements appeared. They mainly developed among the uneducated poor, attracted by the simplest of slogans without understanding their doctrinal subtleties. Such slogans were used by the apocalyptic prophets of those times, itinerant preachers like Peter of Bruys, Henry of Lausanne, or Tanchelm of Antwerp. Some, such as Éon de l'Étoile, even claimed to be new messiahs.

Their religious postulates, however, had certain social consequences. If, for example, one could pray anywhere, and there was no difference between a stable and a church, then churches ought to be torn down. If only itinerants could be preachers, then contemplative orders ought to be done away with and monasteries closed. If the apostles' sharing everything in common is the ideal, then private property ought to be abolished and rich men deprived of their wealth. If Christ forbade taking vows, then vows ought to be invalidated, including marriage vows and fealty oaths (on which the feudal system rested). Hence, a movement that advocated such things had within it an enormous potential for

SECULAR COURTS often used torture, even in matters of heresy.

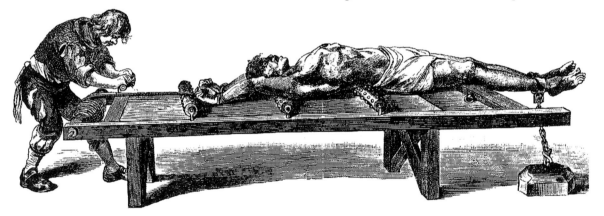

social destruction. In practice, it led to palaces and monasteries being plundered, churches being set on fire, and people, deemed as enemies, being killed.

All this occasioned the secular penal codes' provisions for draconian penalties against heretics, and this happened long before the Inquisition arose. The reign of King Robert II of France saw the first heretics burnt at the stake in Orléans (toward the end of the 10th century), a practice that was primarily opposed by Church hierarchs. Secular courts had conducted heresy trials for decades, frequently inflicting torture and imposing death sentences. The people often demanded such penalties and sometimes took the law into their own hands. Religious conflicts were often an outlet for economic or ethnic tensions. An accusation of heresy

RINO CAMMILLERI, an Italian historian, in conversation with Grzegorz Górny.

became an effective political weapon to destroy an opponent, or at least to justify the use of violence against him.

We had a meeting in Rome with Rino Cammilleri, an Italian historian who wrote a book about the Inquisition.[1] According to him, Catharism was the first great heretical movement in Europe. It encompassed a large part of the continent and was a great challenge to secular and Church authorities for almost three centuries. It was derived from the Armenian Paulicians and Bulgarian Bogomils, appearing in the West

CATHARS EXPELLED from Carcassonne in 1209, after Simon de Montfort captured the city.

CARCASSONNE
in Languedoc
was one
of the main
strongholds
of Catharism
in France.

after the year 1000 and spread mainly in Latin and Germanic cultural circles.

The Cathars' theological doctrine bore a destructive potential for the social order of the time, for it was based on a Manichean vision of the universe, according to which a good god created the spiritual world while an evil demiurge created the material world. This inevitably led to a negation of all that was material. In theology, it meant, for example, the rejection of the teachings on the Incarnation and the Eucharist. But Catharism also had certain social consequences, pertaining not only to religion, but also to government, medicine, marriage, and family life.

According to Catharism, procreation was the gravest sin, as it maintained human bodies in existence. It permitted any form of intercourse, even the most perverse, so long as it was not fecund. The Cathars had but one sacrament, *consolamentum*, which was their form of baptism. It was believed to make a person perfect, and it was usually administered before death. After receiving this sacrament, some Cathars practiced *endura*, a suicide by starvation, so that they could be assured of salvation. Mothers were reported to have starved their children to death, convinced that they would thus be

PRAISE OF THE CREATURES

ST. FRANCIS of Assisi's "Canticle of the Sun", also known as "Praise of the Creatures", is one of the world's best-known medieval literary works. It is impossible to understand this work without seeing it in the context of the struggle with heretics, as St. Francis wrote the work with the Cathars in mind, for they rejected the whole material world as evil in itself, the creation of a terrible demiurge. Yet St. Francis praised all creation as the work of a good Creator. He praised the sun, the moon, and the stars, as well as wind, water, fire, earth, flowers, herbs, and fruit—all that was repugnant to the Cathars. In addition, he wrote the work in Italian, not Latin, in order to make it easier to reach ordinary people, among whom the Cathar heresy spread the most.

ST. HILDEGARD OF BINGEN, Benedictine nun, mystic, composer, and early natural scientist.

ST. BERNARD OF CLAIRVAUX, French Cistercian, theologian, philosopher, and Church reformer.

saved. Since death by starvation is a long and painful process, sometimes Cathars would ask others to suffocate them.

Cathars were divided into two groups: the Perfect and the ordinary unbaptized believers. The former practiced asceticism and veganism, not eating anything that was the fruit of procreation. The latter allowed all manner of wickedness, as everything that existed had no meaning and so deserved to disappear. Hence court judgments, oaths, or agreements had no validity to them. This was a consequence of the logical assumption that every secular power was evil of its nature since it represented the material world. Even medicine was evil, because it saved human life, sinful human bodies. Thus doctors were seen as enemies of the human race.

So it is not surprising that a heresy which proclaimed hate for all creation and undermined the legitimacy of any state authority, met with a decided reaction on the part of secular monarchs. According to Cammilleri, kings and princes fought against the Cathars before the Inquisition was established. Even excommunicated rulers—such as Frederick I (Barbarossa) and King Henry II of England, who had St. Thomas Becket, the archbishop of Canterbury, murdered—imposed death penalties on heretics.

The Church strove to deal with heresy verbally, as recommended by St. Bernard of Clairvaux and St. Hildegard of Bingen. But on the whole, theological arguments did not convince the Cathars. It also happened that heretics who submitted to Church penalties—for

A CROSS
popular in Languedoc,
mistakenly called
a "Cathar cross".
In reality, Cathars
denied Christ's
sacrifice on the Cross.

example, Henry of Lausanne (also known as Henry of Bruys) or Arnold of Brescia —later returned to their former activities and incited riots.

Seeing the Church's weakness in the battle with iconoclastic sects, secular rulers decided on other methods. Experience had shown them that ruthlessness was much more effective than forbearance. In northern France, where secular courts dealt severely with heresies, they were cut to the quick. Meanwhile, in southern France, where decisive measures were not applied, heretics often used force to undermine the existing social order.

Heretics were frequently victims of mob rule. Rino Cammilleri gives some examples. In 1040, there was a conflict between the inhabitants of Milan and some Cathars from Monforte d'Alba. The archbishop wanted to impose a Church penalty on the heretics, but the Milanese burned them at the stake instead. In Soissons in 1114, the locals, fearing that the local bishop would spare some heretics, pulled them out of a prison and burned them. A similar thing happened in Liège in 1135. One can give many more examples. However, one must bear in mind that people in those days saw threats to their souls as more serious than threats to their bodies, as the former

FRANCE

Carcassonne

CARCASSONNE
is medieval
Europe's
largest
fortified city.

153

POPE GREGORY IX
promulgated the code of canon law in the Catholic Church, which remained in force until 1918.

could entail eternal damnation. Hence, heretics were seen as a threat to the whole of society.

Cammilleri has no doubts that the Church was drawn into a legal battle against heresy by secular authorities and public opinion, as the bloody persecutions of heretics were initiated by princes and ordinary people. Collective responsibility was applied during summary and extrajudicial proceedings. Hence people who had joined the Cathars through theological ignorance or in fear of their neighbors, were frequently sentenced to death. Thus arose the idea of an inquisition, which was to prevent such situations.

It came to being gradually, by decisions of successive popes: Lucius III, Innocent III, and Gregory IX. In 1179, the Third Council of the Lateran anathematized heretics who "respect neither churches nor monasteries, and spare neither widows, orphans, old or young nor any age or sex, but like pagans destroy and lay everything waste"[2]. In 1184, an edict was issued during a great assembly of princes and clergy in Verona, which ordered preventive actions against heretics, aiming to expose them and nip the danger in the bud.

Verona

ITALY

THIRD COUNCIL OF THE LATERAN
excommunicated Cathars and their protectors.

The first investigations (Latin: *inquisitio*) pertaining to heresy were launched on the basis of the edict. Penalties were severe. Those who did not show remorse were sentenced to death, while those who did returned to the bosom of the Church. If no crime like plunder or murder had been committed, penance was required, for example, a symbolic scourging, a fine, a recitation of a prayer, or a pilgrimage. Henry Charles Lea, an American historian (a Protestant), wrote that though Inquisition penalties were severe, their purpose was to protect civilization, as the victory of Catharism would have entailed drastic consequences for the whole of Europe.

That was evident at the turn of the 12th and 13th centuries, during the reign of Philip II of France, when southern France was plunged in anarchy and chaos. The Church in particular was attacked. Armed bands robbed churches and monasteries, tortured and murdered priests and monks. Local barons often inspired the attacks, including Raymond VI, Count of Toulouse and Gaston IV, Viscount of Béarn, who used the heretics for their own political aims. Feudal lords often came into conflict with the Church, as it opposed marriage within the family while the lords preferred such marriages, which enabled them to evade the division of their property and depletion of their wealth. Hence, financial issues led magnates in southern France to support Catharism, which, thanks to them spread widely.

Initially, the Inquisition was directed by bishops, but that turned out to be ineffective since it limited their authority to one diocese. All a heretic had to do was move to another diocese to escape being indicted. Those were times when it took months or even years for news to travel between principalities or provinces, allowing fugitives to act with impunity. Apart from that, bishops frequently lacked the theological knowledge to have debates with heretics. Thus the Holy See decided that

RAYMOND VI,
Count
of Toulouse,
was one
of the most
influential
defenders
of the Cathar
sect.

papal legates, specialists in theology and law, directly subordinate to Rome, were to be responsible for inquisitions.

In 1208, Pierre de Castelnau, a papal legate in Languedoc, was murdered due to the influence of Count Raymond VI of Toulouse, a powerful feudal lord who supported the Cathars. His murder caused great indignation and prompted Innocent III to initiate the Cathar Crusade (also known as the Albigensian Crusade, named for the city of Albi, the center of Catharism). It drew many French knights and encompassed almost the whole of Languedoc for two decades (1209–1229), ending in victory for the Christians. The last Cathar fortress (in Montségur) did not capitulate until a nine-month siege in 1242. Its defenders were burned at the stake. It was then understood that to combat heresies, it was necessary to use severe means right from

ALBI'S CATHEDRAL (right) was designed as an architectural symbol of the papacy's triumph over Catharism.

LAST JUDGMENT, mural in the Cathedral of St. Cecilia in Albi (left).

the outset, before they became dangerously strong. Inquisitions were to serve that end.

There are numerous files in the Vatican Secret Archives that confirm the observations of Norman Cohn and Rino Cammilleri concerning the interrogations of medieval sect members. There are also the papal documents that formed the basis of the Inquisition, one of which is the *Capitula contra Patarenos*, promulgated on March 7, 1236, by Gregory IX. The name of the document comes from the armed bands called Patarines (or Routiers or Cottereaux), who attacked churches, murdered clergy, and committed sacrilegious deeds. *Capitula contra Patarenos* was a collection of rules aimed at preventing Catharism from spreading further. It was the

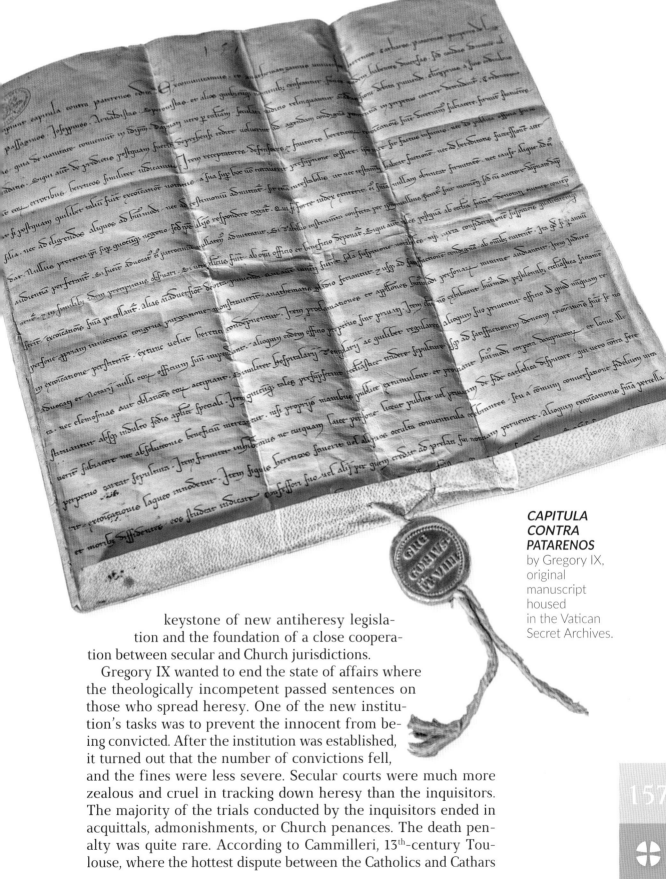

keystone of new antiheresy legislation and the foundation of a close cooperation between secular and Church jurisdictions.

Gregory IX wanted to end the state of affairs where the theologically incompetent passed sentences on those who spread heresy. One of the new institution's tasks was to prevent the innocent from being convicted. After the institution was established, it turned out that the number of convictions fell, and the fines were less severe. Secular courts were much more zealous and cruel in tracking down heresy than the inquisitors. The majority of the trials conducted by the inquisitors ended in acquittals, admonishments, or Church penances. The death penalty was quite rare. According to Cammilleri, 13th-century Toulouse, where the hottest dispute between the Catholics and Cathars

MIRACLE IN FANJEAUX as depicted in Pedro Berruguete's 15th-century painting. According to Jordan of Saxony, St. Dominic had Cathar and Catholic texts cast into a fire, but only the Catholic texts proved resistant to the flames.

occurred, saw only 1 percent of the trials conducted by the inquisitors end in the death penalty.

Initially, the papal legates entrusted the inquisitions to the Cistercians, who had the appropriate theological formation and so could hold debates with the Cathars. They traveled throughout Europe proclaiming the Gospel and held discussions with heretics. At times, they were attacked and killed by their adversaries. St. Dominic de Guzmán, an Inquisition coadjutor, survived several attacks. He came to the conclusion that the Cathars could be overcome by their own weapon. He noticed that the their most effective weapon was the word, coupled with poverty. Their preachers, zealous, eloquent, and poor, walked in pairs from village to village, from town

DOMINICAN RULE, based on the Rule of St. Augustine, has 12 chapters.

to town. They showed by their own example that they were not interested in material goods, as these did not bring true happiness. They thus attracted people.

Hence, St. Dominic decided to found a new order with a preaching mission, one bereft of wealth. Its members were to be educated,

DOMINIC'S HOME in Fanjeaux, where he set off on his missionary journeys throughout Languedoc.

ASSUMPTION CHURCH, in Fanjeaux, where St. Dominic had theological disputes with chief Cathar Guilhabert de Castres.

BEGINNINGS OF THE ROSARY

THE ROSARY developed as a response to the Cathar danger. It recalls the basic truth of the Faith, namely, the Incarnation, in which God (absolute Good) unites himself to matter, which the Albigensians considered evil. The repetition of the Hail Mary—a prayer based on two fragments of the Gospel: the angel Gabriel's words to Mary and St. Elizabeth's exclamation, "Blessed is the fruit of thy womb, Jesus"—consolidated the message in people's hearts and minds. The very existence of Mary, the human Mother of God, was an antidote to the Cathar heresy. The Albigensians were curious about the Rosary, as they themselves used a prayer string with coral beads, called a paternoster, on which they recited the Our Father. It was the only prayer they had retained from the whole of Christian tradition. Hence, it was easier to reach them with another element of the old tradition, the Hail Mary.

St. Dominic did not think up the Rosary himself, but according to tradition received it from Our Lady during a vision, together with a promise of special favors. Dominican testimonies of the time attest to the fact that the prayer turned out to be extraordinarily effective during missions among the Cathars. Since then, it has been universally recognized in the Catholic Church that Mary is the best slayer of heresy, and the Rosary has become the most-used Catholic spiritual weapon. Numerous mystical writings and Marian apparitions, such as at Fatima, testify to its power.

ST. DOMINIC, according to tradition, received the Rosary from Our Lady in 1214 while praying in a forest near Toulouse.

ROSARIUM is the Latin term for "rose garden". In the Middle Ages, prayers were seen as spiritual flowers, and reciting the Rosary was like presenting Our Lady with a bouquet of roses.

pious, and poor, and to devote themselves entirely to an itinerant evangelism. Thus arose the Dominican Order, which was entrusted with supervising the Inquisition. St. Peter of Verona, who came from a Cathar family, became one of its best-known inquisitors. He was very familiar with the Cathar faith, which he compared and contrasted with Catholicism, especially during his theological studies in Bologna, where St. Dominic's sermons inclined him to join the Dominicans in 1221. He was very successful as an itinerant preacher in northern Italy, converting numerous heretics. In June 1251, Innocent IV appointed him as one of the two inquisitors for Lombardy, but he did not participate in any trial. On

MARTYRDOM
of St. Peter of Verona—16th-century painting by Girolamo Savoldo.

April 6, 1252, while walking from Como to Milan, he was murdered by some Cathars.

According to Cammilleri, inquisitors were usually greeted not with fear, but rather with a sense of relief. If the people were unhappy with their verdicts, it was not because of their severity, but rather their leniency. It was not uncommon that defendants were saved from mob rule; counting on fair treatment, many preferred to be under the jurisdiction of the inquisitors rather than that of the secular authorities.

L'INQUISITION,
a study by Jean
and Guy Testas.

Marian Małowist, a Polish historian, wrote that "the Inquisition was not an instrument of a cruel eradication of those who thought differently, but an attempt to rationalize the judicial process, so that it might be conducted according to regulations, as well as an attempt to ascertain the truth."[3] Jean and Guy Testas, French authors and brothers, are of the same opinion, maintaining that against the background of the generally prevailing court customs, the Inquisition was the most objective institution of its time. There was a general conviction that its existence prevented two dangers: the emergence of mass heretical movements and judicial injustice.

The Inquisition took steps to improve the judicial process. Thanks to Pope Gregory IX, defendants had the right to be represented by a lawyer; a judge had to submit his verdict to a jury, made up of the most respected members of the local community; and the defendant and his lawyer had the right to inspect the process files. Thus it is thanks to the Inquisition that contemporary civilization has inherited these civil rights.

**THE PURSUIT
OF THE
MILLENNIUM,**
Norman Cohn's
book about
the millenarian cults
of the Middle Ages.

Norman Cohn, a British historian, wrote *The Pursuit of the Millennium* (1957), one of the best-known books on medieval apocalyptic sects.[4] This classic work pertains to destructive heretical movements that proclaimed the imminent arrival of the Kingdom of Heaven and the Armageddon that would precede it. The protagonists of his work are popular religious leaders in the grip of eschatological obsessions, with a sense of a supernatural mission, such as the Anabaptists Jan Matthys and John of Leiden. In 1534, these two men came to power in Münster, Germany, and the ten thousand inhabitants willingly complied with their orders, proclaiming that Münster was the New Jerusalem. A totalitarian theocracy was established, based on terror and propaganda, and a meticulous control over all areas of life was imposed, with the slightest deviation punishable by death. Despite this, the inhabitants defended their town with an unprecedented fanaticism.

163

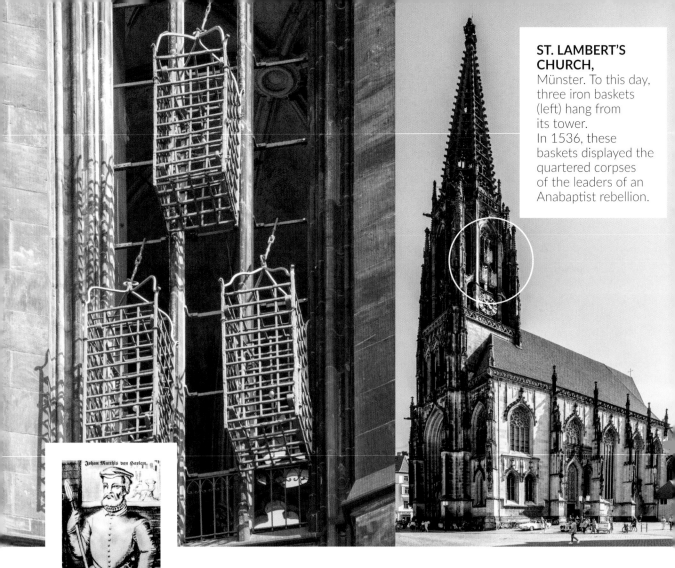

JAN MATTHYS, leader of a theocratic Anabaptist commune in Münster.

JOHN OF LEIDEN, fanatical cult leader and dictator of Münster.

The idea for writing the book came after World War II, when Cohn, as an intelligence officer, was interrogating SS prisoners of war. He was shocked by their worldview, according to which genocide was an inevitable necessity and even the burning of children was deemed good. He mentioned that he then came across a religious fanaticism based on a vision of an apocalyptic struggle on a universal scale, when life or death was at stake. This inspired him to start studying, which resulted in his book that compares National Socialism (Nazism) and Communism with millenarian heretical movements in the Middle Ages, noting an analogy between their respective internal structures and mental frameworks. He defines representatives of Gnostic sects and contemporary totalitarianisms as an "elite of amoral people". Both groups were certain where human history was heading and how the world should be cleansed of that which was destroying it. It always turned out that entire social strata had to be eliminated: sometimes the clergy, sometimes the bourgeois, sometimes the Jews. It was maintained that when it was done, an ideal society would emerge, devoid of internal contradictions and tensions.

Norman Cohn came to a surprising conclusion. If medieval heretics, proclaiming apocalyptic revolutionism, were the counterparts of modern totalitarians, then, perforce, Nazi hunters and the intelligence officers who interrogated Nazi criminals had to bring to mind the inquisitors who conducted investigations against the Cathars, Amalricians, Taborites, and Anabaptists. Such a comparison forces one to see the history of the Inquisition in a somewhat

TORTURE
was ubiquitous in Europe until the end of the 18th century.

different light, as an institution that defended an elemental social order against utopian social engineering projects.

Torture is a separate issue. It was practiced throughout Europe until the 18th century, when King Louis XVI of France was the first ruler to prohibit it. The Magdeburg Law, which was binding in the Middle Ages and the Renaissance, saw an admission of guilt as the only way to prove a crime and understood torture, inflicted up to five times, as the only way to obtain an admission of guilt. In secular

JEAN DUMONT wrote a book on the Spanish Inquisition.

ANDREA DEL COL wrote a book on the Italian Inquisition.

AUTO-DA-FÉ Terreiro do Paço (Palace Yard), Lisbon.

courts, torture was also seen as a kind of punishment. The Inquisition did not provide for corporal punishment in its sentences, which were often delivered in a auto-da-fé.[5] And the Inquisition rarely used torture during interrogations because it regarded it as unreliable; a person who admitted to guilt under torture often retracted his confession when he later had to confirm his testimony in writing before a Church tribunal. Jean Dumont, a French historian, discovered that in Valencia, of the two thousand or so trials conducted by the Inquisition from 1480 to 1530, torture was used in but twelve of them. In Toulouse, from 1309 to 1323, torture was inflicted in but one case out of the 636 trials conducted by the Inquisition.

Some historians who, from 1998 to 2004, went through the Vatican Secret Archives' files on the Inquisition came to the conclusion that only 2 percent or so of all the trials conducted by the

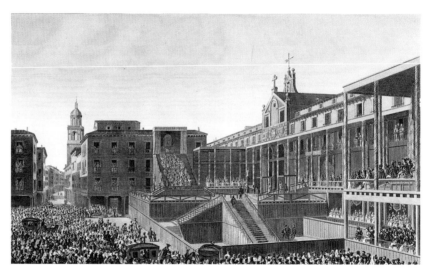

Inquisition in Europe ended in death sentences. Prof. Andrea Del Col, from the University of Trieste, published a book in 2006 on the Inquisition in Italy, which did not contain one illustration depicting an interrogation, a torture session, or a burning at the stake.[6] He maintained that the vast majority of the best-known images pertaining to the subject did not correspond to reality. They mainly arose much later and were influenced by the Black Legend, which was spread about Spain toward the end of the 16th century. The images turned out to be the work of Dutch Protestants who were then at war with Spain over the independence of the Netherlands. They used propaganda weapons, including pamphlets that depicted the cruelty of the Spanish Inquisition. The English, who were at war with Spain over the mastery of the seas, followed

AGOSTINO BORROMEO
noted a difference in the frequency
of torture used by the Inquisition
and that used by the royal and city courts.

RINO CAMMILLERI
explains that the Inquistion, unlike secular
courts, did not see torture as a punishment,
but as an aid in interrogation.

INQUISITION TORTURES

ACCORDING TO

Prof. Agostino Borromeo, torture was used in less than 10 percent of the Inquisition trials, much less than in secular courts, where it was used on a daily basis. Stereotype images of Inquisition prisons as chambers equipped with sophisticated torture devices are also false. According to Rino Cammilleri, torture was only inflicted in cases where there was highly incriminating evidence and all other means had been exhausted. Torture pertained only to adults, but not the elderly, and a doctor had to be present to ensure that prisoners were not maimed. The Inquisition used only one kind of torture, where a man had his hands tied behind his back and then suspended in the air, using a rope that was attached to his wrists. This was done three times, each several days apart. If a prisoner did not confess, he was set free. If he confessed, he had to confirm it in writing. Later, however, prisoners most often revoked their testimony as having been forced. Hence, the inquisitors were not convinced that torture was a reliable means for establishing the truth.

MONUMENT TO THE REFORMATION, Geneva. Left to right: William Farel, John Calvin, Theodore Beza, and John Knox.

suit, and in time so did other opponents of the Catholic Church, for example, representatives of the French Enlightenment.

Maria Elvira Roca Barea, a Spanish historian, draws attention to the disproportionate focus on the victims of religious persecution in Europe. On the one hand, the number of people sentenced to death by the Inquisition is exaggerated; on the other, crimes committed by Protestants are passed over. She gives the example of Geneva, where during John Calvin's time five hundred people perished in a population of ten thousand (5 percent). Despite this, nobody deems the father of Calvinism to be a criminal. The death

MIGUEL SERVET, a Spanish scholar, astronomer, doctor, ethnographer, burned at the stake for heresy in Geneva in 1553 by order of Calvin.

of thousands of English Catholics during the early part of Elizabeth I's reign is similarly ignored, with the queen still seen as a national heroine in Great Britain.

In this context, the findings pertaining to witch-hunts are very interesting. Brian Paul Levack, an American historian, author of one of the most important works on this subject (*The Witch-Hunt in Early Modern Europe*), wrote that about three hundred thousand women perished as witches in 16th-century Europe, of which almost two hundred thousand were in Protestant Germany and seventy thousand were in Protestant England, that is, in countries where the Inquisition did not exist. According to Levack, the

BURNING OF THREE "WITCHES" by Protestants, Baden, Switzerland, 1585.

Inquisition in Catholic countries did not permit societies to succumb to witch-hunt hysteria. Prof. Agostino Borromeo maintains that fifty-nine women perished as witches in Spain, thirty-six in Italy, and but four in Portugal.[7]

Prof. Franco Cardini, an Italian historian and coauthor of a book on the Inquisition, says that witch-hunts arose during the Renaissance, and not in the so-called Dark Ages.[8] He draws attention to the fact that in the Latin translation of the Bible, a person who practiced sorcery was referred to as a *maleficus*, which is a masculine noun meaning "wizard". The Lutheran, Anglican, and

169

COAT OF ARMS of the Spanish Inquisition. The sword to the right of the cross symbolizes the punisment of heretics; the olive branch to the left of the cross symbolizes reconciliation for those acknowledging their error. Inscription around the emblem: *"Exurge Domine et judica causam tuam"* (Psalm 73: "Arise, O God, plead your cause").

THE SPANISH INQUISITION

THE SPANISH INQUISITION, which is considered to have been the cruelest of the Inquisitions, was an institution completely dependent on the royal court in Madrid and independent of Rome. Popes like Innocent VIII, Alexander VI, Paul III, Pius V, Gregory XIII, and Innocent XII protested against many sentences passed by Spanish tribunals, as they saw them as too politicized and unjust. There were even cases where the authorities in Madrid prohibited the promulgation of papal documents due to the differences of opinion between them and Rome.

On the basis of research carried out in the Vatican Secret Archives from 1998 to 2004, it was established that between 1478 and 1834 the Spanish Inquisition conducted about 130,000 heresy trials. Exactly 1.8 percent of the accused were condemned to death, and 1.7 percent were convicted in absentia—those who managed to escape or whose place of residence was unknown—in which case symbolic effigies were then burned at the stake.

According to Prof. Agostino Borromeo, historians from the 19th century onward confused court trials with death sentences, which

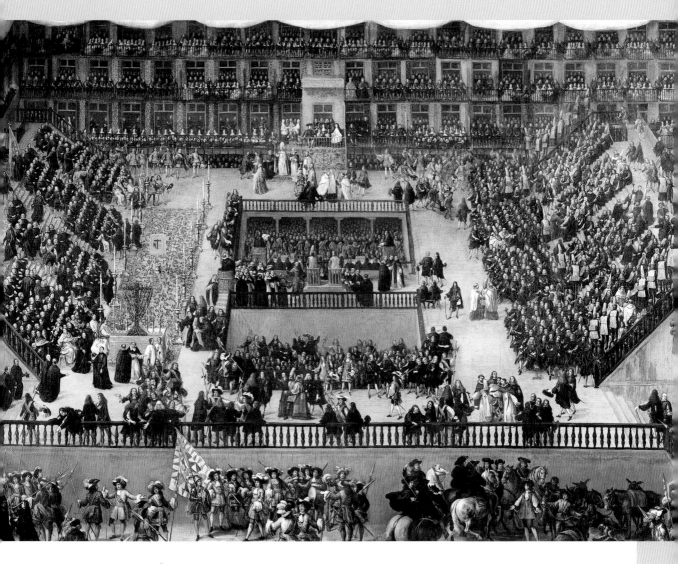

AUTO-DA-FÉ, 1680, in the Plaza Mayor, Madrid, before King Charles II of Spain—painting by Francisco Rizi.

led to a highly inflated estimate of Inquisition victims. Most trials ended in acquittals or temporal punishments, the majority of which were of a spiritual nature, such as pilgrimages, penances, and prayers, with a minority sending to prison or the galleys.

It turns out that the Portuguese Inquisition, also a state institution, was significantly more severe than the Spanish; it condemned to death 5.1 percent of the accused in 13,255 trials from 1450 to 1629. In view of this, why is the Spanish Inquisition seen as having been extremely cruel, while the Portuguese is virtually never mentioned? It is because the English and the Dutch, in a bitter conflict with Catholic monarchs in Madrid, waged a propaganda war against them in the 16th century and beyond. The Anglicans and other Protestants flooded Europe with the Black Legend by spreading pamphlets and books depicting the Spanish tribunals in a bad light; they did not mention the Portuguese, who were their allies.

Calvinist translations feminized the word, and applied to women such terms as witch, hag, and sorceress. In effect, male practicioners of the black arts disappeared, and mostly women were accused of witchcraft.

Women were convicted en masse in Protestant countries for pacts with the devil, night flights on brooms, and ritual infanticide. Inquisitors in Catholic countries, learned theologians, did

JEAN BODIN,
leading proponent of modern absolutism and witch-hunting.

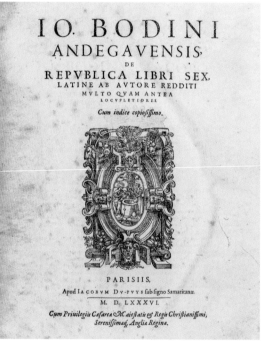

SIX BOOKS OF THE REPUBLIC, 1576, Jean Bodin's main work (right).

not believe in such things. In 1526, there gathered an assembly of inquisitors in Grenada, where it was stated that flying witches were an impossibility; the majority of participants stated that such witches did not even exist.

According to Prof. Marina Montesano, from the University of Genoa, author of two books on the Inquisition, the source of witch-hunts lies in the decline of the medieval political order and its replacement by the absolute state, as the latter required a collective enemy.[9] Hence, modernity brought crimes on a scale unprecedented in prior centuries. It was no coincidence that Jean Bodin, one of the most influential French intellectuals of the 16th century, the main theoretician of the absolute state, was also the author of an extremely popular treatise, *On the Demon-Mania of Witches*, wherein he recommended the most ruthless penalties against witchcraft. No other work exerted

ST. JOAN OF ARC, French national heroine. In 1431, at 19 years old, she was condemned on false charges by a Church court and burnt at the stake. She was rehabilitated 24 years after her death by Callixtus III, who acknowleged that her trial was unlawful. She was beatified in 1909 and canonized in 1920.

a greater influence on the escalation of witch-hunts in Europe than this text of Bodin, a lawyer and politician who, on the other hand, wrote the famous *The Six Books of the Republic*, wherein he formulated a modern theory of sovereignty—the first to do so.

The Inquisition's power occasioned a natural temptation to abuse it. At times, free of the Church's tutelage, it became an instrument of secular authorities, as was the case in the trial of Joan of Arc. The French national heroine was sentenced to death for alleged witchcraft, in complete disregard for Church law and in violation of the inquisitorial procedures on the part of Pierre Cauchon, the bishop of Beauvais, who was obedient to the English and did not have the competence to conduct the trial himself.

The Spanish Inquisition was always a state institution, never a Church one. At the service of the royal court, it sometimes abused its prerogatives, its victims being not enemies of the Church but opponents of the monarchs. There were even times when successive popes condemned the activities of the Iberian inquisitorial tribunals, while Spanish kings prohibited the dissemination and public reading of Roman documents pertaining to the matter. There was also another temptation connected with the activities of the Inquisition. When the beginnings of some dangerous idea are being investigated, every unconventional thought appears to be suspect, since no one knows where it could lead. Thus man's freedom comes under fire, as it poses a threat to rulers and the prevailing system. So the phenomenon of the Inquisition poses a question about human freedom and its limits, for the most monstrous crimes are a consequence of man's free will. Hence the tension between freedom and evil action is an inescapable challenge because men are weak and prone to selfishness.

The Inquisition was one attempt at coping with this problem. It was not a consequence of a totalitarian inclination, but on the contrary, an attempt to prevent the spread of the most destructive ideologies. But is it right to increase control over people at the cost of limiting their freedom? In the face of terrorism, for instance, is it right to keep citizens under surveillance at all times and deprive them of their civil liberties?

DISCOVERY

Conquistadores
and Missionaries

CHAPTER 5

Conquistadores and Missionaries

European conquest of America and the fate of the Native Americans

Vatican

ITALY

There are two documents in the Vatican Secret Archives that were promulgated virtually one after the other by Pope Paul III: the apostolic letter *Pastorale Officium*, of May 29, 1537, and the encyclical *Sublimis Deus*, of June 2, 1537.

Pope Paul III's name has not gone down in Church history in letters of gold.. Alessandro Farnese began his long road to the summit of the Catholic hierarchy thanks to his sister Giulia, Pope Alexander VI's mistress. As a painting by Raphael attests, she was very pleasing to the eye. Her influence occasioned that, at the age of twenty-five, Farnese was appointed cardinal, though he was not even a priest. He lived a worldly, dissolute life, maintaining numerous contacts with humanist scholars and artists from Florence and Rome. He too had a mistress, with whom he had three sons and two daughters. As a layman, he was invested with four bishoprics before being ordained a priest at the age of fifty-one and beginning a celibate life. Five years later, he became dean of the College of Cardinals. During a conclave in 1534, he was elected pope and took the regnal name Paul III. His pontificate, like his predecessors', was characterized by evident nepotism. He was

PAUL III, called the "last Renaissance pope".

MANY FILES in the Vatican Secret Archives deal with the colonization of America.

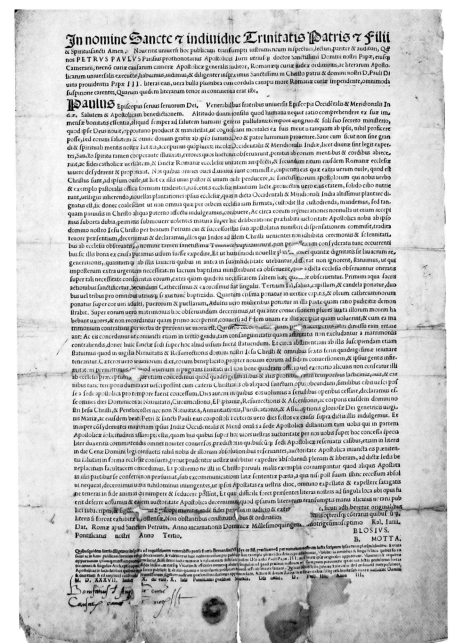

solicitous about the material security of his children and elevated two grandsons to the cardinalate—Alessandro, aged fourteen, and Guido, aged sixteen.

On the other hand, he has also gone down in history as the pope who patronized Michelangelo, excommunicated King Henry VIII of England, approved the Jesuit order, and convoked the Council of Trent to reform the Church, which was going through a grave crisis.

It was during his lifetime that America was discovered and the first native slaves brought to Europe. Contemporary scholars at the universities of Oxford and Salamanca maintained that the natives were not human beings and so were bereft of human rights. Influenced by a Dominican, Bartolomé de Las Casas, who disagreed with such views, the pope commissioned a comparative anthropological study. He also collected reports from overseas missionaries, who saw the natives as human beings.

Hence Paul III sent an apostolic letter (May 29, 1537) to the primate of Spain, Cardinal Juan Pardo de Tavera, archbishop of Toledo, wherein he stated:

SPANISH COLONIZATION of Latin America gave rise to new nations, whose cultures synthesized native and European elements.

These Indians, although they live outside the bosom of the Church, nevertheless have not been, nor are they, deprived of their freedom or of ownership of their own possessions, since they are human beings and, consequently, capable of faith and salvation.[1]

The primate was not a random addressee. Spain spearheaded the conquests in the New World, while some of the Catholic theologians from the Iberian Peninsula, led by well-known humanist Juan Ginés de Sepúlveda, had endorsed an armed conquest of America and the use of force against the natives.

Several days later, Pope Paul III promulgated an encyclical, *Sublimis Deus*, which stated:

> The enemy of the human race, who opposes all good deeds in order to bring men to destruction, beholding and envying this, invented a means never before heard of, by which he might hinder the preaching of God's word of Salvation to the people: he inspired his satellites who, to please him, have not hesitated to publish abroad that the Indians of the West and the South, and other people of whom We have recent knowledge should be treated as dumb brutes created for our service, pretending that they are incapable of receiving the Catholic Faith. We, who, though unworthy, exercise on earth the power of our Lord and seek with all our might to bring those sheep of His flock who are outside into the fold committed to our charge, consider, however, that the Indians are truly men and that they are not only capable of understanding the Catholic Faith but, according to our information, they desire exceedingly to receive it. . . .Indians and all other people who may later be discovered by Christians, are by no means to be deprived of their liberty or the possession of their property, even though they be outside the faith of Jesus Christ; and that they may and should, freely and legitimately, enjoy their liberty and the possession of their property; nor should they be in any way enslaved; should the contrary happen, it shall

PRE-COLUMBIAN AMERICA was dominated by tribal social structures.

179

ST. ADALBERT
ransoming Slavic slaves—bas-relief on Gniezno Cathedral door.

ARISTOTLE
took slavery for granted.

LETTER TO PHILEMON
written by St. Paul in defense of a slave.

180

be null and have no effect. . . . [T]he said Indians and other peoples should be converted to the faith of Jesus Christ by preaching the word of God and by the example of good and holy living.[2]

Why was Paul III's encyclical not to everyone's liking? This was largely due to the fact that slavery was one of the oldest institutions in human history. It was commonplace in almost all civilizations. Aristotle, regarded as one of the greatest philosophers in history, accepted slavery as an outcome of war and stated that men bereft of the capacity for rational thought are natural slaves. In the Roman Empire, a slave was treated as the property of his master, who could do anything to him with impunity, even kill him. The Old Testament did not question slavery, although it required that slaves be treated leniently.

In the statements recorded by the Evangelists, Jesus did not call for the abolishment of slavery. Nevertheless, his teaching and example caused his followers to see each person as a child of God, bestowed with enormous dignity.

St. Paul wrote that in Christ "there is neither slave nor free" (Gal 3:28). "For he who was called in the Lord as a slave is a freedman of the Lord. Likewise he who was free when called is a slave of Christ" (1 Cor 7:22). He appealed: "Masters, treat your slaves justly and fairly, knowing that you also have a Master in heaven" (Col 4:1). "Whatever good anyone does, he will receive the same again from the Lord, whether he is a slave or free. Masters, do the same to them, and forbear threatening, knowing that he who is both their Master and yours is in heaven, and that there is no partiality with him" (Eph 6:8–9).

St. Paul's Letter to Philemon was written in defense of a runaway slave called Onesimus. The apostle begs Philemon to accept Onesimus "no longer as a slave but more than a slave, as a beloved brother" (Philem 1:16). St. Paul uses a telling argument: "Though I am bold enough in Christ to command you to do what is required, yet for love's sake I prefer to appeal to you" (Philem 1: 8–9). He later adds: "I preferred to do nothing without your consent in order that your goodness might not be by compulsion but of your own free will" (Philem 1:14). Hence, according to St. Paul, Christianity is not to be a social revolution, imposed by force, but rather a spiritual and moral revolution, a change of heart.

Fr. Jacek Salij, a Dominican theologian from Poland, writes:

> In a society where such ideas were propagated—frequently by people not at all interested in rebellion—the days of slavery as a social institution were numbered. A common faith usually drew master and slave closer to each other, and relationships of subjection sometimes changed to intimacy and friendship, which often turned out to be stronger even than death. Church martyrology bears testimony to cases where masters were martyred alongside their slaves, such as the well-known martyrdom of St. Blandina and her master in Lyon (177 AD) or the equally famous martyrdoms of Sts. Perpetua and. Felicity in Carthage (203 AD).[5]

The writings of the Church Fathers contain many statements stigmatizing slavery. The sharpest criticism is undoubtedly that of St. Gregory of Nyssa. His commentary on the Book of Ecclesiastes condemns slavery. At the same time, however, some early Christian writers were, in certain cases, for humanitarian reasons, against granting slaves freedom, since some masters were known to rid themselves of ailing, decrepit, or old servants in order to free themselves of their obligation to look after them. St. John Chrysostom wrote that slaves were not to be freed without first teaching them a trade or giving them land otherwise they might end up in poverty or crime.

ST. GREGORY OF NYSSA
wrote fiery works condemning slavery.

ST. PAUL THE APOSTLE
writing his epistles—painting by Valentin de Boulogne.

**ST. CYPRIAN
OF CARTHAGE**
collected 10,000
gold pieces to
ransom prisoners
from the Berbers.

**ST. AMBROSE
OF MILAN**
even sold
liturgical vessels
to ransom slaves.

The decline of the Roman Empire saw a gradual improvement of a slave's legal situation. Masters could not maim or kill them, and they had to look after them in old age. Meanwhile, the material and legal status of the free rural population worsened to the point that in the 5th century both groups were practically on an equal level. During the early Middle Ages, the lives of most slaves were not much different from those of the peasants. The number of slaves steadily decreased, since it simply did not pay to have them—the exception being in sea-faring countries, whose fleets needed oarsmen.

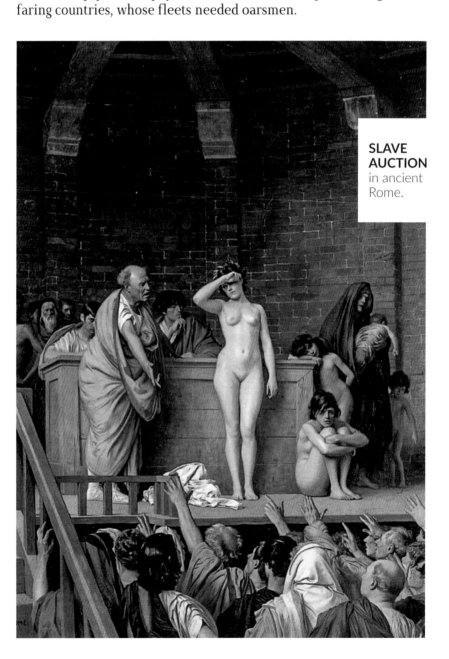

**SLAVE
AUCTION**
in ancient
Rome.

During ancient times, there developed also the practice of ransoming people who had been taken into captivity. St. Cyprian of Carthage, St. Ambrose of Milan, and St. Paulinus of Nola, for example, were famous for ransoming people. The practice took on an institutional form with the Trinitarian and Mercedarian orders, whose mission was to ransom Christians taken prisoner or enslaved by Muslims. The monks made an additional religious vow, namely that in the event of a lack of funds, they would sell themselves in order to save Christians.

European slave ownership flourished again in the 15th century, when Portuguese sailors began trading in black slaves captured in Africa, believing that they had the approval of the pope. During their conquest of America in the 16th century, the Spanish were faced with a tempting vision of cheap labor from the natives in their colonies, in spite of the Crown's objection to their enslavement. Thus began questions and disputations regarding the rights of Native Americans, not only to freedom and property, but even to their humanity.

To settle the matter, Pope Paul III promulgated the encyclical *Sublimis Deus*. What he wrote was obvious to the Franciscan missionaries, who had arrived in Mexico thirteen years earlier (1524).

NATIVE AMERICANS PRAYING before an image of Our Lady of Guadalupe.

183

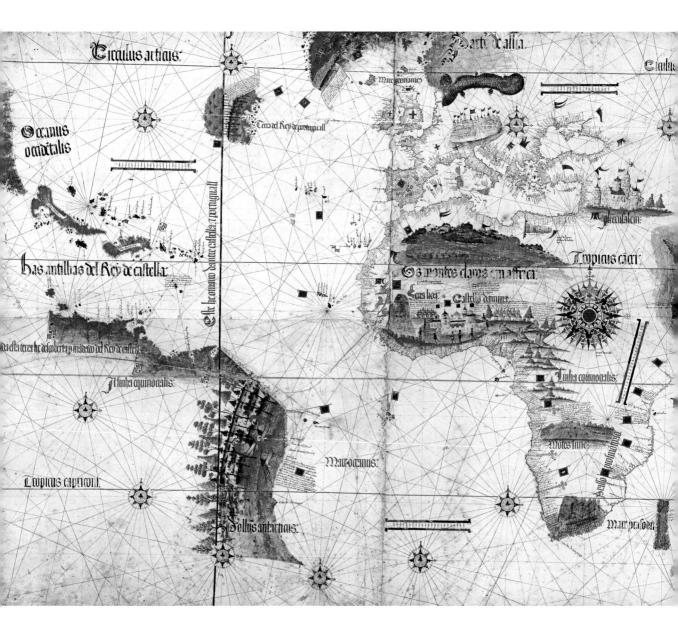

POPE ALEXANDER VI, author of *Inter Caetera*.

DIVISION OF THE NEW WORLD

THERE IS A DOCUMENT in the Vatican Secret Archives that confirms a division of the western hemisphere. It is Pope Alexander VI's bull *Inter Caetera* of May 3, 1493, which divided the spheres of influence in the New World between Spain and Portugal. In those days, both these Iberian countries were leading powers in ocean expeditions, geographical discoveries, and the conquest of new lands. In order to avoid open conflict, Madrid and Lisbon came to an understanding; the pope acted as an arbiter, who, according to the tradition of the time, legalized the right of European monarchs to newly discovered lands. The boundary demarcated by

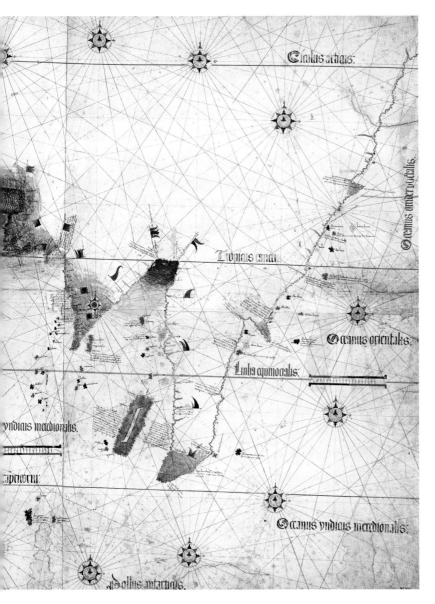

1502 MAP
depicting the division
of the New World
between Spain and
Portugal (indicated by
a vertical line).

A vila de Olinda e o pôrto do Recife no fim do século XVI
Do códice da Biblioteca da Ajuda, História de todos os sítios, embarcamentos, fundos, baixios, alturas que há na costa do Brasil

BRAZILIAN COAST,
shown in this map,
was subject to Portugal.

Alexander VI between the two spheres of influence
ran south, about 342 miles west of the Azores.
Spain had exclusive rights to all the lands it might discover to the west of this boundary, while Portugal had
rights to the east. Over a month later, on June 7,
the rulers of both countries signed the Treaty of Tordesillas, which confirmed the pope's decision, though
it introduced a crucial correction to the benefit
of Lisbon, as the demarcation line was moved over
toward the Pacific, about 1,200 miles west of
the Azores. Thanks to that correction, Brazil was
discovered in the Portuguese sphere.

TREATY OF TORDESILLAS
confirmed the partitioning
of America.

MSGR. EDUARDO CHÁVEZ
with Grzegorz Górny.

HERNÁN CORTÉS,
Spanish conquistadore who conquered the Aztecs.

There are few people who know the history of the first Catholic missions on the American continent better than Msgr. Eduardo Chávez, a descendant of both Native Americans and white newcomers from beyond the ocean. He sees his own country as arising from a synthesis of two cultures: native and European. He studied theology and philosophy at the Pontifical Gregorian University in Rome, defending his doctorate in Church history. He is the cofounder and rector of the Instituto Superior de Estudios Guadalupanos (Higher Institute of Guadalupan Studies), which seeks to bring the phenomena connected with Our Lady of Guadalupe to a broader public.

We met Msgr. Chávez in his office in Mexico City, where he was preparing a work for publication. All told, he has published about thirty scholarly works, both specialized and popular, primarily concerned with the history of the Church in Mexico. He told us about the conflict that arose between the Spanish conquerors and the Franciscan missionaries at the very beginning of the conquest.

FRANCISCO PIZARRO,
Spanish conquistadore, conqueror of the Incas, infamous slave trader.

Before moving on to this confrontation, however, we have to go back in time. Spanish conquistadores, led by Hernán Cortés, were the first white people to appear in the Aztec Empire (1519). Though he had just 566 soldiers, he managed to conquer the most powerful Native American empire, with a population of ten million. That was primarily due to the fact that the Europeans found devoted allies among the neighboring tribes. Take, for instance, the Tlaxcalans, who lived in constant fear of the Aztecs, as the latter fought so-called "flower wars" against them, ritual wars for the sole purpose of capturing prisoners to be sacrificed to the gods.

Sacrificial days were celebrated as feast days. The victim was taken to the top of a pyramid-like temple. Four priests seized the victim by the arms and legs and laid him on a sacrificial stone. A fifth priest split open the living victim's chest with an obsidian glass knife and tore out the heart with his hands. Then he sprinkled the altar with blood, threw the heart into a large stone bowl, and pushed the body down the temple steps. The scale of the proceedings was gigantic. In 1487 alone, during the consecration of a temple in Tenochtitlan, tens of thousands were thus killed over four days; historians estimate the number of victims to be have been between 21,000 and 84,000.

Mass ritual murders were a part of the Aztec religion. They believed that they were the chosen people, that they were responsible for the prolongation of the world's existence. In order that day might follow night, they believed, it was necessary to offer human sacrifices, demanded by Huitzilopochtli, a terrible and insatiable god who directed the movement of the sun. Were there to have been a lack of human hearts in stone bowls and blood flowing down the temple steps, the

TEOTIHUACÁN, a holy city for various tribes in pre-Columbian America, located in what is today Mexico.

RITUAL KNIVES used by Aztec priests to extract the hearts of living victims.

MARTÍN DE VALENCIA, a Franciscan, one of the first 12 missionaries in Mexico.

earth would have been plunged into darkness, and life would have ended forever. So the Aztecs saw themselves as mankind's benefactors.

The Spaniards were convinced that the Aztec religion was a demonic cult. This mobilized them all the more to fight the disciples of a bloodthirsty god. When the Aztecs were defeated and stopped offering human sacrifices, they were overcome by a sense of despair and hopelessness, as the sun still kept rising and the world continued to exist. It turned out that their religion had been an illusion and that the death of countless prisoners had been in vain. The vision on which they had built their lives faded and was replaced by a spiritual, mental, and ideological void.

FLORENTINE CODEX from the 16th century, depicting Aztecs sacrificing human beings.

Apathy among the natives, combined with a mood of profound fatalism, made them quickly succumb to the Spanish invaders. Plunder, violence, slavery, and all manner of injustice became the order of the day. Spain was far away, so the conquistadores felt that they would go unpunished for their evil deeds.

Compared with other conquistadores, Cortés was not cruel or lacking in scruples. In his own way, he respected the natives. A Nahua woman, La Malinche, became his lifelong companion and his chief adviser in negotiations with tribal leaders. He was undoubtedly solicitous about the salvation of Native Americans, since he was the first to invite Franciscan missionaries to Mexico. Hence the first group of religious—twelve men led by Fr. Martín de Valencia —arrived in 1524.

Shortly afterward, disturbing news began to reach the court in Madrid. Rodrigo de Albornoz, an auditor who had returned from Mexico, related that the conquistadores intended to become independent of Spain and that their administration was marked by crime and injustice. Holy Roman Emperor Charles V decided to act, sending new administrators to Mexico, both secular and religious.

FRANCISCAN MISSIONARIES led by Fr. Martín de Valencia, greeted by Hernán Cortés in New Spain.

In August 1528, a ship set sail for America from Seville, with members of the first Royal Audience of Mexico: President Nuño Beltrán de Guzman, Alfonso de Parada, Francisco Maldonado, Juan Ortiz de Matienzo, and Diego Delgadillo (joined later by Gonzalo de Salazar, a tax collector). They made up the highest royal judicial tribunal in New Spain. But in reality, they were a sort of collegiate government. A Franciscan accompanied them, Fr. Juan de Zumárraga, who until recently had been the superior of the monastery in Abrojo. He had been nominated bishop of Mexico by the emperor, but his nomination still awaited confirmation by the pope.

It was a time when Madrid lacked the means to fund overseas expeditions and conquests. Thus these ventures were mainly privately financed. This meant that the conquistadores were not subject to the control of the central authorities and that they themselves established their own order. Being, in the main, troublemakers, desirous of adventure and wealth, they oppressed and exploited the natives, busying themselves with multiplying their fortunes rather than working for the Crown's interests. With this in mind, Charles V sent the first Audience to Mexico.

NUÑO BELTRÁN DE GUZMÁN, Spanish conquistadore, infamous for persecuting the native inhabitants of America.

189

JUAN DE ZUMÁRRAGA,
Spanish Basque Franciscan, first bishop of Mexico, defender of Indian rights.

Unfortunately, the situation was then exacerbated. The new administrators turned out to be worse than their predecessors. They soon came into conflict with Cortés, who shortly afterwards set out for Honduras while they confiscated his property. From then on, they were the only masters in New Spain. A period of even greater oppression of the natives began, marked by murder, violence, and plunder. Nuño Beltran de Guzman had a particularly wretched reputation among the local population, since he organized Indian hunts and sold his captives as if they were but animals.

FIGHTING THE AZTECS
A militia led by Nuño Beltrán de Guzmán, president of the first Royal Audience of Mexico.

Because they were practically beyond the control of Madrid, due to the great distance, the first Audience did not respect the laws enacted by the Spanish Crown. Only Catholic missionaries, including Fr. Zumárraga—upon whom Charles I, the king of Spain, had conferred the title "Protector of the Indians", with a charge to guard their rights—protested against the conduct of the ruthless administrators. Zumárraga was against the Audience's policies, but he did not have the means to counteract them. Neither did he have the authority, as he had not as yet been confirmed bishop by the pope. The Franciscans also publicly condemned the sins of local authorities and so made enemies of the conquistadores themselves.

According to Msgr. Chávez, it would be a mistake to imagine that there were at that time two monolithic blocks opposed to each other, the Native Americans and the Spanish. In reality, both camps were

FIRST CRITIC OF COLONIZATION

The first public defense of Native American rights was a sermon by a Dominican, Fr. Antonio de Montesinos, delivered on December 21, 1511, in Santo Domingo, now the capital of the Dominican Republic. The preacher, turning to the colonizers, said:

> You are all in mortal sin, and live and die in it. . . . Tell me, by what right or justice do you hold these Indians in such a cruel and horrible servitude? On what authority have you waged such detestable wars against these peoples, who dwelt quietly and peacefully on their own land? . . . Why do you keep them so oppressed and exhausted, without giving them enough to eat or curing them of the sicknesses they incur from the excessive labor you give them, and they die, or rather you kill them, in order to extract and acquire gold every day? And what care do you take that they should be instructed in religion? . . . Are these not men? . . .Do they not have rational souls? Are you not bound to love them as yourselves?[24]

The sermon caused a scandal. After the Mass, the incensed viceroy of the Indies Diego Columbus (Christopher Columbus' son) issued the Dominicans with an ultimatum: either Montesinos stopped publicly criticizing the colonizers, or the monks would be expelled from Santo Domingo. But a week later, December 28, Montesinos delivered a yet sharper sermon, wherein he presented five principles that Europeans ought to respect in America: (1) divine law was above private and state law; (2) there was no racial superiority in the eyes of God; (3) slavery and servitude were illegal; (4) freedom and wealth seized from the natives ought to be returned; and (5) Native Americans should not be converted to Christianity by force, but rather by the example of a good and holy life. The Montesinos matter became well known in the Spanish colonies, and news of it eventually reached the royal court. The Dominican had to put his case to King Ferdinand, who not only acknowledged that he was in the right but also summoned a team of theologians and lawyers to draft a code of conduct regarding the natives of the New World. The result was the Laws of Burgos (1512) and the Laws of Valladolid (1513), the first laws in defense of Native Americans. Antonio de Montesinos returned to America, where he ministered until his death in 1540, aged sixty-five and universally respected.

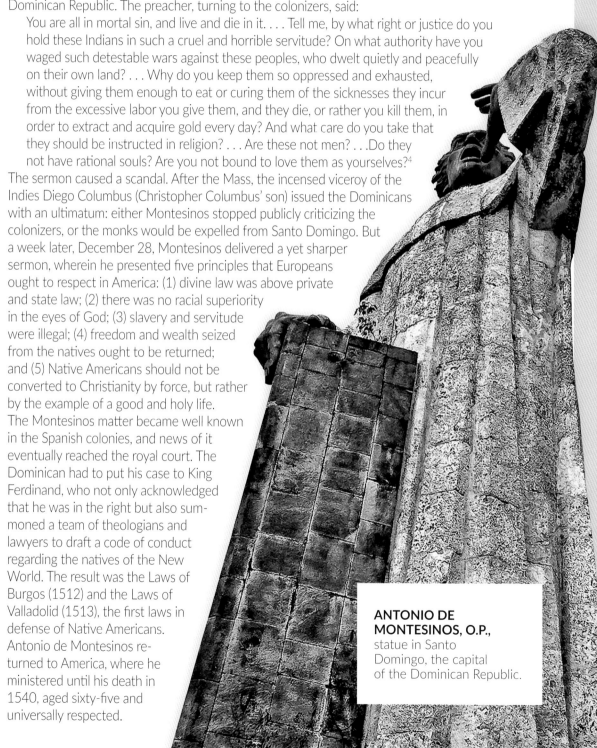

ANTONIO DE MONTESINOS, O.P., statue in Santo Domingo, the capital of the Dominican Republic.

MSGR. EDUARDO CHÁVEZ, Church historian who specializes in the history of the evangelization of Mexico.

MEXICAN CROSS, with the Gospel message expressed through Native American motifs, a symbol of the Christian inculturation of Mexico.

diverse and divided. The natives never constituted a united front, while the tension among them was cleverly exploited by Cortés. There were also serious differences among the Iberians concerning conduct in relation to the Indians. The greatest conflict flared up between the administrators and the missionaries.

The first Audience, as Fr. Geronimo de Mendieta, a 16th-century chronicler of Mexican Church history, relates,

> turned against the friars as if they were capital enemies, not only deprived them of the alms they used to give, but endeavoring to defame them and tarnish them in the eyes of the public, and to punish and disfavor them as much as possible. For fear that the friars might inform the king and his advisers of their abuses, the first Audience used utmost diligence to control the roads and trails by which the missionaries might have sent letters. So they gave orders not to carry the monks' letters until they had been checked. Later, they searched ships, turning everything upside down to the ballasts in search of letters by friars. Not content with that, they decided—just in case—to protect themselves at the cost of the good names of the innocent monks, discrediting them, in the event that they managed to get a letter sent. To this effect, assuming the roles of witnesses and writers, they prepared their own reports, accusing the holy bishop and his friars of things that would never have even entered their imaginations.[5]

The letters to Madrid put not only the Franciscans in a bad light, but also the natives. It was maintained that they were soulless barbarians, which justified subjecting them to pillage and violence. That argument convinced some theologians and lawyers, who supported the first Audience's policies.

According to Msgr. Chávez,, the missionaries, on the one hand, destroyed monuments and objects connected with pagan cults: temples, statues, and codices. But on the other hand, they had great concern for local cultures, in all that did not pertain to the tribal religions. So they were solicitous about the natives' languages, customs, and practices and thus helped to preserve their various heritages. However, they were primarily concerned with saving the natives' souls, wanting to pass on the truths of the Gospel in the most understandable and convincing manner possible, knowing that the best way to do so was to utilize the people's own languages and cultures. But the greatest obstacle to evangelization turned out to be the attitude of the conquistadores, which was a total negation of Christian principles. The natives knew that the Europeans said one thing but did another. At the same time, they observed the ever-increasing conflict among the white newcomers.

Shortly after arriving in Mexico, Bishop Zumárraga summoned the native elders and instructed them to come to him with any complaints

EXPEDITION deep into America, led by conquistadore Cristóbal de Olid (1522).

about the conduct of the administrators. In reply, the first Audience announced that any who did so would be hanged. As the power lay in secular hands, the natives were afraid to complain to the bishop.

The Spanish viceroys felt more and more immune from punishment and were not afraid to challenge the Church directly. On the orders of Diego Delgadillo, an armed unit forced its way into a convent in

EMPEROR CHARLES V, first ruler of "an empire on which the sun never sets".

GONZALO DE SALAZAR, governor of New Spain for over one year.

CAPTURE OF GUADALAJARA, the conquistadores were aided by the Tlaxcala tribe.

194

Texcoco and kidnapped two native novices. Two others were kidnapped in a monastery in Huexotzinco and eventually killed; they had been in hiding as they had angered Guzman by complaining to the bishop about the conquistadores' conduct.

The situation became worse. During a Mass attended by members of the first Audience, Fr. Antonio Ortis began loudly to condemn their ill deeds from the pulpit. Nuño de Guzman sprang to his feet and told him to be silent. Undaunted, the Franciscan continued his homily. So Gonzalo

de Salazar's men forced their way to him and coerced the preacher to be silent. People in the tightly packed church never forgot that demonstration of strength.

Msgr. Chávez, relating those events, helplessly spread out his hands. How could the natives have been evangelized, he asked, when Spanish Catholics gave an antitestimony to the Gospel by not respecting the celebrants of that Mass and even coming to blows with them?

Guzman and his companions continued tirelessly to fabricate false evidence against Cortés, Zumárraga, and the missionaries. They sent reports to Madrid wherein they painted their adversaries in the worst possible light. They also tried to prevent the Franciscans from alerting Charles V about what was happening in New Spain.

According to Joaquín García Icazbalceta, a 19th-century Mexican historian:

> From the very beginning, members of the Audience put a great deal of effort into intercepting correspondence to the royal court. They had agents at ports who scrupulously checked goods and people arriving in Mexico and departing for Europe. They withheld letters they managed to discover, sending them to the capital. Through these letters, the administrators came to know who their hidden enemies were and what their open enemies had written. News of this disgraceful abuse, clear proof of the perpetrators' guilty consciences, reached the king. The indignant monarch issued an urgent directive on July 31, 1529, prohibiting the opening, withholding, and interception of letters in whatever way under pain of a lifelong exile from His Highness' territories. That reprimand, instead of throwing the Audience into confusion, prompted only a gesture of disrespect toward the king; the administrators had the audacity to inform the king that it would be to his benefit to do the opposite.[7]

The Audience ignored the king's prohibition and continued to withhold correspondence. Bishop Zumárraga, however, did not back down. He came to an understanding with a certain Basque sailor, who hid the bishop's report in a barrel of wax. He tied the barrel to the stern of his boat, pulling it along like a buoy, not hoisting the barrel up onto

BIBLIOGRAPHY OF 16TH-CENTURY MEXICO by Mexican historian Joaquín García Icazbalceta.

CHARLES V SURROUNDED by enemies attempting to bind his legs with ropes—a 16th-century engraving.

DISMISSED,
Nuño Beltrán
de Guzmán spent
the last six years
of his life in
Spain, in poverty,
forgotten.

**MAP OF NEW
SPAIN,**
the overseas
province of
Madrid, published
in William
Robertson's
*History
of America*.

the deck until he was on the open sea. It was thus that the bishop's first report reached the king, and it described all the administrators' crimes, evil deeds, and abuses in detail, referring to Guzmán as "a greedy devil from hell".

After reading the report, Charles V immediately dismissed Nuño de Guzman. Guzman had been forewarned. Not waiting for a decision from Madrid, he left Mexico and together with a detachment of five hundred soldiers set out to conquer new territories outside the monarch's control. He founded, for example, the city of Guadalajara, where he became infamous for many cruelties against the local tribes.

One might have expected that after Guzman's departure, the violence would cease and the Spanish administrators would finally listen to the bishop. But it was otherwise. The remaining members of the first Audience were not at all better than their erstwhile superior. There were more conflicts between them and the missionaries, the most serious of which took place on March 4, 1530.

That day, an armed first Audience unit forced its way into the Franciscan monastery in Mexico City and dragged Br. Cristóbal de Angulo out of his cell, along with García de Llerena, Cortés' servant. Both were tortured the next day. Bishop Zumárraga organized a procession demanding their release. A disturbance broke out in the city. Icazbalceta described the events thus:

Insults were hurled by both sides. The bishop, unable to bear Delgadillo's public affronts against the monks, lost patience and responded with the same tenor. When the turmoil was at its peak, the procession was attacked, and the belligerent Delgadillo even struck the bishop with a spear, which fortunately did him no harm.[8]

Msgr. Chávez underlines that this was an unprecedented thing. These Spanish Catholics were not only openly scoffing at the king's orders, but trying to murder publicly the head of the local Church. It seemed that there was nothing sacred to them. So the hierarch declared that he would excommunicate the conquistadores if they dared to harm the two prisoners. The threat of excommunication did not make much impression on them. On March 7, Br. Cristóbal de Angulo was hung, drawn, and quartered, while García de Llerena was given a hundred lashes and had one of his feet cut off.

Bishop Zumárraga excommunicated all the members of the first Audience, suspended Christian liturgical worship in the capital of New Spain, and ordered all the religious to leave the capital. Msgr. Chávez writes that the baptized natives felt they had been abandoned by their gods once again: first by their Aztec deities and now by the Christian God.

FRANCISCAN MONASTERY and Church of St. James in Tlatelolco, 16th-century capital of Mexico.

197

MAIN ENEMY
of the first
Audience, Juan
de Zumárraga.

At that time, according to Msgr. Chávez, the evangelization of Mexico seemed to be a lost cause: just a handful of missionaries—barely forty—an enormous territory, a variable climate, an alien culture, and a great number of languages. The natives, conquered, subjugated, and decimated by the diseases brought by the Europeans, were in a state of despair. They heard that whole generations of their forefathers had served Satan, which only deepened their desolation. In addition, the crimes of the conquistadores, who had proved to be the Gospel's greatest enemies, contradicted the Christian message. Msgr. Chávez poses the question: How, in such a situation, would it have been possible to proclaim God's love and claim that this love was most fully revealed in the Church? In such circumstances, it was a miracle that even some of the natives were converted.

Nonetheless, as many as ten million were baptized over the following decades. Not only individuals and families requested to be baptized, but also whole tribes. People often walked for several days from regions where no missionary had ever been.

Br. Gerónimo de Mendieta, a 16th-century Franciscan chronicler wrote:
> Initially, two or three hundred came at a time. The number of people grew continually; it multiplied until they were coming by

NATIVE AMERICAN BAPTIZED
in José Vivara Valderramy's 18th-century painting.

FRANCISCANS
driving away
demons with
their prayers.
This 16th-century
print from a book
by Diego Muñoz
Camargo.

the thousands. Some came from places a two days' walk away, others, three or four days', and others from yet more distant places. Those who saw this were amazed. There came children and adults, old men and old women, the sick and the healthy. Baptized parents brought their children to be baptized, baptized youth brought their parents, the husbands their wives, wives their husbands.[7]

The Christianization of the natives turned out to be nearly universal, with most of the conversions true and lasting. Historians acknowledge that it was the greatest missionary success in Church history. Henceforward, Mexico has been regarded as one of the world's most Catholic countries. Mexicans stayed true to the Faith even in the face of the bloody persecutions they were subjected to in the 20th century.

How was it possible that such mass conversions—which completely changed the face of the country in just a short time—occurred at a time when evangelization seemed to be a lost cause? Msgr. Chávez, who has dedicated many years to coming up with an answer, has no doubt that it was due to the image of Our Lady of Guadalupe, which to the natives, contained something like a code. Decoding the signs and the symbols that had inexplicably appeared on the *tilma* of a

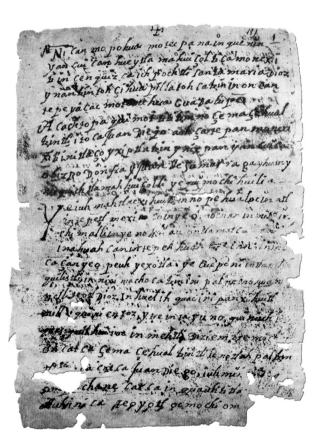

PATRONESS OF MEXICO, Our Lady of Guadalupe (top).

200

***NICAN MOPOHUA* MANUSCRIPT**, discovered in a New York public library toward the end of the 20th century.

native Christian, they became convinced of Christianity's authenticity. No historian has, as yet, come up with any other convincing evidence that might explain such widespread conversions.

Msgr. Chávez points out another fact: the faith of the converts was so strong that not even further crimes committed by the conquistadores were able to shake it. The natives could separate the essence of Christianity from the evil committed by Christians—of which there was no lack. The struggle between the oppressors and the defenders of the native population of the Americas continued. Catholic religious in particular played a great role in that struggle.

DISCOVERY OF MANUSCRIPTS

FOR THE GREATER part of the 20th century, many critics questioned the authenticity of the Guadalupe apparitions (1531) and even denied the existence of its main hero, Juan Diego, a Native American. They argued that the oldest document on the matter was from 1649 and that there were no earlier written sources. Hence it was suspected that the whole matter might well have been concocted a hundred years later.

The situation changed due to two discoveries. The first, towards the end of the 1980s, was a manuscript entitled *Nican Mopohua*, which was discovered in a public library in New York. It was written (1553–1554) by a Native American, Antonio Valeriano, who knew Juan Diego personally. It turned out that the manuscript had been stolen by American soldiers during the war with Mexico in 1847 and then taken to the United States. The second discovery, in 1995, was of the so-called

Codex Escalada, the oldest historical account of the Guadalupe apparitions (1548). Thus it was proven that Juan Diego really did exist and that his experiences were already known of in the mid-16th century.

FIRST EDITION
of *Nican Mopohua* (1649).

CODEX ESCALADA, discovered in 1995.

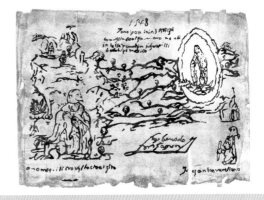

BP. ZUMÁRRAGA KNEELING before Juan Diego and the image of Our Lady that appeared on his tilma.

One of the most important figures in that struggle was Vasco de Quiroga, a Galician lawyer who was sent to Mexico by the royal court after the dismissal of the first Audience. On hearing of the mistreatment of the natives, he volunteered to help them even though he was sixty years of age. A member of the second Audience, he became known as a great benefactor of the natives, a defender of their rights, establishing mission settlements called *pueblas*, which

VASCO DE QUIROGA
in a *puebla*,
a missionary
settlement.

FIRST BISHOP OF MICHOACÁN,
Vasco
de Quiroga,
a great defender
of Native
American rights.

were located in enclosed and guarded areas beyond the reach of the conquistadores. Each settlement had homes, a school, a hospital, an inn for guests, and craft workshops. Both men and women were taught to read, write, and count, and they were also familiarized with the achievements of European civilization. In 1538, at the age of sixty-eight, de Quiroga was ordained a priest and appointed the bishop of Michoacán. He personally funded the building of hospitals, orphanages, shelters, and schools. He also wrote a special catechism for the natives. He died in 1565, at the age of ninety-five, in the odor of sanctity.

It was also necessary to take up the struggle for Native American rights in Europe. Fr. Francisco de Vitoria, a Spanish Dominican, distinguished himself in that struggle. In 1532, he gave a series of lectures at the University of Salamanca that sent great shock waves throughout Europe. He maintained that the natives had the same rights as other people and that no higher civilization or religion could justify a violation of those rights. He argued against the view that the natives were bereft of reason: "In essence they are not irrational; they just use reason in their own way."

Fr. Bartolomé de Las Casas, a Dominican, turned out to be the best-known defender of Native American rights. His father was one of the sailors who accompanied Columbus on his ocean expeditions. In 1502 eighteen-year-old Bartolomé sailed to America to participate in the conquest and colonization of first Hispaniola and then Cuba. While a priest, he became an owner of land and slaves and grew rich. However, he experienced a conversion, after which he gave up his wealth and his slaves and became a Dominican. He spent the rest of his life advocating for the rights of the natives. He ministered in Cuba, Peru, Nicaragua, and Mexico, where he was the bishop of Chiapas (1543-1547). He gained friends and respect everywhere, defusing tension between the foreign administration and the local population. He frequently sailed to Spain to plead for the natives at the royal court. Thanks to his efforts, Pope Paul III promulgated the encyclical *Sublimis Deus*, while Emperor Charles V issued Las Leyes Nuevas (the New Laws), which prohibited the enslavement of Native Americans.

Las Casas incurred the disdain of many influential officials and had to meet the criticism of numerous scholars. An Andalusian Dominican, Juan Ginés de Sepúlveda—a humanist and the tutor of Philip II, the successor to the throne—turned out to be his best-known

BARTOLOMÉ DE LAS CASAS, Spanish Dominican, spokesman for Native American rights.

SHORT ACCOUNT OF THE DESTRUCTION OF THE INDIES Las Casas' main work: Spanish edition, 1552 (left); French edition, 1620 (right); Italian edition, 1643 (above).

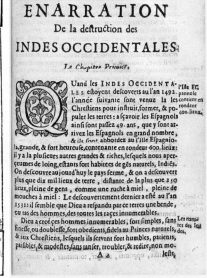

**LAS CASAS
SAYING MASS**
for natives.

**JUAN GINÉS DE
SEPÚLVEDA,**
Las Casas'
main intellectual
opponent.

intellectual opponent. Sepúlveda was the first to translate Aristotle into Spanish and adopted his views on slavery. He maintained that some people were destined to that state because they were unable to distinguish between good and evil or between truth and falsehood, and thus they had no right to happiness. This particularly pertained to barbarians and idolaters, who were to be combated, conquered, and converted. If they resisted, this only testified to their perversity, in which case they should be destroyed.

As the matter evoked a great deal of emotion and controversy in Spain, the authorities enjoined the adversaries to hold a public debate, which took place at the Colegio de San Gregorio in Valladolid, presided over by Cardinal Salvatore Roncieri, the pope's representative .

The difference between Sepúlveda and Las Casas was immediately apparent. The former had never been overseas. He was a cold theoretician, substantiating the facts of history; for him, Aristotle's *Politics* was the starting point for debate. The latter had spent several decades in the Americas. He spoke passionately

COLEGIO DE SAN GREGORIO, Valladolid, where the famous theological debates about native rights were held in 1550.

VALLADOLID DEBATE first edition, record of the 1552 theological debate between Sepúlveda and Las Casas.

about his contacts with the natives, whom he saw as equals. For him, the Gospel was the basic point of reference.

Las Casas advocated a peaceful Christianization, seeing a declaration of war on the natives as unjustifiable.

He concluded his speech with the following words: "The Christian religion treats all nations justly and equally. It does not deprive anyone of freedom, nor does it take away anyone's due rights

205

PROTECTOR OF
THE INDIANS

remains
Fr. Bartolomé
de Las Casas'
moniker
to this day.

THE NEW LAWS

(Las Leyes
Nuevas) were
issued in 1542
by Charles V,
prohibiting the
enslavement
and forced
labor of Native
Americans.

under the pretext that nature itself has destined him for the state of slavery."

After the debate, both sides claimed victory. But the royal court decreed that Las Casas was in the right. The authorities prohibited the publication of works by Sepúlveda justifying slavery, whereas the works of his adversary were approved, with Las Casas' *Short Account of the Destruction of Indies* circulated throughout Europe.

For almost three centuries, the Catholic Church in Latin America cultivated the tongues of the indigenous tribes, the Nahuatl, Guarani, Quechua, and Purépecha languages, developing their grammar, syntax, and orthography, publishing dictionaries, and even founding special philological departments at universities. The standardization of languages in South and Central America did not occur until the 20th century, under the influence of the Enlightenment. It was then that the actual Hispanization of the continent occurred.

Let us return to Bartolomé de Las Casas. The Dominican's success had an unexpected side effect. The defense of Indian rights saw the colonizers turning to Africa for cheap labor. They began to bring black slaves to the American continent, and they were physically stronger and hardier than the Indians. Initially, Las Casas supported the practice as the lesser evil, but he changed his mind and regretted his attitude for the rest of his life.

There were significantly more defenders of Indians on the Iberian Peninsula. It is thanks to them that the coloniztion of Latin America, occupied by Catholic Spaniards and Portuguese, occurred otherwise than in New England, conquered by Protestant Anglo-Saxons. The latter saw the continent as the Promised Land, and the Indian tribes as Canaanites to be wiped out. So it is no surprise that in the United States there are barely one-and-a-half million "members of Indian tribes" (people who have at least one-quarter Indian blood), many of whom live on reservations. A different situation prevails in Latin America, where the decided majority of the inhabitants are Indians or Mestizos. This fact speaks volumes about the colonization of the New World.

PEOPLE OF MEXICO today includes Mestizos (60%), Indians (30%), and Caucasians (9%), with an 89% Catholic population. The Basilica of Our Lady of Guadalupe is the Mexican Catholics' national shrine.

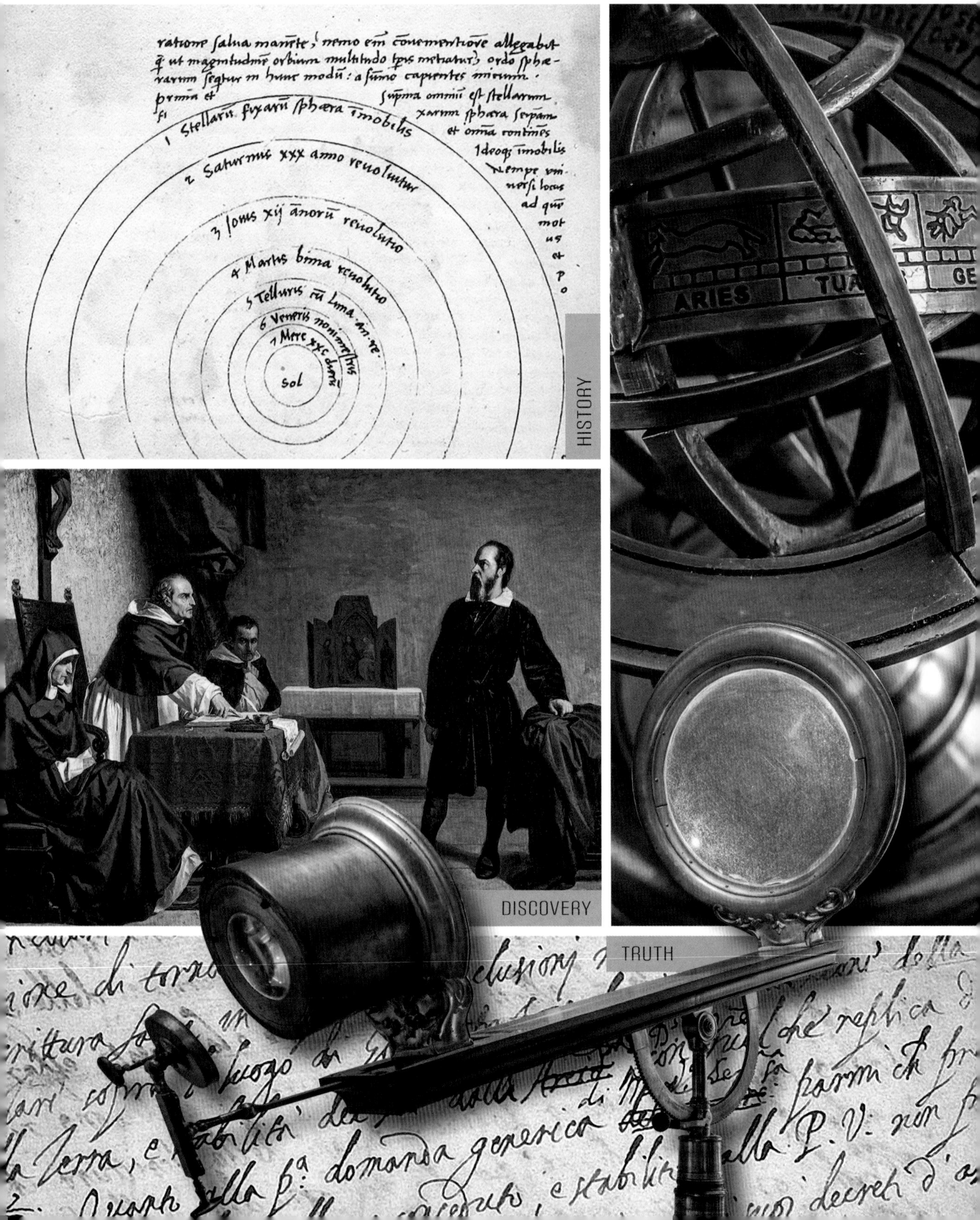
HISTORY
ARIES
DISCOVERY
TRUTH

The Trial of Galileo

Trial of Galileo

The most famous scholar condemned by the Inquisition

The Galileo Galilei affair had preoccupied Karol Wojtyła for a long time. He particularly pondered the relationship between faith and reason, which has come into question during the numerous debates concerning the trial of the 17th-century scholar. To many people, this affair is the most conclusive proof of the impossibility of reconciling science with religion. Wojtyła, shortly after becoming Pope John Paul II, decided to clarify certain issues connected with the trial of Galileo, which still arouses such strong emotions.

Vatican City

ITALY

SOUTHERN HEMISPHERE
through animated constellations—illustration in Andreas Cellarius' *Harmonia Macrocosmica* (1661).

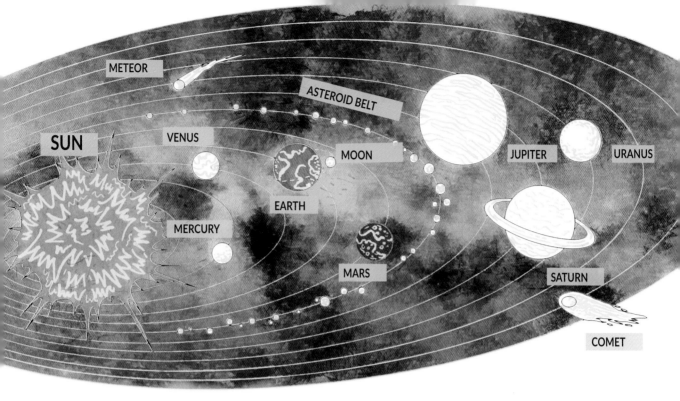

On November 10, 1979, when the Pontifical Academy of Sciences was celebrating the hundredth anniversary of Albert Einstein's birth, John Paul II said:

The greatness of Galileo is known to everyone, like that of Einstein; but unlike the latter, whom we are honouring today before the College of Cardinals in the apostolic palace, the former had to suffer a great deal—we cannot conceal the fact—at the hands of men and organisms of the Church.[1]

Further in the address, the pope spoke of intensifying research on one of the most notorious trials in history. To that end, he established (July 3, 1982) a special scientific commission, composed of both clerical and secular researchers and gave them access to all the documents on the subject housed in the Vatican Secret Archives. The researchers were divided into working groups to deal with separate fields: exegesis, science and epistemology, history and culture. Eleven years of research bore fruit in numerous publications that help one to see the Galileo affair a subject around which so many misunderstandings had arisen over the centuries—in the right light.

HELIOCENTRIC SYSTEM
holds that the earth and other planets orbit the sun. In the 17th century, Johannes Kepler discovered that the planets orbit not in a circle, but in an ellipse.

211

**GALILEO
GALILEI**
showing
the doge
of Venice how
to use his
telescope—fresco
by Giuseppe
Bertini.

In a survey by the European Parliament of students from member countries of the European Economic Community, almost 30 percent were convinced that Galileo was burnt alive at the stake by the Church, and virtually all (97 percent) believed that he was tortured in various ways. Some of the few who said something specific about Galileo claimed he said the following in response to the inquisitors who sentenced him: *"Eppur si muove"* ("And yet it moves"). The students said Galieo's accusers used religious beliefs to deny scientific facts about the earth's rotation around the sun.[2]

In reality, the "And yet it moves" statement was thought up by Giuseppe Baretti, a journalist in London in 1757. Contrary to popular belief, Galileo died in his bed, not at the stake. He did not spend a single day in prison. He was never tortured, which was first alleged as late as 1841 in *The Martyrs of Science, or the Lives of Galileo, Tycho Brahe, and Kepler*, a book by Sir David Brewster, a Scottish physicist.

Even those who are familiar with the above facts are inclined to see Galileo's trial as a conflict between science and religious superstition, between freedom of inquiry and a repressive system that suppressed research. That dispute, according to numerous commentators, has created an unbridgeable abyss between science and religion.

Prof. Franco Cardini, one of the most distinguished contemporary Italian historians, awarded the Galileo Prize by the Grand Orient of Italy in 2013, disagrees with this view, which he sees as a gross simplification. In reality, it was not a conflict between faith and reason, since most scholars in Europe at that time were opposed to some of Galileo's theories. Lutheran professors at the Protestant University of Tübingen, though bitter antipapists themselves, raised triumphant toasts on hearing of Galileo's conviction. On the other hand, some Catholic scholars had openly voiced views similar to those of Galileo, yet did not run into trouble, for example, Pierre Gassendi, who even held several Church positions.

In order to get to the crux of the 17th-century scientific controversy, we must go back to ancient times. Since the dawn of time, mankind has wondered about the structure of the universe. In antiquity, the theory of geocentrism was popular, for it certainly appeared as though the sun, the moon, and the other celestial bodies orbited around the earth. The geocentric theory was first formulated in the 4th century BC by Eudoxus of Cnidus, an astronomer, mathematician, and philosopher, and six centuries later, Claudius Ptolemy from Alexandria gave it its final form, which came to be known as the Ptolemaic geocentric model and was accepted for the next 1,600 years.

The longevity of the geocentric model was connected not only with the limitations of scientific equipment, but also with a philosophy that saw the earth as being in a privileged position in the

FRANCO CARDINI, Italian historian, leading expert on Galileo's life.

JESUS CHRIST as the architect of the universe.

PTOLEMAIC COSMOLOGY, modelled in a picture of the solar system with the earth in the center, from Andreas Cellarius' *Harmonia Macrocosmica.*

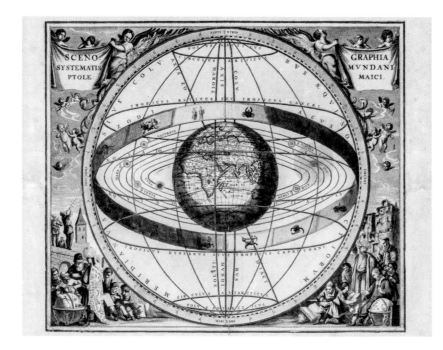

universe, which was perfectly compatible with the Christian vision of the world, where man, created in the image and likeness of God, was the crown of creation.

Nicolaus Copernicus, a Polish astronomer, was the first publicly to contest the geocentric theory. In 1543, he published his *On the Revolutions of the Celestial Spheres*, wherein he formulated a

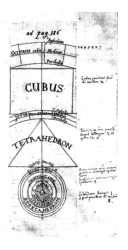

ASTRONOMIAE PARS OPTICA
by Johannes Kepler, 1604 (top).

GEOMETRIC HARMONY
in Kepler's *Harmonices Mundi*, 1619.

SOLAR SYSTEM
drawn by Nicolaus Copernicus.

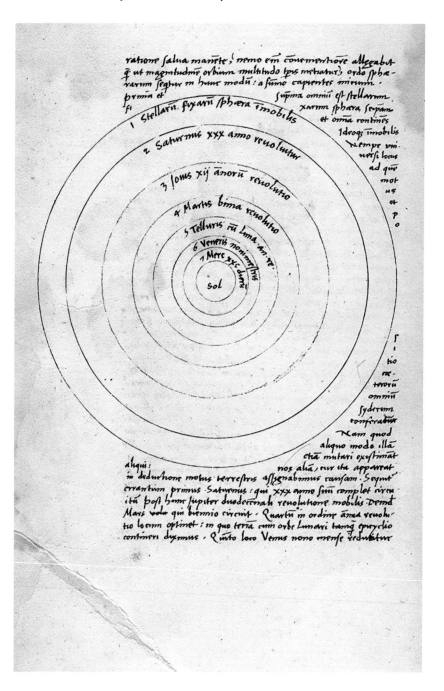

new theory that saw the earth orbiting the sun; the sun was at the center of the universe. He published his work at the instigation of two Catholic hierarchs, namely, Bishop Tiedemann Giese and Cardinal Nikolaus von Schönberg. The latter wrote to Copernicus: "Therefore with the utmost earnestness I entreat you, most learned sir, unless I inconvenience you, to communicate this discovery of yours to scholars."

But Copernicus did not provide irrefutable evidence to confirm his theory. Hence, in the following decades, the Ptolemaic geocen-

NICOLAUS COPERNICUS, statue, Polish Academy of Sciences, Warsaw.

tric and Copernican heliocentric theories were seen as two equivalent hypotheses, though the former had significantly more supporters in academic circles. Protestants were usually more critical of heliocentrism than Catholics. Martin Luther said of Copernicus: "The fool wants to turn the whole art of astronomy upside-down." Philipp Melanchthon followed suit: "We will not tolerate similar fantasies." The Catholic Church, however, did not condemn Copernicus, but recommended that his theory be seen solely as a probable hypothesis and not as a scientific certainty.

215

GENIUS FROM TORUŃ

ASTRONOMER COPERNICUS, *or Conversations with God*, painting by Jan Matejko, 1873.

TITLE PAGE of Copernicus' *On the Revolutions of the Celestial Spheres*, second edition, Basel, 1566.

Nicolaus Copernicus, a Polish scholar, was born in Toruń in 1473. He was truly a Renaissance man: astronomer, mathematician, lawyer, economist, physician, cartographer, military strategist, translator. He studied in Kraków, Bologna, and Padua. After receiving minor orders, he fulfilled many functions in the Church in such places as Lidzbark Warmiński, Wrocław, Frombork, and Olsztyn. For many years, he was the right-hand man of his uncle Lucas Watzenrode, the Prince-Bishop of Warmia. He therefore participated in many religious and politi-

Frombork
Lidzbark Warmiński
Toruń
Olsztyn

Wrocław

POLAND

TORUŃ, birthplace of Copernicus.

cal events, diplomatic missions, and administrative works. Having proved himself, his uncle wanted him to take over as bishop, but Copernicus preferred to devote himself to learning. From 1510, he lived in Frombork, where he built his own observatory. He discovered, for example, that the earth's orbit is eccentric and that the sun's apogee moves in the same direction as the fixed stars.

In 1520, during the Polish-Teutonic War of 1519–1521, Olsztyn was successfully defended by the Poles under Copernicus' command. In 1522, at the instigation of King Sigismund I, "the Old", he wrote a treatise on the value of money, wherein he formulated an early version of what is now called Gresham's Law—the notion that "bad money drives out good", a central concept in economics to the present day—and also advanced a quantity theory of money.

COPERNICUS' LAST MOMENTS,
drawing by Aleksander Lesser, 19th century.

But his greatest achievement pertained to astronomy, that is, the elaboration and propagation of his heliocentric theory, expounded in his *On the Revolutions of the Celestial Spheres*, which he dedicated to Pope Paul III. The book was published in Nuremberg on March 21, 1543, exactly two months before he passed away at his home in Frombork. According to legend, a copy of the work was presented to him on the very day that he died.

Galileo Galilei, a distinguished Italian scholar, entered the scene. He was born in Pisa in 1564, into a family that originated from a Florentine patriciate. Vincenzo Galilei, his father, was a wool merchant and a composer. Galileo Galilei went to a Jesuit school and then studied at the University of Pisa. Initially, he studied medicine but gave it up to study mathematics, geometry, mechanics, and physics. He made several scientific discoveries, combining empirical and deductive methods. His genius was quickly noticed. Though he never earned a doctorate, he was entrusted with university chairs at Pisa (1589–1592), Padua (1592–1610), and Florence (1610–1632).

GEODETIC COMPASS
for measuring horizontal angles, 16th century.

WINDOWS, HOUSE IN PISA,
Galileo's birthplace.

PORTRAITS OF SCIENTISTS
Nicolaus Copernicus, Jacopo Mazzoni, and Johannes Kepler.

In letters written to Giacopo (Jacopo) Mazzon and Johannes Kepler in 1597, Galileo Galilei declared that he was in favor of Copernicus' theory of the solar system, as it was a better depiction of the universe than the Ptolemaic geocentric theory. He also questioned Aristotle's physics, mechanics, and cosmology.

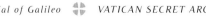

✢ Pisa

ITALY

In July 1609, Galileo constructed a telescope that allowed him to observe astronomical phenomena better than any other existing optical device. He perfected his telescope and so made new discoveries. He was the first to observe sunspots, the rings of Saturn, the mountains on the moon, the moons of Jupiter, and the phases of Venus. He gradually came to the conclusion that

TELESCOPE constructed by Galileo.

the phenomena he had observed supported the heliocentric theory more than the geocentric theory.

In the spring of 1610, Galileo went to Rome, where he was received with honors by the scholars of the Jesuit Roman College, which had the world's most renowned astronomical observatory. He became a member of the elite Accademia dei Lincei, which had been established seven years earlier during Clement VII's pontificate. The academy attracted scientists who propagated experimental natural sciences. Their coat of arms depicts a lynx, whose sharp vision symbolizes the observational prowess that science requires.

According to Italian historian Rino Cammilleri, Galileo's meteoric career, and the fact that he had not even gained a doctorate, aroused the envy of other scholars. His new functions and honors, the favors he enjoyed at the papal court, were coveted. In time, envy turned into hate, the more so as Galileo openly scoffed at his adversaries, resorting to offensive epithets. Hence his enemies decided to circulate his private letters, which were interpreted as an attack on the veracity of Holy Scriptures. The statement in question pertained to a passage from the Book of Joshua, where Joshua stops the sun at Gibeon until the final victory of the Israeli army over the Amorites (cf. Josh 10:12–15). Galileo

SHARP-EYED LYNX, coat of arms of the Accademia dei Lincei, Rome.

219

thought that, from a scientific point of view, the depiction was mistaken. For this, he was attacked by some preachers.

In November 1613, Niccolò Lorini, a Dominican friar, started to castigate supporters of the Copernican heliocentric theory during sermons in Florence, calling them "the devil's sect of mathematicians". A year later, he was joined by another Dominican, Fr. Tommaso Caccini, who maintained that the heliocentric theory defended

VILLA IN ARCETRI, Florence, where Galileo spent the last years of his life.

MARINER'S ASTROLABE, a navigational aid for sailors.

and propagated by Galileo contradicted the Bible, as proved by the aforementioned passage from the Book of Joshua; other clergy also criticized Galileo.

In 1615, Galileo wrote three letters (the Copernican Letters), wherein he put forward his views on the relationship between religion and science. Two of the addressees were the Benedictine monk Benedetto Castelli and Archbishop Piero Dini, to whom he wrote that he would sooner have his eye plucked out than to be the cause of scandal in being disobedient to the Church. The best-known letter is the one addressed to Christina of Lorraine, Grand Duchess of Tuscany. She thought that Galileo's theories were suspect, in contrast to her husband, Ferdinando I de' Medici, Grand Duke of Tuscany, who saw himself as a pupil of Galileo and even granted him a lucrative position at the Medici court in Florence.

In his letters, Galileo distinguished between two kinds of knowledge, namely, theological and scientific, stressing both their autonomy and their complementarity and recalling Cardinal Cesare Baronio's famous formula that the intention of the Holy Spirit, who inspired the Bible, was to teach us how to get to heaven, not how heaven moves. He also wrote that if one found a contradiction between scientific knowledge and Scripture, it meant that one has misunderstood Holy Scripture. Hence the problem was not the credibility of the Bible, but its erroneous interpretation.

CHRISTINA OF LORRAINE,
Grand Duchess of Tuscany, addressee
of Galileo's famous letter.

COSIMO II DE' MEDICI,
Grand Duke of Tuscany from 1609 to 1621.
He was Galileo's tutor from 1605 to 1608.

But things did not turn out to Galileo's liking. In 1615, Fr. Niccolò Lorini's allegations pertaining to the heliocentric theory ended up at the Supreme Sacred Congregation of the Roman and Universal Inquisition (Holy Office). They were reviewed by eleven theologians, who on February 24, 1616 issued a statement regarding two theses:

> First thesis: The sun is the center of the world and completely devoid of local motion.
> Assessment: All said that this proposition is foolish and absurd in philosophy, and formally heretical since it explicitly contradicts in many places the sense of Holy Scripture.

**LUNAR ECLIPSE
PHASES,**
drawn by Galileo.

**LIST OF
PROHIBITED
BOOKS,**
part of the title
page (1564
edition).

Second thesis: The earth is not the center of the world, nor motionless, but it moves as a whole and also with diurnal motion.
 Assessment: All said that this proposition receives the same judgment in philosophy and that in regard to theological truth it is at least erroneous in faith.[3]

The Holy Office did not agree with the theologians' assertion that heliocentrism is heretical and had the word removed from the decree before its publication. The document officially referred to three works that propagated the new astronomical system. The Carmelite Fr. Paolo Antonio Foscarini's book was "totally banned and condemned", while Nicolaus Copernicus' *On the Revolutions of the Celestial Spheres* and

Diego de Zúñiga of Salamanca's *In Job Commentaria* were banned until corrections were made. They could be printed if it was stated in the introduction that they presented a scientific hypothesis and not an absolute truth. *On the Revolutions of the Celestial Spheres*, which had not encountered any reaction from the Church for seventy-three years, was suddenly included on the *List of Prohibited Books*.

The Holy Office adjudicated that the Copernican heliocentric theory was erroneous from a philosophical and theological point of view, not a natural sciences point of view. The censors did not want the unconfirmed heliocentric theory to be used to interpret Holy Scripture, as it contravened the commonsense view of the world, which was supported by the authority of the majority of the scientific centers of learning. It is worth adding that not only theologians but also famous scholars, such as Tycho Brahe (alongside Johannes Kepler the most distinguished astronomer of the time), René Descartes (one of the greatest scholars of the 17th century), and Francis Bacon (sometimes called the father of modern science), thought that the Copernican theory was false. Others, how-

ENGRAVING
from the 19th century, inspired by Aristotle's cosmology—a man reaches the edge of the earth.

ST. ROBERT BELLARMINE, Italian Jesuit, cardinal, scholar, Doctor of the Church.

ever, thought it was true. One could find many supporters of Copernicus among influential clergymen, for example, Cardinal Alessandro Orsini; Piero Dini, archbishop of Fermo; Fr. Paolo Antonio Foscarini, a Carmelite provincial; and Fr. Giovanni Ciampoli, later secretary chamberlain to Pope Urban VIII. So the dispute about the heliocentric theory was not a conflict between religion and science, but between two natural science camps and two camps of theologians.

One must remember that Galileo questioned not only the Ptolemaic geocentric theory, but also Aristotle's physics. Both scientific systems arose in ancient Greece and dominated Christendom for several centuries, creating a vision of the universe that was strongly interwoven with religion. To many people, the undermining of those paradigms signified a destabilization of the whole theological structure on which their faith was based. John Donne, an Anglican clergyman and a pre-eminent metaphysical poet, lamented that the new science had caused irreversible damage, burying the eternal order of the world. Papal theologians maintained that one could not cause such spiritual havoc on the basis of an uncertain theory. In those days, research was on such a level that neither side could provide compelling evidence to prove its case.

Some people are of the opinion that Galileo was the only accused party in the whole affair, which was not so. On February 26, 1616, Galileo received an invitation from Robert Bellarmine, one of the most influential cardinals in the Roman Curia (canonized in 1930, and named Doctor of the Church), who also had an unpleasant experience at the hands of the Holy Office when his *Disputationes de Controversiis Christianae Fidei* was included on the *List of Prohibited Books* in 1590 until corrections had been made. He received Galileo sympathetically and was even prepared to accept the heliocentric theory if irrefutable evidence were provided.

Cardinal Bellarmine received Galileo in the name of Cardinal Giovanni Garzia Mellini, prefect of the Holy Office. Church law at that time provided for three stages in proceedings against those who defied the institution's bans. First came a warning, then, in the case of disobedience, a formal instruction, and finally a charge and a trial. The hierarch applied the first point, cautioning Galileo not to present the heliocentric theory as a scientific certainty but as a probable hypothesis, especially since he had no proof as to its veracity. Galileo agreed to comply.

A Dominican, Fr. Michelangelo Seghezzi, commissioner general of the Holy Office, expecting Galileo's opposition, prepared a formal instruction of silence prior to Galileo's meeting with Cardinal Bellarmine. It turned out that the document was not needed, yet

POPE PAUL V
was kind to Galileo.

BASILICA DI SANTA CROCE
in Florence.

nonetheless it was added to the files on the matter. Years later, the document, which Galileo had not laid eyes on, turned up during his trial.

Two weeks after the meeting, Galileo was received by Pope Paul V. The audience lasted forty-five minutes in, according to Galileo, a congenial atmosphere, with the pope expressing his appreciation of his guest's scientific achievements. Galileo returned to Florence content.

Galileo submitted to Rome and did not propagate or publicly defend the Copernican theory, busying himself with astronomical research, which led to a bitter dispute with two Jesuit scholars. One was Fr. Christoph Scheiner, known for, among other things, his invention of the pantograph, the creation of one of the three earliest maps of the moon, his helioscope, and his discovery of several laws of optics. Independently of Galileo, he discov-

FR. CHRISTOPH SCHEINER, German Jesuit and astronomer.

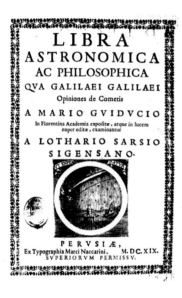

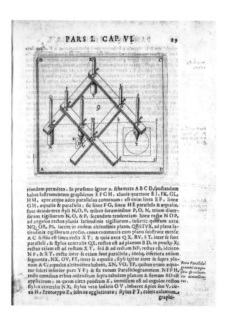

LIBRA ASTRONOMICA AC PHILOSOPHICA by Orazio Grassi, 1619, arguing against Galileo's views (left).

A WORK BY SCHEINER, 1631, with a drawing of the pantograph he invented (right).

ered sunspots, though they differed as to the nature of the phenomenon: Scheiner maintained that sunspots were produced by asteroid swarms, while Galileo was of the opinion that they were the result of processes within the sun. In this case, Galileo was right.

But Galileo was not correct regarding the origin of comets. The Jesuit Fr. Orazio Grassi maintained that comets were celestial bodies, while Galileo insisted that they were a meteorological phenomenon, the result of solar rays falling on high parts of the atmosphere.

There is nothing unusual about scientific disputes. But in this case, the conduct was uncommon. Galileo, of a fiery temperament, did not mince words, calling his adversary "an imbecile", "a beast", "a snake", "a scorpion", "a stain on the honor of mankind", or someone whom "you can hardly see as a man". In effect, he needlessly aroused ill will and hostility toward himself, in both academic and Church circles.

**POPE
URBAN VIII,**
Galileo's friend
and patron.

Even Kepler, who was well-disposed toward Galileo, severed contacts with him on account of their differences of opinion on scientific issues.

August 16, 1623, turned out to be a crucial day, as Cardinal Maffeo Barberini was elected pope, taking the regnal name Urban VIII. Galileo came to the conclusion that the time had come to rehabilitate the heliocentric theory, since the newly elected pope had been his friend for years and supported his work. In 1611, he had even written an ode in honor of Galileo, while in 1616 he was Galileo's informal advocate in Rome. Shortly after being elected, he emphasized that the Church had never deemed the works of Copernicus to be heretical and that she would never do so. Moreover, Cardinal Francesco Barberini, Urban VIII's nephew, had gained influence in the curia; he had been Galileo's colleague and great admirer at the Accademia dei Lincei. It would have been difficult to find a more opportune moment.

**PANORAMA
OF FLORENCE,**
where Galileo
spent many
years of his life.

Taking advantage of the favorable circumstances, Galileo decided to publish a book in defense of the Copernican theory. As he was elderly, work on the text was long and drawn-out (finished in 1630). It was titled *Dialogue Concerning the Two Chief World Systems* (comparing the Copernican system with the traditional Ptolemaic system).

Galileo sought to obtain a Church imprimatur (let it be printed) through Niccolò Riccardi, a Dominican friar at the Vatican. He obtained it on April 25, 1631, but on the condition that he make several corrections, the most important of which pertained to presenting the heliocentric theory as a hypothesis and not as a proven scientific truth. Furthermore, the pope asked him to mention God's omnipotence in the summary. Galileo agreed. After the corrections had been made, the book was to have been published in Rome.

But Galileo left Rome for Florence, where he had the *Dialogue* published by Giovanni Battista Landini in 1632 without the corrections he had agreed to make. When Urban VIII received a copy, he was outraged and felt that he had been cheated, as his friend had neglected to write a paragraph about God's omnipotence; further, in the book, Galileo even put some advice the pope had given him on the lips of one of the book's characters, namely, Simplicius, the fool.

There was an immediate reaction by the Holy See. The imprimatur was withdrawn, the worked banned, and the author was urgently summoned to Rome, to be questioned by the Holy Office commissioner. In response, Galileo sent a certificate, signed by three doctors, to the Vatican, stating that he was seriously ill and unable to make such a tiring journey. But the pope was uncompromising and threatened to have him brought by force. Galileo appeared in Rome on February 13, 1633.

He was not thrown into prison, but took up residence in a five-room apartment, with a view of the Vatican Gardens and a servant at his disposal, all at the Holy See's expense. In all, there were four hearings, during which Galileo talked with scholars who worked in the same disciplines as he did. Two charges were brought against him, both of which were upheld.

DIALOGUE CONCERNING THE TWO CHIEF WORLD SYSTEMS, Galileo's most famous work.

CARD. FRANCESCO BARBERINI, Urban VIII's nephew, a great admirer of Galileo.

The first charge concerned his disobedience regarding the decree of 1616, by presenting the heliocentric theory as an axiom and not as a hypothesis. He defended himself by claiming that he had received only a caution and not a formal instruction from Cardinal Bellarmine. His arguments were acknowledged. It was true that a document drawn up by Fr. Seghezzi years ago had been found in the case files, but as it had not been signed by Bellarmine or Galileo, it was seen as having no evidential value. But that did not change in any way the fact that Galileo was aware that he was defying a Church ban, since he, after all, had agreed to make corrections and did not do so.

GALILEO BEFORE THE INQUISITION
by Cristiano Banti, 19ᵗʰ century.

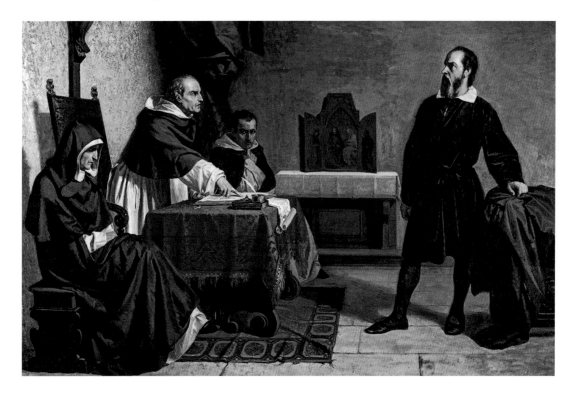

The second charge was based on the fact that he propagated false evidence as to the motion of the earth around the sun. Here again the prosecution was in the right. Galileo's problem lay in the fact that he deduced true theses from false premises. He rightly defended Copernicus, but the only evidence that he set forth in his work and during the trial—that is, the ebb and flow of the tides—turned out to be easy to rebut. The real reason was not discovered until 1728, when James Bradley observed the aberration of light phenomenon. According to Georges Bené, Galileo's biographer, a Church commission's decision to withdraw the *Dialogue* from circulation was completely justified from a scientific point of view.

On June 22, 1633, Galileo was pronounced guilty of the charges brought against him at the convent of Santa Maria sopra Minerva in

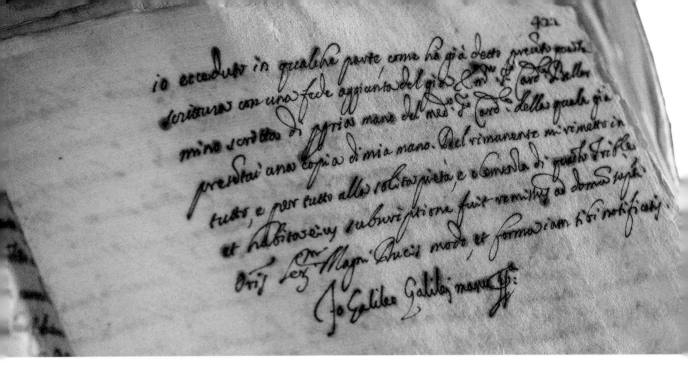

Rome, the seat of the Holy Office. Of the ten cardinals who made up the tribunal, three refused to sign the guilty verdict, namely, Francesco Barberini, Gaspar de Borja y Velasco, and Laudivio Zacchia. Documents housed in the Vatican Secret Archives show that Galileo was charged with an offense of a disciplinary and not of a doctrinal nature. The Church did not resolve which theory was true, charging the defendant solely of not submitting to the Church ban and of presenting heliocentrism in a categorical way rather than *ex suppositione* (as a hypothesis). The Holy Office decree, like a prior one of 1616, was but a Vatican congregation document, which did not have the dogmatic status of the infallible teaching of the Church.

The hotheaded Galileo incurred discipline largely due to his inappropriate behavior, not by what he propounded. Not only the pope, but

SANTA MARIA SOPRA MINERVA, Rome. Galileo's trial was held in the adjacent Dominican convent.

LAMP OF GALILEO
in the Pisa Cathedral, a massive brass chandelier whose oscillations, according to legend, turned Galileo's attention to the spinning of the earth.

WIND ROSE,
Galileo Galilei Museum, Florence.

also scientists who defended the Ptolemaic system felt offended by him. The author of the *Dialogue* mocked their views by attributing them to the fool Simplicius. Astronomers connected with the Roman College were particularly aggrieved. Fr. Christoph Scheiner, whom Galileo had treated brusquely during a dispute about sunspots, attacked Galileo very strongly. Another Jesuit, Fr. Melchior Inchofer, a mathematician and philosopher, presuming the negative verdict, wrote a withering appraisal of the *Dialogue* for the Holy Office. Lodovico delle Colombe, an Italian physicist, stood at the head of scientific circles that criticized Galileo, defending Aristotle's static cosmology against new theories. He too had a reason for revenge, as he had been the object of Galileo's countless taunts and jokes.

Prof. Franco Cardini points to yet another aspect of the case. The year 1633 came in the middle of the Thirty Years' War (1618–1648), the greatest religious conflict in European history. It marked the climax of hostilities that had started over a hundred years before Martin Luther's Ninety-Five Theses. The breakup of Christianity had been fomented by differences of opinion over Scripture. Some of the clergy in Galileo's time feared that his views, published in a simple and accessible way in Italian, and not Latin, the language of contemporary science and theology, could contribute to the further erosion of public acceptance of the Church's authorative interpretation of the Bible, which had been worked out in subtle formulas and distinctions over the centuries.

The trial ended with Galileo being sentenced to house arrest for life, which was commuted to three years. He spent that time at the Villa Medici on the Pincian Hill in Rome, then at the Sienese palace of Archbishop Ascanio Piccolomini—a great admirer of Galileo—and finally at the Villa il Gioiello, near Florence. The ban on leaving his residence was lifted, but he could not change his place of residence without the consent of the Inquisition. During his house arrest, he was visited by numerous scholars and Church dignitaries, with whom he had long debates. He could also carry on his research and write more works. He was solely prohibited from talking about Copernicus' theory. It was then that he published *Discourses and Mathematical Demonstrations Relating to Two New Sciences* (1638), his most fundamental work, which was about the principles of a new mechanics.

The second part of the punishment was a weekly recital of the Penitential Psalms for three years, which he continued later of his own

LETTER BY GALILEO to Leonardo Donato, doge of Venice.

PORTRAIT OF GALILEO by Peter Paul Rubens.

231

✠

INDEX LIBRORUM PROHIBITORUM SS^{mi} D. N. BENEDICTI XIV. PONTIFICIS MAXIMI JVSSV Recognitus, atque editus.

ROMÆ M. DCC. LVIII.
Ex Typographia Rev. Cameræ Apostolicæ.

CUM SUMMI PONTIFICIS PRIVILEGIO,

TITLE PAGE
of the *List of Prohibited Books*, 1758 edition, published during the pontificate of Benedict XIV, who removed heliocentric works from the list.

POPE PAUL III
established the Supreme Sacred Congregation of the Roman and Universal Inquisition in 1542.

LIST OF PROHIBITED BOOKS

The introduction of movable-type printing by Johannes Gutenberg, as well as the Reformation, occasioned that 16th-century Europe was flooded with literature that undermined the official teaching of the Catholic Church. Because the Church saw herself as the sole depository of orthodox Christian truths, she decided to respond forcefully.

In 1542, Pope Paul III established the Roman Curia, which was to coordinate activities to stop the spread of heresy. Hence the

POPE PAUL IV,
initiator of
the *List of
Prohibited Books*.

Holy Office, which was headed by Cardinal Gian Pietro Carafa, who was elected pope in 1555 and took the regnal name Paul IV. He was the first to order the compilation of a list of works that could not be disseminated, possessed, or read since they contained matter that was not in accord with the teaching of the Church (*List of Prohibited Books*). The works were divided into three groups: heretical, obscene, and occult. People were liable to excommunication if they defied the ban. The first such list appeared in 1559, the last in 1948. Works by, for example, Francis Bacon, Daniel Defoe, Alexander Dumas, Erasmus of Rotterdam, Edward Gibbon, Victor Hugo, Immanuel Kant, René Descartes, John Locke, Adam Mickiewicz, Montesquieu, Blaise Pascal, and many other prominent writers were included on the list at some time. The list even included works by authors whom the Church later raised to the altars, such as St. Robert Bellarmine and Bl. Antonio Rosmini-Serbati.

According to Fr. Jacek Salij, a Polish theologian, the *List of Prohibited Books* was an example of how evil ideas may arise from good intentions. In his opinion, the Church, in thus defending herself against dangers, drifted further and further away from the mainstream of European culture. According to British historian Henry A. Kamen, the actual possibility of enforcing the ban turned out to be severely limited, while the damage it caused was considerable, as the intellectual elite began to identify the Catholic Church with the suppression of freedom of speech and the prohibition of intellectual research. In 1966, the *List of Prohibited Books* was abolished.

PALACE OF THE HOLY OFFICE,
Vatican, which now houses the Congregation for the Doctrine of the Faith.

free will. Nobody questioned Galileo's faith or his religious convictions, neither during the trial or before nor after; he stressed throughout his life that he was a faithful son of the Catholic Church. Not one of the inquisitors expressed any reservations as to Galileo's morality in his personal life, though it was widely known that in Padua he lived with Marina Gamba, a laundress, with whom he had three illegitimate children, but whom he did not marry because of her low social status. Because he knew that he would be unable to have two of his daughters appropriately married, he placed them in a convent before they were of age. Virginia, the elder, who took the name Maria Celeste, was in her element as a nun, whereas for the younger Livia, Sr. Arcangela, religious life was the source of mental and spiritual suffering throughout her life.

Galileo died on January 8, 1642, in the Villa il Gioiello at the age of seventy-five. After his death, he became the hero of countless works,

GALILEO'S TOMBSTONE, Basilica di Santa Croce, Florence.

which depicted him as a victim of the Catholic Church and embellished his biography with numerous fictional details. Protestant and Enlightenment authors excelled in this. In time, the fictional elements began to obscure Galileo's real biography.

But the matter was not closed in the Church. In 1664, during Alexander VII's pontificate, the Holy Office revoked the decree of 1616 that condemned the works of Copernicus, Paolo Antonio Foscarini, and Diego de Zúñiga. In 1757, after James Bradley's discoveries, which confirmed the veracity of the heliocentric theory, the Holy Office removed works propounding the Copernican theory from the *List of Prohibited Books.*

Of all the popes, John Paul II showed the greatest interest in the the Galileo matter. After the special scientific commission that he

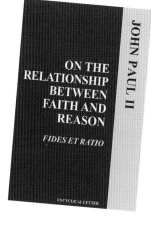

FIDES ET RATIO, John Paul II's encyclical on the conformity of faith with reason.

CREATION OF ADAM, fresco by Michelangelo in the Vatican's Sistine Chapel.

set up had presented the results of its research, he decided to do justice to Galileo. On October 31, 1993, during a plenary session of the Pontifical Academy of Sciences, he publicly acknowledged that Galileo was correct about the relationship between faith and reason. He noted that "the problem that the theologians of that time posed to themselves was that of the compatibility of heliocentrism and Scripture." According to John Paul II, the new science forced them to resolve the issue on the basis of their own criteria regarding the interpretation of the Bible, which the majority of them were incapable of doing. Paradoxically, Galileo, a person of deep faith, showed more insight in the matter than his adversaries. The majority of the theologians did not sense the formal difference between Holy Scripture and its interpretation, which led them to consider scientific issues inappropriately in the context of the Church's doctrinal teaching.[4]

In 1998, John Paul II issued an encyclical *Fides et Ratio.* It began with a sentence that Galileo would have subscribed to: "Faith and reason are like two wings on which the human spirit rises to the contemplation of the truth."

235

DISCOVERY

HISTORY

TRUTH

The French Revolution

CHAPTER 7

The French Revolution

The first systematic genocide
in the history of modern Europe

Vatican City

ITALY

**PIUS VII
ARRESTED**
by Gen. Étienne
Radet and
transported
to France.

There is a shortage of archival material in the Vatican Secret Archives from the revolutionary and imperial periods of France. Reports from France stopped arriving at the Vatican in the late 18th century, because in the grip of a revolutionary fever, she had severed diplomatic contacts with the rest of Europe, including Rome. In 1781, the Apostolic Nunciature in Paris closed, and its head, Archbishop Antonio Dugnani, departed for Milan. One could lose one's life for corresponding with the papacy, as the authorities in Paris saw contacts with the Holy See as treasonous. Several years later, the Eternal City was occupied by French troops. The head of the worldwide Catholic Church lost control of the Vatican. From then until 1814 papal diplomats on various continents did not have anywhere to send their reports.

PIUS VI, whose pontificate lasted 24 years.

Napoleon's forces entered Rome on February 15, 1798, when the twenty-third year of Pius VI's pontificate was being celebrated in the Papal States. Gen. Louis-Alexandre Berthier announced the dethronement of the pope, proclaimed Rome a republic, personally erected a "Tree of Liberty" on Capitoline Hill, ordered a thanksgiving service to be celebrated in St. Peter's Basilica for the establishment of the new system, and gave Pius VI three days to leave the city.

GEN. LOUIS-ALEXANDRE BERTHIER arrested Pius VI.

DEATH OF PIUS VI, under house arrest in Valence.

Though the pope was eighty-one years of age, partly paralyzed, and unable to walk, he categorically refused. He was therefore arrested and transported to Siena, then to Florence. Rome was without a bishop for the first time since the Avignon Papacy. The exile of the head of the Church lasted eighteen months. He was transported on a stretcher from Italy to France: to Briançon, Gap, Grenoble, and finally to Valence, near Lyon, where as "Citizen Pope", a prisoner of the French Republic, he died on January 29, 1799, praying for his enemies.

POPE PIUS VII,
whose pontificate
lasted 23 years,
almost as long as
his predecessor's.

People bid farewell to the pope, but also to the papacy in general. Supporters of the French Revolution were convinced that Pius VI would be the last pope. But three months later, a conclave was held at a Benedictine monastery (San Giorgio Maggiore) in Venice, under the protection of Austrian soldiers. The cardinals debated from December 1, 1799, to March 14, 1800. They finally elected as pope Cardinal Gregorio Barnaba Niccolò Maria Luigi Chiaramonti of Turin, who took the regnal name Pius VII in honor of his predecessor. In the opinion of the College of Cardinals, the new pope brought fresh hope of coming to an understanding with France, as he maintained that democracy not only could be reconciled with Catholicism, but would need Christian virtues to survive. On the other hand, he was intransigent in matters pertaining to the Faith and supported the popular uprisings that broke out in the Apennine Peninsula against anticlerical aggressors.

MONASTERY OF SAN GIORGIO MAGGIORE,
Venice, where a conclave elected Pius VII.

Napoleon, then the first consul of the Republic, who aspired to be emperor, needed to come to an understanding with the Church. Hence he signed the Concordat of 1801, which gave Catholics the right to practice their faith within limitations determined by the authorities in Paris. Bonaparte believed that people ought to have the freedom to exercise their religion, provided it was regulated by the state. Thus the Organic Articles were added to the concordat, stipulating that the Church could not make important decisions without government consent.

In 1804, Bonaparte summoned Pius VII to Paris to celebrate his coronation Mass in Notre Dame Cathedral. The pope agreed, hoping

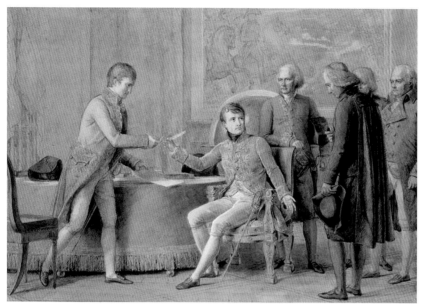

CONCORDAT between the Holy See and the French Republic, 1801.

that, in meeting Bonaparte personally, he would obtain some concessions from him. But Bonaparte treated him as a subordinate. He ostentatiously displayed his contempt for the pope by making him wait for him in the cathedral for an hour and then by taking the crown from him in order to crown himself, proclaiming himself emperor of the French. He thus showed that he did not owe his power to anyone but himself, not even to God. He also crowned Joséphine, his wife. He categorically refused to have a Church marriage, just as he had earlier refused to go to confession and receive Holy Communion. The pope swallowed the humiliation in silence.

At the beginning of 1808, Bonaparte, strengthened by his military successes in Europe, demanded further concessions of Pius VII: the right to nominate the patriarch of France and to assign French

NAPOLEON BONAPARTE, emperor of the French.

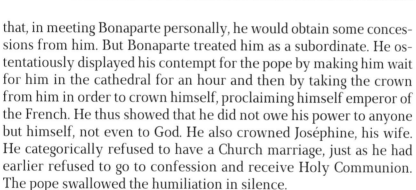

CORONATION OF NAPOLEON, Notre Dame Cathedral, Paris, 1804.

241

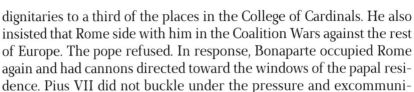

Paris

FRANCE

**GEN. ÉTIENNE
RADET**
arrested Pius VII.

dignitaries to a third of the places in the College of Cardinals. He also insisted that Rome side with him in the Coalition Wars against the rest of Europe. The pope refused. In response, Bonaparte occupied Rome again and had cannons directed toward the windows of the papal residence. Pius VII did not buckle under the pressure and excommunicated Bonaparte.

Gen. Étienne Radet, invoking the emperor's will, demanded that the pope surrender temporal power over Rome. The pope informed him that it was impossible, as that power did not belong to anyone but the Church. So on July 5, 1809, the pope shared the fate of his predecessor: he was kidnapped and transported to France, where he spent five years as a prisoner of the empire.

Once Rome was occupied by the French, papal institutions ceased to function, including the Vatican Secret Archives, which were taken over and emptied of their contents. All the files and artifacts were transported to Paris in 1810. Bonaparte believed that they would never be returned to Rome, while many supporters of the new order thought that Rome would never again see a Vicar of Christ. Yet both returned several years later.

**HÔTEL DE
SOUBISE**
in Paris.
All the Vatican
Secret Archives'
collections were
transported
here in 1810.

It is not surprising that the papal archives from this period are insubstantial. A historian studying the history of the French Revolution on the basis of documents housed in the Holy See faces an insurmountable difficulty. The lack of reports from the Apostolic Nunciature in Paris spans the period from spring 1791 to December 1819, as at that time the pope did not have a representative in France. Raging terror, the persecution of Catholics, severed diplomatic relations, and a communications blockade on the part of the revolutionaries—all this caused a huge gap in the papacy's information system. An unimaginable situation arose. There broke out in the most powerful state in

Europe—called the eldest daughter of the Church, the very heart of Christian civilization—bloody and brutal persecutions of Christians, massacres and slaughters, on a scale unseen since ancient times, while Rome, about six hundred miles from the French border, received but bits of news about the situation. In effect, the pope was not even aware that Vendée, a province of France, had become an arena of genocide (1793–1794), the victims of which were mainly local Catholics.

One of the few written historical accounts of that time in the Vatican Secret Archives is a letter from Queen Marie Antoinette of

FRANCE

LETTER FROM PRISON
by Queen Marie Antoinette
to her brother-in-law—Vatican Secret Archives.

France to her brother-in-law, composed while she was in prison in January 1793. The content is brief. It does not contribute much to our knowledge about the French Revolution or the queen. It is not of as much import as, for example, Mary Stuart's letter (also housed in the Vatican Secret Archives) to Pope Sixtus V, sent on October 23, 1586, from her cell in Fotheringhay Castle just before the announcement of her death sentence (the Queen of Scots wrote that she was departing this world faithful to the Catholic religion, that she forgave her enemies, and that she entrusted her soul to God). The significance of Marie Antoinette's letter is that it was one of the few that ended up in the Vatican.

Marie Antoinette also wrote a farewell letter to Élisabeth of France, her sister-in-law, on October 16, 1793, the night before her

MARIE ANTOINETTE,
queen of France, was the 15th child of Holy Roman Emperor Francis I and Maria Theresa of Austria

243

execution. The letter still bears traces of her tears, which blurred the ink here and there. The queen confessed that she would die in the apostolic Roman Catholic faith, trusting in the mercy and goodness of God, forgiving her enemies, and asking to be forgiven by all those she might have wronged in life. The letter never reached the addressee. It was discovered years later among Maximilien Robespierre's documents.

One can learn more about the violence of the Revolution in the documents written by those who inspired and perpetrated it than in the few documents from this period housed in the Vatican Secret Archives. French historian Reynald Secher made a breakthrough discovery about the victims in Vendée on March 4, 2011, at the Archives Nationales in Paris.

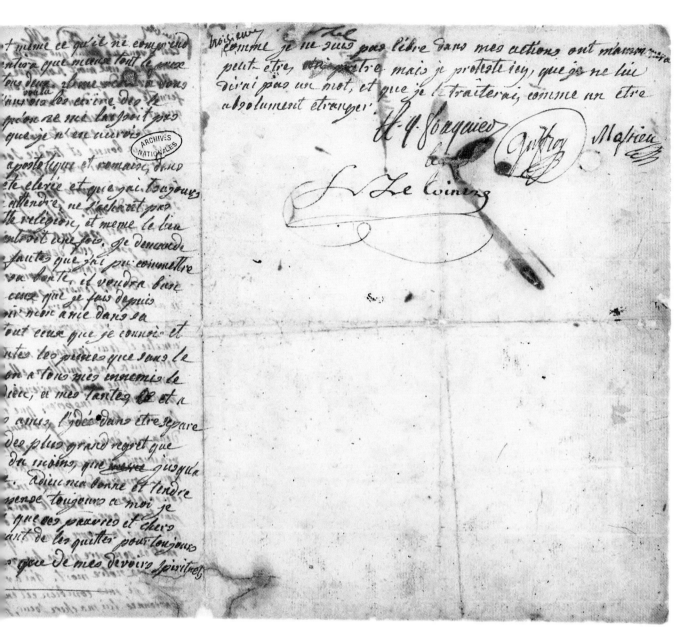

TO THE GUILLOTINE, Marie Antoinette led by revolutionary troops on October 16, 1793.

EMBLEM
of the Vendean insurgents.

We met him in Acigné, a small town near Rennes in Brittany. His home reminds one of a museum, full of mementos from the tragic events in Vendée towards the end of the 18th century. He related that when he was at school, the official version spoke of a counterrevolution, an antirepublican uprising, a civil war. The issue was treated in a general way, without going into detail.

At the same time, the events of two centuries ago were still present, passed on from generation to generation, as in the Secher family, whose ancestors perished during the massacres in Vendée. They kept alive the memory of those days in a closed circle, limited to their neighborhood, their experiences being completely unknown in other parts of France.

When Reynald Secher began to study history at the University of Rennes, he met Prof. Jean Meyer, who expressed his amazement at

REYNALD SECHER,
a French historian, during a discussion with Jan Kasprzycki-Rosikoń and Grzegorz Górny.

MEMORIAL ROOM
dedicated to the victims of the Lucs-sur-Boulogne massacre in Vendée.

encountering the inhabitants of Vendée: whenever the Revolution was mentioned, a wall of distrust, silence, and secrecy arose. Meyer discovered that no one had yet calculated exactly the number of victims, the economic losses, and the extent of physical destruction in the region. Hence he suggested that Secher, his student, write about the uprising on the basis of research in La Chapelle-Basse-Mer, his hometown. Since he was a local, he was welcomed everywhere; he had access to family archives and heard oral accounts that were shared with nonrelatives for the first time.

The young historian had hundreds of discussions between 1978 and 1982. He saw that he had arrived on the scene just as a certain era was ending. Secher was in time to talk to the remaining representatives

La Chapelle-Basse-Mer
✛

FRANCE

PATCHES
worn by Vendean insurgents.

of the last generation. He then compared everything they told him with what he found in archives—state, Church, and private. He discovered that the accounts of the Vendeans agreed with what he found in documents.

In 1983, Secher defended his doctoral thesis at Sorbonne University. Prof. Meyer was his supervisor, and the examiners were Profs. Pierre Chaunu and André Corvisier, famous French academics. Secher demonstrated that in just two days, March 10 and 17, 1794, the revolutionaries murdered 850 of the 3,250 inhabitants during a massacre in La Chapelle-Basse-Mer. About 40 percent of the victims were women, children, or elderly. Of the 980 houses, 363 were burned down, and the remaining farms were plundered. Material losses were as high as 81 percent of the value of La Chapelle-Basse-Mer's total assets.

It was the first research in France on the extermination of the civilian population in Vendée. The reviewers stated that Secher had discovered a new research area and urged him to extend his studies over the whole region that was encompassed by the civil

247

✛

MASSACRE IN LYON

Initially, the inhabitants of Lyon supported the Revolution. They primarily counted on the abolition of the unjust tax system, which favored a small group of the wealthiest citizens. In time, discontent increased because of the direction taken by the new authorities. Opposition was particularly aroused against the centralism of Paris. Most key decisions occurred in the capital, and the solutions worked out there were imposed heavy-handedly on the whole country. A sense that state matters were heading in the wrong direction increased particularly after the execution of Louis XVI. Many important cities rebelled against the centralizing inclinations of Paris, for example, Nîmes, Marseille, Rennes, Caen, and Bordeaux. The bloodiest events of the royalist uprising occurred in Lyon in the summer of 1793. It was surrounded, bombarded, and captured by Gen. François Christophe Kellermann's soldiers. Later, at the request of Bertrand Barère from the Committee of Public Safety, a decree to destroy the city was passed, commanding forces to burn it to the ground and erect a commemorative column with the inscription:

"Lyon made war on liberty: Lyon is no more!"
Ultimately, the demolition of the city was called off, but a repression of the inhabitants commenced. An extraordinary commission was established that issued death sentences en masse, not only to insurgents, but especially to random, innocent people. They had 1,600 people executed. Some of the executions were carried out using cannons loaded with grape shot.

CI GIT

LOUIS FRANÇOIS PERRIN COMTE DE PRECY
GENERAL DES LYONNAIS EN MDCCXCIII
DÉCÉDÉ LE XXV AOUT MDCCCXX
À MARCIGNY SUR LOIRE OÙ IL FUT INHUMÉ
ICI RELIGIEUSEMENT DÉPOSÉ LE XXIX SEPT MDCCCXXI

1. **OSSUARY** in a Lyon crypt, containing the bones and skulls of French Revolution victims.

2. **CHAPEL OF THE HOLY CROSS,** Lyon, which houses the crypt.

3. **PLAQUE** commemorating the victims of the massacre in Lyon.

4. **EXPIATORY CHAPEL** formed like a pyramid, where the remains of the victims in Lyon were kept from 1823 to 1906.

5. **SKULLS AND BONES** of those murdered in Lyon were moved in 1906 from the Expiatory Chapel to the Chapel of the Holy Cross.

6. **JEAN-FRANCOIS DE FEYDEAU,** whose ancestor perished in the Lyon massacre.

DOCTORAL DISSERTATION by Reynald Secher, 1983, on the massacre in La Chapelle-Basse-Mer.

FIELD MASS celebrated for Vendean insurgents by an "unconstitutional" priest.

ANTONIO DUGNANI, archbishop, apostolic nuncio in Paris.

war. Secher took on the task, which lasted thirty-five years. A completely different picture emerged from his research than the official one; the religious dimension, often ignored by scholars, came into view.

At the beginning of the Revolution, nothing indicated that it would become so bloody or that it would assume a clearly anti-Christian character. Peace had reigned in France for six years, and there were no famines or plagues. There was no organized opposition or a political republican force, and no anticlerical incidents had been observed for a long time. The reports sent to Rome by Antonio Dugnani, the apostolic nuncio, were reassuring.

When Louis XVI of France announced (January 24, 1789) that he intended to convoke the Estates General, which had not assembled for 175 years, no one expected the storm that it was to bring. The king made the decision mainly to gain public support for new taxes, as there were large debts to pay after participating in the American War of Independence. King Louis XVI was also prepared to carry out important reforms in his administration. Things got out of control when

a large swath of discontented commoners (Third Estate) broke out in open war against the royal and clerical classes (First and Second Estates) in order to form a new government. Eventually, the affair slid into chaos and frightened even those who had instigated the Revolution, such Jean Joseph Mounier, its first leader, who organized riots in Grenoble in 1788 and was the main initiator of the famous Tennis

Court Oath in Versailles (June 20, 1789), which became a turning point in French history.

Initially, the inhabitants of Vendée supported the French Revolution, as they were particularly unhappy with the prevailing system, which—unlike in England—blocked the advancement of those of the Third Estate: the bourgeoisie, burghers, officials, representatives of various professions, craftsmen, and peasants. In order to become an officer in the French Army, it was necessary to prove one's nobility at least four generations back. The aristocracy was jealous of its privileges and prevented people of a lower rank from rising to a higher one. The Revolution abolished such barriers.

KING LOUIS XVI, famous for being a very inept politician.

JEAN-JOSEPH MOUNIER, president of the National Assembly, October 5–6, 1789.

TENNIS COURT OATH in Versailles (June 20, 1789).

251

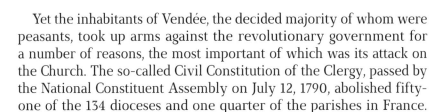

Yet the inhabitants of Vendée, the decided majority of whom were peasants, took up arms against the revolutionary government for a number of reasons, the most important of which was its attack on the Church. The so-called Civil Constitution of the Clergy, passed by the National Constituent Assembly on July 12, 1790, abolished fifty-one of the 134 dioceses and one quarter of the parishes in France. Thus the parish system, which underpinned the state administrative structure, was destroyed. The rural population was attached to the

SEWING
badges of the Sacred Heart of Jesus onto clothing.

parish structure and identified with it to a large extent. In Vendée, the majority of parish priests, who lived on the same material level as the peasants, represented their interests before the state. Without them, the sphere that for generations had assured peasants of protection and security disappeared.

The Civil Constitution of the Clergy also dissolved all male and female orders with the exception of those that provided education or were involved in charity work. It also reduced the status of bishops and parish priests to that of state officials who were to be elected not only by the Catholics of a given department, but also by other citizens, including Protestants, Jews, and atheists. A property qualification was also introduced that favored those voters who paid higher taxes. In effect, it was not the inhabitants who elected the parish priest of a given village, but wealthy burghers, and often even dissenters. The revolutionaries announced that they intended to respect the new law rigorously. They demanded that all the clergy swear an oath of loyalty to the state. Whoever refused was deprived of the right to exercise his pastoral ministry.

The Civil Constitution of the Clergy aroused the vehement opposition of Pius VI, increasingly alarmed by frightening reports from the Apostolic Nunciature in France. In the spring of 1791, Pius VI issued two papal briefs, stating that the Civil Constitution of the Clergy was a sacrilege and a heresy and calling on the clergy not to swear an oath to it, under pain of suspension. The tension between Paris and Rome came to a head, and Antonio Dugnani, the apostolic nuncio, fearing for his own safety, fled to Milan.

VENDEAN INSURGENT entrusting his life to Our Lady before setting out to fight government soldiers.

FRENCH CONSTITUTION of 1791 briefly transformed absolute monarchy into a constitutional monarchy (until 1793).

The overwhelming majority of the bishops, and over half of the parish priests, did not accept the new law. Hence the state subjected them to bloody repressions. Three bishops and three hundred priests were shot in Paris in 1792, and many were killed in other regions. As many as forty thousand clergy were exiled. In the autumn of that same year, a concentration camp for priests was established in Rochefort-sur-Mer, where 829 were interned, of which 547 perished in inhumane conditions (John Paul II beatified sixty-four of them in 1995).

In Vendée, the majority of priests refused to take the antipapal oath of the Civil Constitution of the Clergy. The poor peasants—and so representatives of the Third Estate, theoretically supporters of the Revolution—raised a militia, the Catholic and Royal Army. They did not create any counterrevolutionary doctrine. Their protest was a spontaneous response to defend the Catholic faith and the traditions of their ancestors. Reynald Secher states that the insurgents stood in defense of liberty, particularly religious liberty, and that in reality they

SACRED HEART OF JESUS, symbol of the Vendean insurgents.

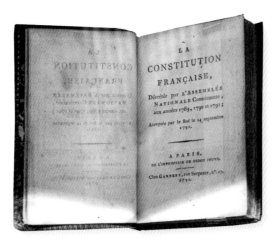

RED PHRYGIAN CAP, symbol of the French Revolution.

acted in accord with article thirty-five of the 1793 Declaration of the Rights of Man and of the Citizen: "When the government violates the rights of the people, insurrection is—for the people and every part of the people—the most sacred of rights and the most inalienable duty." Though the revolutionary authorities theoretically proclaimed that right, in practice they denied it to others.

The uprising began when the French government made military service compulsory. In a statement of grievances—that is, demands made prior to the convocation of the Estates General in 1789—peasants had demanded that the authorities cease the recruitment of all those who worked on the land. The National Convention, the revolutionary parliament created in 1792, ignored these original demands and ordered the largest mobilization in history in March 1793. The Vendean peasants were forced to join the French Revolutionary

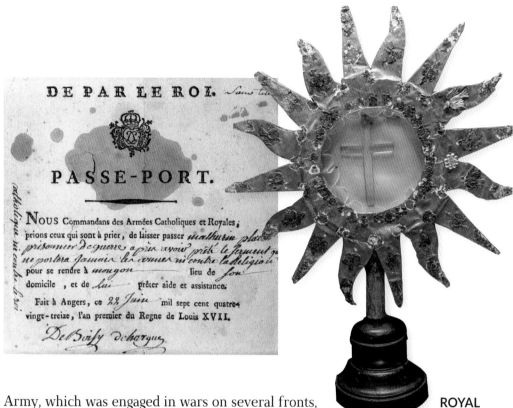

Army, which was engaged in wars on several fronts, in order to fight for a regime they hated. They revolted, refusing to serve in the military. This uprising occurred in area encompassing about 3,600 square miles.

The Vendée insurrection was of a peasant character. The Catholic and Royal Army, mainly made up of peasants, was not well armed and lacked experienced officers. It was only after some time that the nobility began to join it. The memory of brave leaders in the revolt is still alive in Vendée to this day, for example François-Athanase de Charette de la Contrie; Charles-Melchior Artus, Marchess of Bonchamps; Henri du Vergier, Count of La Rochejaquelein; Louis-Marie Joseph, Marchess of Lescure; Maurice Joseph Louis Gigost d'Elbée; and Jacques Cathelineau.

ROYAL PASSPORT
for prisoner of war Mathurin Placé (left).

MONSTRANCE
of wood, cardboard, and paper, used by Fr. Louis-Robert Duguet, chaplain to the insurgents' army.

CHÂTEAU D'ANGERS,
captured by the Vendean insurgents on June 18, 1783.

255

KEY LEADERS of the Vendée uprising did not live long:

The fighting raged with mixed fortunes, defeats intertwined with victories. The Vendean resistance provoked the fury of the central authorities. On April 4, 1793, Bertrand Barère de Vieuzac presented a plan for the "total destruction" of Vendée, maintaining that it was in the national interest, a necessary condition for saving the homeland. On August 1, 1793, the National Convention approved the plan:

GEN. FRANÇOIS-ATHANASE DE CHARETTE DE LA CONTRIE (1763–1796).

CHARLES-MELCHIOR ARTUS, MARQUESS OF BONCHAMPS (1760–1793).

HENRI DU VERGIER, COUNT OF LA ROCHEJAQUELEIN (1772–1794).

LOUIS-MARIE JOSEPH, MARQUESS OF LESCURE (1766–1793).

GEN. MAURICE JOSEPH LOUIS GIGOST D'ELBÉE (1752–1794).

JACQUES CATHELINEAU, "SAINT OF ANJOU" (1759–1793).

GRACE AUX PRISONNIERS !

deforestation, rebels' houses demolished, property and cattle confiscated, crops harvested and taken away, and women, children, and the elderly deported to other regions (this marked the first time the term "deportation" was used in official documents). The decree did not mention men in their prime—a silence that, to the enforcers, was tantamount to a death sentence.

As the Vendeans fought bravely, and even had successes, on November 1, 1793, a new law came into force providing for the extermination of all the inhabitants of the unruly region, including women, children, and the elderly. People were murdered not for what they had done, but for who they were. Secher suggests that behind the massacres lay a revolutionary logic, which held that a man cannot be against the rights of man, of which the Revolution was an expression. If one was against those rights, then one was not a man. And if one was not a man, then he should be treated as an animal, the killing of which was normal and did not need to be justified.

One of the most significant incidents of the war in Vendée occurred on October 18, 1793. The Vendeans, withdrawing under the pressure of the prevailing enemy forces at the Battle of Cholet, decided to break through to the northern bank of the Loire, to Brittany. They set off on a long march—tens of thousands of people, three quarters of whom were elderly, women, or children fleeing from certain death at the hands of revolutionary troops. At the last moment, they managed to cross the river and escape with their lives. But prior to that, they faced a dilemma—they had to decide what to do with their five thousand prisoners, who were kept in a church in Saint-Florence-le-Vieil. Most thought that they ought to be killed, to avenge their commander Charles-Melchior Artus, Marchess of Bonchamps, mortally wounded during the Battle of Cholet. Moreover, they saw the prisoners as criminals who murdered civilians and so did not deserve a trial.

When the dying general heard of this, he summoned his closest colleagues and asked them to fulfill his last wish: to pardon all the prisoners and set them free. The general said that he did not want to stand before God with a conscience burdened by such a monstrous crime. Shortly afterwards, Bonchamps died, and the Vendeans crossed to the right bank of the Loire, leaving the pardoned revolutionary troops on the left bank.

GEN. LOUIS MARIE TURREAU, an executioner of the Vendée, organizer of the "infernal columns".

When information about this event reached Paris, members of the Committee of Public Safety flew into a rage. They decreed that the story should never see the light of day, and gave instructions to disseminate another version of the event, namely, that the prisoners were treated in a cruel manner, condemned to death, but then rescued at the last moment by government soldiers. But that was not all. The authorities ordered all those who had been taken prisoner to kill all the witnesses and take revenge on the civil population in order to "wash away the shame". Shortly afterward, the soldiers released from captivity, en route to Nantes, murdered two thousand helpless people.

Gen. Louis Marie Turreau became commander of the French Revolutionary Army in Vendée on November 27, 1793. He formed twelve large detachments called "infernal columns", which plundered property and carried out a systematic extermination of the civilian population. The commander ordered his subordinates not to spare women,

PACIFICATION OF THE VENDÉE, depicting an agreement signed April 20, 1795.

as they were the "reproductive soil" out of which rebels arose. Vendée, as he was wont to say, ought to become one large cemetery.

The civil war ended on December 21, 1793, when the Vendeans were defeated at the Battle of Savenay. However, the systematic extermination of the civilian population lasted from August 1793 to July 1794, ending with the execution of Maximilien Robespierre, the leader of the Reign of Terror. Secher defines the crimes of this period as genocide, as they fulfil the United Nation's criteria of 1948.

FRANÇOISE DE CHABOT-DARCY during a discussion with Grzegorz Górny.

AVENGED MASSACRE

The Parc Soubise in Vendée's Mouchamps is the property of Françoise de Chabot-Darcy's family. We met her in front of her ancestors' palace, which was ruined toward the end of the 18th century and has not been restored to this day. Her ancestors fled to Hungary during the Reign of Terror, leaving peasants on the estate. During the war in Vendée, the local men took up arms, while the women, children, and elderly stayed at home. When the French Revolutionary Army entered the Parc Soubise, all the inhabitants were gathered in front of the palace and murdered. The only survivor was a teenage boy who, pretending to be dead, spent several hours under a pile of corpses. When it was dark, he fled to a wood, where he came across a detachment of insurgents. The men decided to avenge the slaughter, which was not difficult since the perpetrators were fast asleep, blind drunk. The insurgents hanged them all.

DEVASTATED PALACE in Parc Soubise, Mouchamps, unrestored since the Vendée uprising.

Besides, it is no coincidence that the term "genocide" first appeared in the context of the Vendée uprising. The term was used by François-Noël Babeuf, called the "First Revolutionary Communist", to describe what had happened in Vendée. In 1795, he wrote a pamphlet entitled *The System of Depopulation, or The Life and Crimes of Carrier*, devoted to one of the main organizers of the atrocities.

BATTLE OF SAVENAY, where Vendean insurgents were defeated.

Towards the end of 1793, Gen. François Joseph Westermann wrote a report to the central authorities in Paris that reflects the French Revolutionary Army's mentality and aims:

Citizens of the Republic, Vendée is no more. It fell—along with its women and children—under our free saber. I have just buried it in the mud and forests of Savenay. Following the orders I received from you, I crushed children under the hooves of our horses, and I massacred women, who—at least those—will not give birth to any more bandits. I do not have a single

PRINCESS DE LAMBALLE, murdered by revolutionaries on a Paris street September 3, 1792, simply for her friendship with the queen.

prisoner to reproach me. I have exterminated them all. . . . The tails of all my hussars' horses hold shreds of the bandit banners. The roads are littered with bodies. There are so many of them that in several places, they form pyramids. In Savenay, we fired without stopping, because bandits were coming up constantly to surrender. Klèber and Marceau are not with us. We did not take prisoners; we would have had to grant them the bread of freedom, and pity is not a revolutionary virtue.[1]

From the contents of the letter, it would seem that the revolutionaries had achieved their aim. Nothing could be further from the truth! After overcoming the insurgents, when the civil population in Vendée was defenseless, the forces began the genocide. Because the murders became so numerous, the army utilized science in the service of genocide, perhaps for the first time in history. Industrial means of the extermination of people began to be considered. Two French chemists, Antoine François, Count of Fourcroy, and Joseph-Louis Proust

VENDEAN VOLUNTEERS defending themselves against revolutionary soldiers.

attempted to produce a lethal nerve gas, but they failed. They contemplated landmines and water poisoning as well, but the ideas were abandoned, since they endangered both sides.

Reynald Secher closely studied the long discussions pertaining to this question within the National Convention and the Committee of Public Safety. He told of the dilemmas that prevailed in the revolutionary camp. Those responsible for the extermination complained that the traditional methods of murder were too long and costly. There were not enough bullets; besides, they were needed elsewhere. Bayonets and sabers quickly broke, as did rifle butts after smashing skulls. Moreover, soldiers who carried out serial murders showed symptoms

261

SAINT GUILLOTINE

The guillotine, undoubtedly the most spectacular instrument of terror, became a symbol of the French Revolution. Guillotines were erected in all the main squares of larger towns in France. Executions attracted crowds, who had a sense of participating in an extraordinary spectacle. People even fought among themselves for the best places to observe the executions.

The new order that was to replace Christianity created its own sacred sphere. The guillotine was part of it, as a "redemptive instrument", as a "high altar" at which a "red Mass" was celebrated. Covered with blue velvet and showered with roses, it occupied the central place during the Festival of the Supreme Being, the most important holy day established by the revolutionaries. All the National Convention members paraded in front of it. Songs and prayers were written mockingly in its honor, like the following litany:

Saint Guillotine, protector of patriots,
pray for us.
Saint Guillotine, scourge of aristocrats,
pray for us.
Amiable Machine,
have pity on us.
Admirable Machine,
have pity on us.
Saint Guillotine,
protect us from tyrants.[2]

Traitres regardez et tremblez elle ne perdra son activité, que quand vous aurés tous perdu la vie.

PUBLIC EXECUTIONS by guillotine took place in France from 1792 to 1939.

PLACE DU BOUFFAY in Nantes, site of a guillotine during the French Revolution.

of mental deterioration. The guillotine also turned out to be an expensive instrument, as an executioner received fifty-nine livres for each head (a teacher's monthly pay was one hundred livres). Each guillotine provided for about seventy-five victims daily, but the need was significantly more. Apart from that, it needed conservation, sharpening, and general upkeep. Then there was the maintenance of prison cells, the transport of prisoners, and the payment of guards. Eventually, it was decided that the victims themselves had to pay for their own executions. Prior to execution, their money and valuables were taken, even their clothes, their hair cut off, and their teeth pulled out, which were put up for auction. In Les Ponts-de-Cé, human skin was tanned for trousers for officers. In Clisson, fat was melted out of the victims' bodies.

The authorities thought up a new method of extermination, which was mainly implemented in Vendée and neighboring Brittany. It was first used in Nantes on November 16, 1793, when ninety priests who refused to take the oath were led to the Loire and, tied together in pairs, loaded under the decks of the barges that were moored there. Then the barges were towed to the middle of the river and sunk. This practice lasted until January 31, 1794, and has gone down in history as "vertical deportation" or the "drownings at Nantes". In all, about five thousand victims perished in that way—four hundred children on one of the barges, three hundred women on another. At the edge of

Nantes

FRANCE

QUAY ON THE LOIRE in Nantes, where barges were loaded with prisoners and sunk to drown them.

J.B. CARRIER.
Né à Yolet dép. du Cantal en 1756.
Député à la Conon Natle de Revolution
le 5. Fr.e Condamné à mort le 26 frimaire.

the river, they were stripped of their clothes (which were sold) and pushed naked onto the deck. Driven towards the river, women tried to hand their children over to people standing silently along the streets, but such help was punishable by death. People were drowned in other cities too, such as Angers, Les Ponts-de-Cé, Le Pellerin, and Bourgneuf, where children in particular were killed in this way, including infants.

However, that extermination method evinced more and more reservations among the revolutionary camp because of its cost, as the sunken river vessels could have been used for other purposes. So attempts were made to suffocate people in tightly sealed rooms below the decks, but that sometimes ended in failure.

So the Committee of Public Safety and the National Convention decided to revert to traditional ways of murdering people. Jean Baptiste Carrier wrote that one could not show the slightest sign of humanity towards the Vendeans, or spare any of them. The extermination was entrusted to General Turreau's "infernal columns", which crisscrossed the Vendée, killing those they came across. One symbol of their genocidal activity is Les Lucs-sur-Boulogne, where the French Revolutionary Army murdered all of its 560 inhabitants, including the elderly, women, and children, on February 28, 1794.

Reynald Secher had access to numerous documents that show the sort of deeds committed under the banners of the Republic. Many of the testimonies were written by the perpetrators themselves. Thus we learn, for example, that the defeated Vendeans had their genitals cut off and made into earrings, which were pinned to belts as trophies. Women were gang-raped, and explosives inserted into their wombs and detonated. Pregnant women were crushed in wine presses.

After of many years of research, Secher established that 117,000 people out of the 815,000 inhabitants of Vendée perished in the persecution. As many as 80 percent of the victims were women and children.

VENDEAN YAD VASHEM

On September 25, 1993, a mausoleum dedicated to the victims of genocide was opened in Les Lucs-sur-Boulogne, thanks to Philippe de Villiers, chairman of the Vendée General Council. At times, it is called the "Vendean Yad Vashem". The site of the monument was not chosen by accident, as it was at this spot that the French Revolutionary Army murdered all of the town's 564 inhabitants, including Reynald Secher's ancestors. Aleksandr Solzhenitsyn, a Russian writer, a former prisoner of Soviet labor camps, and the recipient of the Nobel Prize in Literature in 1970, gave the inaugural talk at the opening of the mausoleum. He compared the French Revolution with the Bolshevik Revolution, noting that in both cases there prevailed the utopian idea that a revolution could improve human nature. Instead, he said, people's most primitive and barbaric instincts

YAD VASHEM means "place and name" in Hebrew, which reflects the essence of the mausoleum in Les Lucs-sur-Boulogne, since it commemorates the names of the victims of the genocide.

were aroused, and the malevolent powers of jealousy, greed, and hate were released.

According to Solzhenitsyn, the motto of "Liberty, Equality, Fraternity" was also utopian, as liberty and equality are mutually exclusive in social life. Liberty by its very nature results in social inequality, while equality is unachievable other than by the suppression of freedom. Solzhenitsyn also drew attention to the mistaken understanding of fraternity, which is only achievable spiritually and not by social methods.

Of its 53,270 buildings, 10,300 were destroyed. Vendée was erased from maps of France. On November 7, 1793, the National Convention voted for a new name for the department: Vengé (Avenged).

Because of the information blockade, the inhabitants of other parts of France had no idea of what was happening in Vendée. It was not until Robespierre's death, and the end of the Reign of Terror in July 1794, that reports of the murders and plunders began to circulate. Turmoil prevailed in Paris. Most of the criminals still held high positions. In order to avoid responsibility and to calm the people, it was decided to sacrifice some of the leaders of the Republic, blaming them for the massacres in Vendée. Hence Jean Baptiste Carrier was guillotined by order of his former friends in December 1794. Earlier (April), another criminal, François Joseph Westermann, was guillotined, not for his crimes but for his close relationship with Georges Jacques Danton;

PRINCE OF TALMONT INTERROGATED
Prince Antoine Philippe de La Trémoïlle, one of the leaders of the Vendée uprising, was guillotined on January 27, 1794.

the Revolution devoured its own children. But most of the criminals avoided punishment, particularly Louis Marie Turreau, commander of the "infernal columns", whose name is inscribed on the Arc de Triomphe de l'Étoile in Paris to this day.

It is said that the popes had the world's best intelligence service. But that is not true. Pius VI, completely cut off from information, knew nothing of the genocide in Vendée. Reports from France were sporadic and only contained bits of information about some events in the country called the "eldest daughter of the Church". One thing in Rome was certain: that the Revolution had declared war on Catholicism and tried to replace it with a new religion.

The Civil Constitution of the Clergy was but a prelude to further activities. On November 10, 1793, the National Convention abolished Catholic worship. That day, Notre Dame Cathedral in Paris was rededicated to the Cult of Reason. In the chancel was erected an imitation of Mount Olympus, upon which stood Mademoiselle Maillard, an opera house soprano, as the Goddess of Reason, clothed in a white dress, a blue mantle, and a red cap. When she sat down on the throne, a hymn in praise of liberty was sung. Portraits of new saints were on display, namely, Maximilien Robespierre, Jean-Paul Marat, and other leaders of the Revolution.

Everything associated with Christianity was done away with. About eight hundred priests, monks, and nuns were murdered, the priesthood abolished, religious symbols removed, churches destroyed, cemeteries devastated, holy days abolished, even Sunday (a month earlier, the Catholic calendar had been replaced with a revolutionary one, which started not with the birth of Christ, but on September 22, 1792, the day Louis XVI was arrested). Jean de Viguerie, a historian, writes that during the last decade of the 18th century every church in France was closed for a certain time (several weeks to several years), and some were demolished or converted into stables, barracks, and warehouses.

MAXIMILIEN ROBESPIERRE, main architect of the Reign of Terror.

JEAN-PAUL MARAT, murdered by Charlotte Corday, proclaimed a martyr of the French Revolution.

MADEMOISELLE MAILLARD, a Parisian dancer, worshipped as the personification of Reason in Notre Dame Cathedral.

LA CARMAGNOLE by Charles Richefeu, 1923—a satirical depiction of a revolutionary dancing with the head of an aristocrat.

The destructive fury of the Revolution affected not only people. It is estimated that about one third of France's works of art were damaged or lost for good during the Revolution. Catholic buildings were the main objects of attack—churches, monasteries, chapels, seminaries, bishops' palaces, church libraries and archives—along with the objects found in them, such as gravestones, sculptures, religious paintings, liturgical vessels, organs, church bells, reliquaries, and book collections.

The aim of the French Revolution was to create a new man, a new nation, and a new world free from inequalities. But, first, the pillars of the old order had to be destroyed, of which religion was the most important. In that sense, the struggle with Catholicism was a logical consequence of the philosophical assumptions adopted from Voltaire, Jean-Jacques Rousseau, and Marie-Jean-Antoine-Nicolas de Caritat, Marchess of Condorcet. In place of Christianity, they proposed a "civil religion" wherein the state was the supreme value (in this context Maximilien Robespierre alone stood out, promoting the Cult of the Supreme Being, an undefined deity).

Terror brought the desired results. Almost half of the diocesan priests signed the Civil Constitution of the Clergy. Later, 50 percent of these, under pressure from the authorities, gave up the priesthood. For a dozen or so years, people became accustomed to foregoing Mass and the sacraments. In 1789, 90 percent of Frenchmen celebrated Easter, in 1801, only 50 percent did so. Bloody persecutions undoubtedly contributed to a rapid secularization of France.

Prof. Jean de Viguerie maintains that the dechristianization could well have been greater, had it not been for the resistance of masses

FESTIVAL OF THE SUPREME BEING, revolutionary state holiday celebrated on June 8.

VUE DU JARDIN NATIONAL ET DES DÉCORATIONS,

Le jour de la fête célébrée en l'honneur de l'Être Suprême le Decadi 20 Prairial l'an 2 de la République Française.

of Catholics. Though leading a religious life was punishable by death, nuns formed clandestine convents, which sometimes cost them their heads, as was the case with the sixteen Carmelite nuns from Compiègne and the thirteen Ursulines from Valenciennes. One could end up on the guillotine for attending an illegal Mass, yet people still assembled at secret liturgies. One woman, called Bergeron,

269

POPE PIUS X
beatified sixteen
Carmelite nuns
from Compiègne,
guillotined simply for
living in a convent.

**ANTOINE
LAVOISIER,**
scientific genius,
guillotined in
1794.

**GEN. DE
CHARETTE**
before
a firing
squad.

270

a shopkeeper, had a secret chapel where Mass was said daily for eighteen months, even though the chapel was opposite the Revolutionary Tribunal.

There was no lack of paradoxes. The Revolution, though it invoked reason, executed scholars whose sole crime was their independence of thought. Antoine Lavoisier, for example, the most famous physicist and chemist of the time, was guillotined in Paris. The tribunal chairman, when passing sentence, stated: "The Republic does not need scholars."

Paweł Jasienica, a Polish historian, pointed out another paradox:

Half of the death sentences carried out during the Reign of Terror occurred in Vendée and Brittany. Of the victims, 2 percent were of the nobility, 2 percent were of the clergy, and 6 percent were of the middle class, while 48 percent were peasants, and 41 percent were craftsmen and common laborers.[3]

So the Third Estate, in the name of which the Revolution broke out, made up 95 percent of its victims.

Fighting did not cease in Vendée until 1796, when Gen. François de Charette, the last uprising leader, was shot. But peace did not come to the region until the time of Napoleon, whose name has gone down gratefully in the memory of the department's inhabitants. He refused to participate in the repression of the Vendeans, admiring the insurgents' fortitude. Later, he granted compensation to victims and supported the rebuilding of the ruined province.

Today, Frenchmen are but dimly aware of the truth about the genocide in Vendée, whereas they were keenly aware of it at the beginning of the 19th century, during the reigns of Louis XVIII and Charles X of France. In 1819, Victor Hugo even wrote an ode entitled "In the Vendée", wherein he praised the bravery of the insurgents. The situation

DESCENDANT OF THE "KING OF VENDÉE"

There are many descendants of Vendée war heroes still alive today. One of them is Alain de Charette de la Contrie, a descendant of the brother of General François-Athanase de Charette de la Contrie, the last leader of the uprising. His family has always kept alive the memory of the brave general, who was presented to the children as a model of fortitude and dedication, often recalling his life motto: "I often fought, sometimes I was beaten, but I have never been killed off." Some of his keepsakes are kept at his home.

Some exhibits pertaining to the general are kept in the Logis de la Chabotterie manor, where he lay wounded and was captured by revolutionary soldiers. Today, the manor has a museum dedicated to the war in Vendée and the crimes of the Revolution.

1. **ALAIN DE CHARETTE DE LA CONTRIE,** descendant of the brother of the last leader of the Vendée uprising.

2. **SABRE HILT** of Gen. de Charette.

3. **INTERIOR, CASTLE** where Gen. de Charette was captured and imprisoned.

4. **XAVIER DE MOULINS,** director of the museum in the Logis de la Chabotterie manor house, in discussion with Grzegorz Górny.

5. **MUSEUM** in the Logis de la Chabotterie manor house.

PUBLIC EXECUTION
of Gen. François-Athanase de Charette in Place Viarme, Nantes, on March 29, 1796.

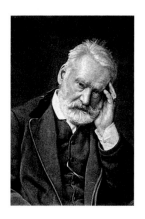

VICTOR HUGO,
a great admirer of the Vendean insurgents.

JULES MICHELET
wrote a historiography of the French Revolution that is still in use today.

began to change after the July Revolution in 1830, but particularly after the February Revolution in 1848 and the proclamation of the Second Republic. It was then assumed that the new founding myth of the state was to be the French Revolution. During 1847 to 1853, Jules Michelet wrote his monumental seven-volume History of the French Revolution, which shaped historiography in France for many decades. Whatever did not accord with that paradigm was marginalized or removed. Reynald Secher calls that process *mémoricide*—the "annihilation of memory". That also pertains to the victims of the genocide in Vendée.

Jules Verne's case is an illustration of this. In 1863, as yet a little-known writer, he published a serial novel in a Paris magazine about the war in Vendée, entitled *The Count of Chanteleine: A Tale of the French Revolution*. Once he was famous, he decided to publish the novel as a book. Publishers rejected his proposition, as his heroes were insurgents who had defended their faith against the terror of the Revolution. It was at the time of the Third Republic, so the novel would have been unequivocally seen as an attack on the ideological foundations of the secular state. The ideological guideline at that time was Georges Clemenceau's declaration of 1891: The French Revolution is *un bloc*—a unit—therefore it must be accepted completely, along with all of its episodes. Hence Verne's novel was not published in France until 1971.

The situation gradually began to change due to Secher's research, and that of other historians who followed in his footsteps. But for some time, he could not establish the origins of the plan to murder the inhabitants of Vendée—until he made a discovery on March 4,

2011, while poring over Committee of Public Safety documents in the National Archives in Paris.

During the French Revolution, a select executive body played the role of the present-day Council of Ministers, only with significantly more power. It was established by the National Convention in April 1793.

OFFICIAL EMBLEM
of the Committee of Public Safety.

COMMITTEE OF PUBLIC SAFETY
meeting in Tuileries Palace.

Officially, the National Convention did not have a chairman. Georges Danton had the greatest influence, followed by Maximilien Robespierre, who wanted to transform France into a "Republic of Virtue".

Robespierre thought that it could be done only through terror. That did not just mean murders and executions. Historians estimate that of the twenty-seven million inhabitants of France, about half a million ended up in prison, while several hundred thousand were under surveillance. An atmosphere of fear surrounded government officials, who issued "certificates of civic virtue" and decided who lived or died. The authorities appealed for "revolutionary vigilance" and information about anything that was suspect. Hence people were afraid of even their closest neighbors. Fear and suspicion were omnipresent. Bloody persecutions of real or alleged enemies continued through the duration of the Revolution. They escalated particularly after the Law of Suspects was passed on September 17, 1793, on the basis of which not only clergy and nobility ended up in prison, but above all townspeople and peasants. People were arrested on the grounds of a political joke, a letter from abroad, or a tip from a neighbor.

At the request of the Committee of Public Safety, a new law came into force on June 10, 1794, which provided for only two verdicts, that is, acquittal or death. Trials were mainly collective. The accused did not have the right to a lawyer or witnesses, and

REYNALD SECHER
claims Lenin visited Vendée in 1919 to learn methods of terror and genocide. When he took over power in Russia, he said: "We must exterminate the Cossacks. They are our Vendée."

273

ROBESPIERRE ARRESTED with his associates during the coup on July 27, 1794.

LOUIS DE SAINT-JUST, the so-called "Angel of Death" or "Archangel of Terror".

GEORGES COUTHON, one of the fathers of the Reign of Terror.

"moral proof" was enough to convict him. Not only opponents of the Revolution were guillotined, but also its fervent supporters if for some reason they seemed to waver in their zeal. The fanaticism of Robespierre and his closest associates, Louis de Saint-Just and Georges Couthon, led other members of the Committee of Public Safety to fear that they too could end up on the scaffold. Hence they organized a conspiracy, and on July 27, 1794, they pulled off a coup. The next day, the three present leaders of the Committee of Public Safety were guillotined without a trial, which was met with enthusiasm by the Parisians, who had had enough of the Reign of Terror. Succumbing to public pressure, the conspirators, who themselves had blood on their hands, were forced to limit persecutions. The Committee of Public Safety gradually lost its prominence and was abolished in 1795.

After Robespierre's execution, all the Committee of Public Safety's documents were thrown into trunks. Ten years later, Napoleon had them sorted out. They were arranged into eight files and sent to an archive. The files were accessible to historians, but nobody examined them thoroughly for over two hundred years. Then on March 4, 2011, digging through the archives, Reynald Secher discovered among the files some wrinkled scraps of paper that turned out to be of fundamental importance. The small, inconspicuous cards attest to measures that decided the fate of thousands of people. The Committee of Public Safety was made up of twelve members, four of whom dealt with the Vendée matter: Maximilien Robespierre, Bertrand Barère, Lazare Carnot, and Jacques Nicolas Billaud-Varenne. Their signatures appear under various proposals of genocidal measures, which were presented to the National Convention and passed.

L. N. M. CARNOT.

LAZARE CARNOT
served the king,
the Revolution,
the Republic,
and the emperor,
dying in 1823
at age 70.

Reynald Secher's case shows that great discoveries can still be made in places where everything seems already to have been sorted, studied, and described. Could researchers of the French Revolution make a similar discovery in the Vatican? The revolutionaries themselves tried to make sure that there would be no documents pertaining to the Revolution in papal archives. But one cannot exclude the possibility of some researcher suddenly coming across a document that may prove to be an intriguing missing link. Such cases occur in the Vatican Secret Archives.

DISCOVERY

War in Spain

CHAPTER 8

War in Spain

The religious dimension of the bloodiest civil war in the history of the Iberian Peninsula

There are not many historians outside Italy who have spent as much time in the Vatican Secret Archives as Fr. Vicente Cárcel Ortí, who was the first to discover many unknown documents that help to understand better the history of the Spanish Civil War (1936–1939).

We met him in the Pontifical Spanish College in Rome. He comes from Valencia but has lived in Rome almost forty years. He studied Church history at the Gregorian University, specializing in the 19th and 20th centuries, and he gained insight into the bloodiest conflict in his country's history by going through documentation in the Vatican Secret Archives.

STREET FIGHTING in Madrid during the Spanish Civil War.

Nobody before him had ever examined the documents, which had not even been catalogued. The Apostolic Nunciature in Madrid housed two hundred boxes, each containing six to eight hundred pages of unexamined documents. He spent years in the Vatican Secret Archives laboriously copying reports, letters, accounts, and testimonies. From 2011 to 2018, he published seven thick volumes of files, containing as many as 2,889 documents.

Thanks to his work, the religious dimension of those events has emerged. Thirteen bishops, 4,184 priests and seminarians, 2,365 monks, 283 nuns, and about 4,000 lay people who aided religious

VOLUME 6
of Fr. Vicente Cárcel Ortí's *Second Republic and Civil War in the Vatican Secret Archives.*

FR. VICENTE CÁRCEL ORTÍ with the fruit of his work in the Vatican Secret Archives: seven volumes containing documents about Spain 1931–1939.

✠

RUINED SEPULCHER
of Card. Carrillo de Acuña, Alcalá de Henares Cathedral.

SALVAGING A BISHOP'S TOMB,
Alcalá de Henares Cathedral.

were murdered during the Spanish Civil War. In all, 12 percent of the Spanish clergy perished; in areas occupied by the Left, the number of clergy killed approached 80 percent, and the revolutionaries forbade pastoral work altogether. All the churches were closed, and property was confiscated. Anything that was connected with the Church was destroyed, burned, or looted—bishops' palaces, monasteries, seminaries, and the headquarters of Catholic organizations. It is estimated that about twenty thousand churches were destroyed, that is, almost half of the churches in Spain, and many priceless works of art were lost. Numerous historical documents housed in archives, libraries, and museums met a similar fate. The devastation was conscious, planned, systematic, yet bereft of military justifications.

But that which most moved Fr. Ortí was the cruelty that accompanied the crimes. Catholics were spared no kind of martyrdom,

including crucifixion. Many victims were tortured, urged to renounce their faith.

They were urged to curse God, spit on images of Christ, or to tread on the crucifix. Despite that, Fr. Ortí, a Spanish historian, did not come across a single documented case of apostasy. Instead, he found numerous testimonies about the contrary, about people who remained faithful to God despite being tortured. In Valencia, for example, a Catholic Action activist, eight months pregnant, had her stomach ripped open and her baby killed, just because she refused to deny Christ. In Rafelbunyol, in the same diocese, nine brothers were murdered because they were too religious.

Pope Pius XI, on hearing terrifying news from the Iberian Peninsula, could not understand why Catholics murdered Catholics, why brothers killed brothers. After all, most of the killers had been baptized.

In order to understand the historical background of that conflict, we have to remember that the fratricidal war began in a country that was politically divided long before Gen. Francisco Franco swung into action. After the fall of the Bonapartist regime, there was a civil war (1814–1833) between conservatives and liberals. Then, from 1833 to 1868, there were two civil wars, the overthrow of the monarchy, fifteen military coups, two uprisings in Cuba, numerous revolts and assassinations (including priests), forty-one different governments, and three constitutions. After the fall of the monarchy in 1868 until the coronation of Alfonso XIII in 1902, the country was torn apart by constant uprisings and revolts, including another seven-year civil war and the murder of two presidents. Later, before the proclamation of the Second Spanish Republic in 1931, there were numerous military revolts, three attempts to assassinate the king, and a seven-year period of dictatorship. During the republic of 1931 to 1936, there were twenty-two cabinet changes, a constitution was adopted and annulled, religious persecution and terror were daily occurrences, while a communist-anarchist revolution broke out in Asturias.

Such was the situation in Spain over the one hundred twenty years prior to the Spanish Civil War, which claimed several hundred

POPE PIUS XI
mentioned the persecution of Christians in Spain in his 1937 encyclical *Divini Redemptoris*.

ALFONSO XIII
became king of Spain upon birth; his mother, Maria Christina, served as regent until he assumed full power in 1902.

281

ISABELLA OF CASTILE
and husband, Ferdinand, received the title Reyes Católicos (Catholic Monarchs) from Pope Alexander VI.

CAPTURE OF GRANADA
in 1492 marked the end of the Reconquest.

FERDINAND II OF ARAGON,
whose marriage to Isabella of Castile gave rise to the Spanish Empire.

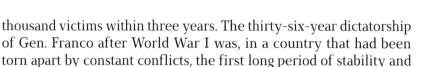

thousand victims within three years. The thirty-six-year dictatorship of Gen. Franco after World War I was, in a country that had been torn apart by constant conflicts, the first long period of stability and internal peace in one hundred fifty years.

The Spanish Civil War, which broke out in 1936, revealed widespread hostility towards the Church, leading to mass crimes. According to historians, the sources of Spanish anticlericalism are diverse, reminiscent of separate streams that when flowing separately do not constitute a deadly threat, but when they merge into one river, can turn into a raging torrent that obliterates everything in its path.

Over the centuries, a particular kind of regalism—that is, a system of royal domination over the Church within a Catholic

state—prevailed in Spain. It was so ingrained that bishops appointed by the king often took up office before the papal appointment. The state and the Church, however, maintained this symbiosis on the grounds that it was necessary to preserve the Catholic unity of the nation. That conviction arose from the Reconquest, the several centuries of war to reclaim the country from the Muslim Moors, who had ruled over much of Spain from 711 to 1492. But regalism occasioned that the monarchy was identified with Catholicism, so much so that King Ferdinand and Queen Isabella were named the Catholic Monarchs of Spain in the 15th century. Ever since, hostility toward the king often signified an attack on Catholicism. Hence the republican aversion to royalism turned into hate for the Church.

Reforms modeled on those carried out by Emperor Joseph II in Austria were introduced during the Enlightenment, especially during the reign of King Charles III and Manuel Godoy, his prime minister, during the period of called enlightened absolutism. The Spanish version of Josephinism entailed a further subordination of religious life to the state. In the 19th century, nationalist and liberal governments used this mechanism to carry out several waves of secularization of ecclesiastical property, especially the wealth of monasteries.

MANUEL GODOY, prime minister of the Kingdom of Spain from 1792 to 1797.

ALLEGORY OF MADRID by Francisco Goya.

Liberal rulers appropriated the goods of religious congregations. On the one hand, they were financially motivated to fight the Church, as they drew from her wealth, while on the other, they were ideologically motivated, as they were convinced that a rejection of religion was a necessary condition of modernizing the country. In order to survive, the state had to be modernized. Hence the struggle against the Church was in the national interest—a position accepted even by many nationalists.

By the end of the 19th century, many Spanish intellectuals, including José Ortega y Gasset, sought to de-Catholicize Spanish culture through, among other things, educational reforms implemented in the 1890s. Also active were Masonic lodges, which sought to destroy the old order, the main pillar of which was still the Catholic Church. Suffice it to say that in the first Cortes Generales, after the proclamation of the Second Spanish Republic in 1931, over 60 percent of the parliamentarians were Freemasons.

JOSÉ ORTEGA Y GASSET, Spanish thinker, author of *The Revolt of the Masses.*

By the 1930s, Spanish society was deeply divided. The only common ground for cooperation between various factions turned out to be their aversion to the Church, an aversion that was capable of uniting anarchists, communists, socialists, Freemasons, republicans, liberals, and nationalists. Thus a popular anticlericalism was launched by multiple groups vying for power at the same time.

In Madrid, we had a meeting with Spanish historian Pío Moa, a leading expert on the Spanish Civil War and the author of numerous books on the subject. He opposes the prevailing, simplified view of the conflict, according to which nationalists and fascists were on one side, called the Nationalists, and communists, republicans, and democrats were on the other, called the Republicans. In reality—he explained—it was much more complex. Gen. Francisco Franco Bahamonde led the monarchists (divided into loyalists and Carlists), conservatives, Christian democrats, nationalists, and some liberals; while

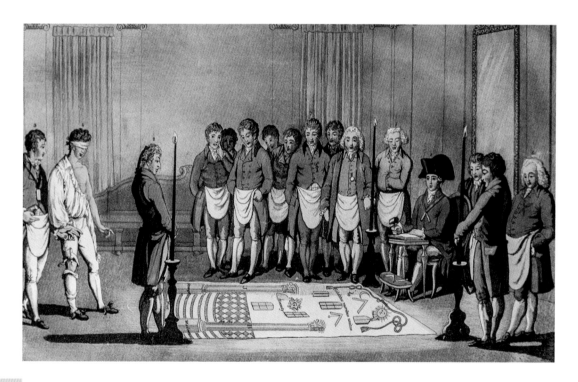

284

INITIATION RITUAL at a Masonic lodge.

in the other camp were various communists and socialists, anarchists, and republicans, as well as Catalan and Basque nationalists.

Moa took a closer look at the leftist camp in terms of its aversion to Catholicism, since this was the main link between the various factions. The first element of the coalition was composed of "Jacobin" republicans, led by Manuel Azaña Díaz, who was fascinated by the French Revolution. He declared, "At the height of power, I would be

PÍO MOA, Spanish historian, in conversation with Grzegorz Górny.

more like Robespierre than Marcus Aurelius." In his opinion, the task of building a new social order rested on the intelligentsia. But it was necessary first to demolish the old order, and this required an alliance of leftist forces, of "powerful peasant battalions" that would help to destroy the historical Catholic heritage of Spain, which he compared to syphilis. So it is not surprising that when anticlerical militias burned many churches in May 1931, he was against punishing the perpetrators, saying, "All the monasteries in Madrid are not worth the life of one republican." When he was prime minister (1931–1933), he legalized the secularization of cemeteries, dissolved the Jesuit order, closed Catholic schools, and justified violence against Christians.

Madrid

SPAIN

GEN. JOSÉ SANJURJO, seasoned commander who was supposed to lead the uprising, but died in a plane crash, leaving Gen. Franco to take charge.

FROM TERRORISM TO HISTORY

Pío Moa was born in Vigo (in Galicia, Spain) in 1948. From as early as he remembers, he was against Gen. Francisco Franco's regime. As a young man, he became fascinated with Marxism, especially with Maoism, its Chinese variant. He became a member of the reactivated Communist Party of Spain and one of the founders and leaders of the left-wing terrorist organization GRAPO (First of October Anti-Fascist Resistance Groups). His organization was responsible for many assassinations and attacks, in which about eighty people were killed. He participated in the group's first major action (October 1, 1975), where four Civil Guard policemen were shot. Moa was expelled from GRAPO two years later.

He changed his views about the Spanish Civil War when he began to study history. It turned out that the view of the armed conflict he had been taught was distinctly different from the one that emerged from his research. In time, he became one of the world's leading experts on the subject, publishing numerous books, including *The Origins of the Spanish Civil War* (1999), *Myths of the Civil War* (2003), *The Collapse of the Second Republic* and the *Civil War* (2001), and *Franco: A Historical Assessment* (2005).

GRAPO, the First of October Anti-Fascist Resistance Groups.

The second element of the leftist camp was the Spanish Socialist Workers' Party, led by Francisco Largo Caballero and Indalecio Prieto. Marxism was its official doctrine, and its goal was the dictatorship of the proletariat, entailing the abolition of private property and religion, which Karl Marx called the "opium of the people". The socialists believed that they should first be allied to the republicans in order to destroy the monarchy and the Church, and then abolish bourgeois democracy as well as proclaim a new order. So it is not surprising that members of the socialist militia and the Guardia de Asalto (Assault Guard) participated in numerous attacks on Catholic churches before the Spanish Civil War broke out.

The third major element in the left-wing camp was that of the anarchists, represented by the Confederación Nacional del Trabajo, which numbered as many as 750,000 members at its peak. While the socialists were Marxists, the anarchists were Bakuninists, who also called for the overthrow of capitalism. Their leader, José Garcia Oliver, wrote that they supported any revolution that would sweep

FRANCISCO LARGO CABALLERO, a leader of the Spanish Socialist Workers' Party (PSOE).

MANUEL AZAÑA, reviewing troops in Alcalá de Henares.

away the old bourgeois institutions (including the Church), break with democracy, and create an egalitarian system called anarcho-communism. The future society was to consist of communes, wherein there would be no place for religion, money, political power, or social differences resulting from work or sex. To achieve that goal, the anarchists agreed on a tactical alliance with the republicans, seeing democracy as a kind of transitional form on the way to a new system.

The fourth element of the left-wing coalition was the Communist Party of Spain, led by José Díaz and Dolores Ibárruri. It was a Stalinist group, the ideal of which was the political system prevailing at the time in the Soviet Union. Its approach to the Catholic Church

INDALECIO PRIETO, a leader of the Spanish Socialist Workers' Party (PSOE).

287

"WIN OR DIE"
A poster for POUM,
the Workers' Party
of Marxist Unification
(Trotskyists).

was similar to the one the Bolsheviks adopted toward the Russian Orthodox Church—that is, exterminating the clergy, destroying objects of worship, and persecuting Christians.

During the civil war, Trotskyists in the Workers' Party of Marxist Unification took on a certain significance. They were supporters of a permanent revolution and were also antireligious, particularly anti-Catholic.

The last element of the left-wing camp was made up of Catalan and Basque nationalists, the only groups that did not programmatically seek to fight the Church. They aimed either to gain autonomy or to break their provinces away from Spain and establish their own independent states. Both the Catalans and the Basques saved many priests and even some bishops.

LEADERS OF THE LEFT
in Spain:
1. José Díaz,
2. José Garcia Oliver,
3. Dolores Ibárruri.

The other camp was made up of an eclectic alliance of various right and center forces, united in their aversion to revolutions and their attachment to traditional culture and the Catholic faith. The alliance was of a reactionary nature, a response to left-wing activities.

Fr. Vicente Cárcel Ortí points out that the Church's problems did not arise because she sided with the Francoists, as the persecution of Catholics began long before Gen. Franco appeared on the scene. The beginning of the repressions was connected with the proclamation of the Second Spanish Republic, which occurred under quite unusual circumstances

KING ALFONSO XIII
abdicated, then
went to France
and eventually
to Italy.

On April 12, 1931, local elections were held in Spain. They were won by the monarchists, who obtained 40,324 councilors' mandates throughout the country. The republican-socialist camp came in second with 40,101, while the members of the Communist Party were third with barely sixty-seven mandates. The monarchists were victorious in the provinces, the republicans in large cities, particularly Madrid. The following day, large demonstrations were staged in the capital demanding the king's resignation. Wanting to avoid bloodshed, Alfonso XIII abdicated on April 14 and departed for France. Thus arose the Second Republic.

The Church quickly came to terms with the change and did not even try to defend the monarchy. The Spanish hierarchy appealed to the faithful to respect the new authorities, while the Holy See immediately recognized the new government. According to Fr. Ortí, there were many supporters of democracy among Catholics

MADRID STREET
in April 1931,
during the
proclamation
of the Second
Republic.

at that time, but unfortunately, they were rejected by the Second Republic. The Jacobin conception of the relationship between the state and the Church held sway.

In May 1931, barely a month after the king's abdication, anticlerical militias burned down about one hundred churches in Madrid, Valencia, Barcelona, Alicante, Murcia, Málaga, Cádiz, and other cities, while police and firemen looked on. Attacks on priests multiplied, but the central authorities did not react, though they forced Primate Pedro Segura y Sáenz to leave the country for criticizing the government.

**FR. VICENTE
CÁRCEL ORTÍ**
in conversation
with Grzegorz
Górny (left).

On June 28, 1931, elections to the Cortes Generales were held, and republican and left-wing forces triumphed. On December 9, they passed a constitution that was anticlerical, anti-Catholic, and antireligious. Well-known thinker José Ortega y Gasset, though generally in favor of the constitution, thought that it also contained some articles that were akin to dynamite on the verge of detonation, as they limited religious freedom, removed catechesis from schools, banned priests from the teaching profession, and limited the possibility of organizing processions. The Second Republic introduced a total secularization in the Jacobin spirit. Religious symbols were removed from schools, and there were fines for ringing church bells. The Jesuits were expelled from Spain.

Political action was accompanied by a press campaign accusing the Church of indecent wealth, decadence, and insensitivity to the plight of the poor. Magazines like *La Traca* and *Fray Lazo* excelled at this.

CARD. PEDRO SEGURA Y SÁENZ, primate of Spain, arrested by the Civil Guard. He was expelled and lived in France, then Rome.

A book series was published, the Library of the Godless, based on the Soviet pattern, wherein Christ was depicted as an evil man and the apostles as having concubines.

The later minister of justice Manuel de Irujo Ollo, in a memorandum submitted to his government on January 7, 1937, wrote self-critically that the Second Republic, proclaimed in 1931, was "a system in the full fascist sense, as believers' consciences were daily violated by public authorities".

How did the Church react? The most important document was the Spanish bishops' pastoral letter of December 20, 1931, expressing disappointment with the government's policies but at the same time a readiness for future cooperation. In their letter, the hierarchs noted that after the proclamation of the Second Republic, the Church had avoided any acts that could have been seen as hostile to the new system, and still she was not treated as a normal institution, but as a threat that must be destroyed by any means necessary, even by breaking the law and violating religious freedom.

SPANISH CONSTITUTION, adopted in 1931, was anticlerical.

PROCLAMATION OF THE SECOND REPUBLIC, Madrid, April 1931.

LA TRACA, anticlerical leftist magazine.

The results of the parliamentary elections held on November 19, 1933, gave some hope for an improvement of the situation, as the right-wing forces were triumphant. The situation did indeed improve somewhat.

In October 1934, a revolution fomented by communists and anarchists broke out in Asturias. It was bloodily crushed by government

JOSÉ MARÍA GIL-ROBLES, Catholic politician, active during the Second Republic, exiled during the Spanish Civil War.

SECOND SPANISH REPUBLIC marked a period of constant social unrest, riots, and violence.

authorities, who were afraid that Spain might be transformed into a Stalinist dictatorship. Several thousand people were killed during the fighting, including thirty-four priests, monks, and seminarians, among others, including eight members of the Institute of the Brothers of Christian Schools, which provided free education for children of poor miners in Turón. Just as during the French Revolution, they were killed not for what they did, but for who they were. They were Catholic religious, which was enough reason for them to perish. So

the first martyrs for the Faith, Fr. Ortí stresses, were murdered two years before the outbreak of the Spanish Civil War.

In July 1935, the Seventh World Congress of the Comintern (Communist International) took place in far-off Moscow. It drew up a new strategy that was to bring about dire consequences for Europe, including Spain.

What actually happened at the congress? According to Pío Moa, it was Stalin's response to events that had occurred in Germany, particularly the dissolution of Germany's Communist Party. The largest Leninist organization in Western Europe had been wound up overnight by the National Socialists (Nazis). Hitler did not hide the fact that he saw Bolshevism as his archenemy, and his offensive against the Communist Party caused the Soviet Union to seek new methods of self-defense. Hitherto, the Communist Party had attacked all political groups that did not completely share its views. They even called the social democrats "social-fascists"

REVOLUTIONARIES arrested in Asturias by members of the Civil Guard (1934).

and forbade forming coalitions with them. The party decided to change its strategy, calling for an alliance of all those forces for whom "fascism" was the number-one enemy. Thus arose, at Stalin's instigation, the idea of popular fronts, which brought various leftist groups together. In Spain, such an alliance—named the Popular Front—was forged by Communists, socialists, Trotskyists, leftist republicans, and center-left Catalan nationalists. On February 16, 1936, they took power as a result of snap parliamentary elections. It is true that more voted for the center-right, but as the results were strongly divided, most of the mandates were won by the Popular Front, which formed a new government.

The left wing decided the time had come to move to the next stage of taking power. Having overthrown the monarchy with the help of republicans and other liberals, leftists moved to rid Spain of its bourgeois democracy and to set up a dictatorship of the proletariat. They sought to foment a revolution similar to the one the Bolsheviks had unleashed in Russia. A week before the elections of February 9, 1936, *El Socialista* reported: "We are determined to do in Spain that which was done in Russia. The plan of Spanish socialism and Russian communism is the same." Some even thought that Lenin and Stalin were not radical enough. Margarita Nelken, a socialist deputy, stated in the Cortes Generales: "We want a revolution, but the Russian revolution cannot serve as a model for us, as a huge revolutionary fire must break out here that will be seen throughout the world, and the country must be flooded by waves of blood that will color the sea red."

These were not idle words, for churches were burning again soon after the elections. On March 8, a Catholic school, a religious house, and five churches were set on fire in Cádiz. Priests, nuns, and even lay Catholic activists died in the attacks. The police and the Republican Guard did not react to the attacks by left-wing militias. According to official sources, from February to July 1936, 170 churches were burnt down, with 330 people killed and 1,511 wounded. Progovernment newspapers *El Libertad, El Liberal*, and *El Socialista* urged a crackdown on Catholics. The country was plunged into anarchy and internal struggles. The largest Catholic daily, *El Debate*, which informed readers about what was happening, was repeatedly suspended by the authorities.

JOSEPH STALIN, who promoted popular fronts in Europe.

293

SACRILEGIOUS behavior by Spanish revolutionaries, Madrid, 1936.

"WE SHALL JUDGE GOD"

Below is a passage from an article published in July 19, 1936, in *Solidaridad Obrera*, a daily newspaper connected with the National Confederation of Labor (CNT):

> The Church continues along her own way, still our great enemy. We know her by her works. Because of what she does, she will be hated by all Spaniards worthy of the name. We will destroy her by putting an end to the formation of the "blacks". People should not forget. People must not forgive the unforgiveable, never, never, never.
>
> We are combatting the priestly profession because it is useless and harmful, as are so many other professions related to capitalism. We understand that due to the necessity caused by war, we should combat them all the more, since we need to increase production, eliminate unnecessary industries, and put an end to unproductive activities.
>
> We are the same atheists we were yesterday, which is why we light up the sky with the flames of burning churches of obscurantism. The sky is the only place where God causes us trouble. If anyone wanted to bring him here, on earth, we would fight him and destroy his churches, convents, etc., again. And we shall judge him.

The murder of José Calvo Sotelo, a monarchist and the leader of the parliamentary opposition, dramatically changed the situation. On July 13, 1936, members of the socialist militia and the Guardia de Asalto kidnapped him from his home and killed him. According to American historian Stanley G. Payne, such an execution of an opposition leader by government police was an unprecedented crime in the history of Western European parliamentarism. The murder, according to him, showed that respect for civil rights and constitutional freedoms under left-wing rule was but a fiction in Spain.

Ángel Galarza, one of the Socialist Party leaders, said of the murder: "The assassination of Calvo Sotelo made me sorry. I regretted that I did

ALCALÁ DE HENARES CATHEDRAL, destroyed by anticlerical militants in 1936.

not participate in the execution." Many Spaniards, however, felt otherwise. The killing turned out to be the straw that broke the camel's back, the spark that ignited the civil war. A military group led by the generals Francisco Franco Bahamonde and Emilio Mola y Vidal decided to stage an uprising. On July 17, 1936, the anti-Left anti-Left rebellion broke out in Morocco, which was then a Spanish colony. A day later, fighting began in the Iberian Peninsula.

The Church did not participate in the Francoist plot. Clergy did not take part in the right-wing military coup. Nonetheless, it became

295

JOSÉ CALVO SOTELO, leader of the parliamentary opposition, murdered by members of a leftist militia group in July 1936.

one of the main victims of revolutionary terror. Wherever the leftist forces gained power, bloody campaigns ensued against representatives of the Church. Catholics were murdered, churches set on fire, religious objects profaned, sacrilegious processions organized (wherein prostitutes with Marian symbols flaunted themselves on floats), Masses parodied. Even the tombs of nuns were opened, their remains pulled out to be mocked by the rabble. In Huesca, for example, corpses were removed from graves and arranged in pairs in copulatory positions.

GEN. EMILIO MOLA, Gen. Franco's comrade-in-arms.

REVIEW OF TROOPS by Gen. Mola before they went to the front.

The greatest terror reigned during the first three months of the war, when most mass murders were carried out and with impunity. On August 24, 1936, people's tribunals were established, creating the appearance of a rule of law, but they were of an ad hoc nature, issuing death sentences for trivial allegations, just as it was once done in revolutionary France and Russia.

Fr. Vicente Cárcel Ortí draws attention to the difference between religious persecution and political repression. Catholics were often sentenced to death not for political but religious reasons, out of

BARRICADE on a Barcelona street, July 1936.

hatred for the Christian faith and the Church. Statements by numerous left-wing leaders attest to the fact that exterminations were intentional. For example, Andrés Nin Pérez, chairman of the Trotskyist Party, spoke thus of the Church problem (Barcelona, August 8, 1936): "We have resolved it completely, reaching its roots, eliminating priests, churches, and worship." On March 5, 1937, in Valencia, José Díaz, secretary general of the Spanish section of the Cominform (Communist Information Bureau), declared: "The Church no longer exists in the provinces where we had power. Spain went a little further than the Soviets, as the Church in today's Spain has been destroyed."

Manuel de Irujo Ollo, the leader of the Basque Nationalist Party, who became minister without portfolio in the republican government, attempted to change the religious policy of the left-wing camp. On January 7, 1937, during a cabinet meeting in Valencia, he submitted a memorandum on religious persecution. His speech was one long accusation against his own political camp, and parts of it are worth quoting:

WOOL BALACLAVA of a political commissar from the time of the war.

297

MARTYRS OF THE SPANISH CIVIL WAR

So far, the Holy See has raised over one thousand Spanish Civil War martyrs to the altars. No other military conflict in history has brought the Church so many blesseds and saints who were murdered out of hatred for the Faith.

Particularly noteworthy are four great collective beatifications:

- 122 martyrs on October 25, 1992 (Pope John Paul II—Vatican)
- 233 martyrs on March 11, 2001 (Pope John Paul II—Vatican)
- 498 martyrs on October 28, 2007 (Pope Benedict XVI—Vatican)
- 522 martyrs on October 13, 2013 (Pope Francis—Tarragona)

One of the victims of anti-Catholic persecutions was Ceferino Giménez Malla, called El Pelé (the Strong One, or the Brave One). A drover and dealer in mules, donkeys, and horses, he was the first Romani (Gypsy) to be canonized by the Church. He was arrested because he stood up for a young priest who was being dragged along a street. His interrogators found a rosary on him, which was enough to condemn him to death. He was shot on August 8, 1936, at the cemetery in Barbastro, at the age of seventy-five. On May 4, 1997, over forty thousand Gypsies attended his beatification Mass in Rome, which was celebrated by Pope John Paul II.

BUS BARRICADE on a Barcelona street, by anarchist groups CNT and FAI.

The current situation of the Church since July of 1936 throughout areas that remained faithful to her is, except in the Basque provinces, as follows:

– all altars, paintings, and objects of worship, with very few exceptions, have been destroyed, mostly with contempt;

– all churches have been closed to worship, which has been suspended in a total and absolute manner;

– most churches have been burned down, which in Catalonia has become the norm;

– the depots and public institutions have taken in bells, chalices, monstrances, candelabras, and other objects of worship, melting them down and even using the materials for war or industrial purposes;

– various warehouses, shops, car workshops, stables, apartments, and shelters, as well as various service and public institutions, have been set up in churches; the public institutions that have taken them over have built permanent works,

– all monasteries have been dissolved and their religious life suspended. Their buildings, objects of worship, and goods of every kind have been burned, plundered, taken over, or destroyed;

– priests and monks have been arrested, locked up in prisons, and shot without trial by the thousands. Such things, though in smaller numbers, take place not only in the villages (where priests and monks are hunted and then killed in a barbaric way), but also in towns. Madrid, Barcelona, and other large cities have seen hundreds of arrests and imprisonments on no grounds other than the fact of being a priest or religious;

– people have even been absolutely forbidden to have images and objects of worship. Police—searching houses, rummaging through people's homes and intimate personal or family belongings—have scornfully destroyed pictures, holy cards, religious books, and anything connected to or recalling religion.[1]

FR. JOSEMARÍA ESCRIVÁ DE BALAGUER, founder of Opus Dei, had to hide from the Republicans during the Spanish Civil War.

Manuel de Irujo Ollo demonstrated that anticlerical activities led the government to lose the world's sympathy and respect. He suggested, among other things, that the clergy should be released from prisons, religious freedom restored, and the requisition of Church property terminated. Two days later, the Council of Ministers unanimously rejected his proposals. Juan García Oliver, the justice

"¡NO PASARAN!"
"They shall not pass!": Spanish Left battle cry, slogan of the defenders of Madrid during the civil war.

"¡PASAREMOS!"
"We shall pass!": the Francoists' response, presaging the capture of Madrid. In his first speech after the victory, Gen. Franco said, "¡Hemos pasado!" (We passed!).

minister, criticized them for showing "excessive respect towards the Church". The project was also condemned by the left-wing press, including the PSOE's daily *El Socialista*, which wrote that such a measure would evoke within its own ranks an indignation that would be difficult to oppose.

In May 1937, Manuel de Irujo Ollo became the minister of justice. He held the office for seven months, trying to normalize the relations between the government and the Church, but without much success. He failed to have priests released from prison and to have public worship

C-3 SUBMARINE, part of the fleet loyal to the government at the Cartagena Naval Base.

restored. But thanks to him, the number of religious persecutions fell sharply, though murders and desecrations still occurred.

At the beginning of the Spanish Civil War, the odds were in favor of the government. It had a distinct military advantage in terms of personnel and equipment, with an overwhelming superiority in the air and at sea. It also had the majority of the country's strategic resources–controlling almost all of the large cities, the industrial sector, the main communication hubs, and the state treasury. Victory seemed to be within reach. Two weeks after the beginning of the fighting, Diego Martínez Barrio, mayor of Valencia, announced that the war was over—the rebels against the Republic had been defeated.

Yet it turned out to be otherwise. The basis of the Nationalist forces was the Spanish Legion. Though small, it was well trained and maintained high morale. It also turned out that Gen. Franco was a much

REPUBLICAN SAILORS from the Jaime I battleship anchored in Almería.

DEFENSE OF TOLEDO

After the outbreak of the civil war, Toledo (thirty thousand inhabitants) was quickly captured by the Republicans. The Nationalists retreated into the alcazar, a stone fortress set on high ground overlooking the Tagus River and the city. There were not many of them—about thirteen hundred men, five hundred fifty women, and fifty children. They withstood a siege for seventy days, under the command of fifty-eight-year-old Col. José Moscardó Ituarte. On July 23, 1936, he received a call from Commissar Candido Cabello, the chief of the Worker's Militia, who gave him an ultimatum: either he would surrender in ten minutes or Cabello would kill Luis Moscardó, the colonel's son. Wanting to show that he was not bluffing, he handed the phone to the twenty-four-year-old captive:

TOLEDO
1 Alcazar after liberation,
2–3 Col. Moscardó's study,
4 Francoist patches,
5 panorama of the city, with the towering alcazar.

"What is happening, my son?" asked the colonel.

"Nothing," answered Luis. "They say they will shoot me if the alcazar does not surrender."

"If this is true," replied Moscardó, "then commend your soul to God, shout 'Viva España', and die like a hero. Good-bye, my son."

"That I can do," answered Luis. "Good-bye, my father."

A month later he was shot.

During the defense of the alcazar, the Nationalists enjoyed some successes. When they took Maqueda, they had to decide whether to march to Madrid or Toledo. Gen. Francisco Franco was urged to take the capital, as it seemed to be an easy target, but he decided to go to the rescue of Col. Moscardó. Despite the lack of food and ammunition, the Nationalists managed to hold out until Franco relieved them. Toledo was taken by José Enrique Varela on September 29, 1936.

better military commander than any of the Republican officers. Another advantage was that many Catholics, terrified by the religious persecutions, supported the uprising.

On the basis of his research, Pío Moa stated that simple people dominated among the conservatives who opposed the Left in defense of faith, family, property, and country. The revolutionaries sought to abolish these things because they believed they were bourgeois instruments of domination, which led to the exploitation and the alienation of the individual. Their goal, as is the case with other utopian movements, was the creation of a "new man".

He rejects the argument that the Church became the object of leftist attacks because of its enormous material wealth and its insensitivity to the plight of the poor. If that had been so—he argues—then mainly hierarchs and priests from the rich districts would have

GEN. FRANCISCO FRANCO BAHAMONDE, leader of the national uprising.

FRANCO ENTERS REUS, Catalonia.

been murdered. In reality, priests, nuns, and monks who ministered among the poor, often living under the same conditions of poverty as they did, were most often killed. Moreover, at a time when there was no social welfare system, it was the Church who maintained hospitals, orphanages, nursing homes, shelters, and schools for workers and the poor. Perhaps that was not enough, says Moa, but no one except the Church undertook such works in Spain.

In his opinion, hatred for Catholicism stemmed from the ideological belief that religion is one of the chief obstacles to the realization of a new age of equality and social liberation. Cruelty to Catholics attested to one's determination in pursuing a noble goal; thus it was seen as meritorious and not as a proof of depravity.

Despite the persecutions, both the Holy See and the Spanish episcopate recognized the legality of the left-wing government for quite some time. It was not until July 1, 1937, almost a year after the outbreak of the civil war, that Spanish bishops published a letter condemning the government for the first time and supporting

FRANCO'S BELONGINGS: binoculars, walking stick, and coat.

Gen. Franco's troops. This was in large measure connected with the fact that in areas captured by the Nationalists, religious freedom had been restored, whereas the government had no intention of ceasing repressions.

Meanwhile the Communist Party violently purged the leftist coalition of non-Stalinists, such as Trotskyists and anarchists, and took over the Republican camp. When the Spanish government decided to deposit its gold reserves in another country for safekeeping, under Communist influence it agreed to move the gold to Russia. On October 25, 1936, 510 tons of gold departed on ships for Odessa, and it was never returned to Spain.

Thanks to the gold, the Kremlin was able to provide the Communists with weapons and take full control of the Spanish Republican Army.

PUENTE DE LOS FRANCESES (Bridge of the Frenchmen) over the Manzanares, a strategic military asset during the Battle of Madrid.

It came to the point where key decisions were made by Soviet advisers, not by Spanish officers and politicians, while the country's internal security was subordinated to the Soviet secret police. The infamous Cheka was established in all the places under Republican control. Had the Republicans won the civil war, Europe would have been hemmed in by the Communists: Russia from the east and Spain from the west.

The Republicans benefitted from Stalin's aid, while the Nationalists were aided by Hitler and Mussolini. Gen. Franco accepted military

support from the Third Reich and Italy, neither of which wanted to see the victory of Bolshevism in the Iberian Peninsula. The difference was that the Nationalists were independent of the Axis powers, while the Republicans were dependent on the Kremlin.

The spring of 1938 saw the last wave of persecutions, murders, and profanations. It was not until the outcome of the war was virtually decided in favor of the Nationalists that the Left decided to change its religious policy somewhat. On December 8, the General

NAZI AND BOLSHEVIK patches and badges. Both the Third Reich and the Soviet Union used Spain as a testing ground during the civil war, supporting the two warring parties.

Commission of Cults was established to normalize relations with the Church. But the Catholics were not won over by the gesture. On March 28, 1939, the Nationalist forces entered Madrid. On April 1, the war was over.

BUNKER IN MADRID, part of the capital's defense system during the civil war.

After the Nationalists won, whenever they came across traces of crimes committed by the Republicans, they very often sought revenge, and in the name of justice, they committed many crimes. For instance, while soldiers who were taken prisoner were tried, the left-wing militia members were shot without trial—as rebels captured with weapons in their hands. As is often the case during a war, the most primitive instincts were aroused, and personal scores were settled. The Church

307

**MADRID
AFTER
THE WAR**
was one of the
most devastated
cities in Spain.

**KSAWERY
PRUSZYŃSKI,**
Polish
reporter, war
correspondent
in Spain, author
of *Garnet Rosary*.
The photos on
this page come
from his reports,
published in
*Wiadomości
Literackie*
in 1936.

tried to calm the situation, calling for murders to cease, for enemies to be forgiven. Her appeals for peace and forgiveness turned out to be largely unsuccessful.

A white terror followed the red terror, but Pío Moa points to clear differences between them. The spiral of violence was compounded by the revolutionaries who, in the name of building a bright future, decided to cleanse the world of "reactionary elements". In the wake of the Nationalist victory, the response of the people who had been terrorized was of a vengeful nature, which often got out of control. Moa confesses that although there were some in both camps who called for more compassion, they were largely ignored.

Both sides minimized their own crimes and exaggerated their losses. Simone Weil and Georges Bernanos' correspondence is an example of an effort to rise above the political sympathies of their own camps. Although both came from France, they found themselves in Spain on two opposite fronts: she actively committed to the Republicans and he wholeheartedly on the Nationalist side. Their idealism, however, collided with the savagery of war. They

**LEFTIST
MILITIA**
members, from
the Socialist
militia and the
Assault Guard.

were unable to close their eyes to the cruelties that were committed by the camps with which they had identified. In their writings, they expressed the terror and the disgust that seized them at the sight of those who ought to have represented the forces of good but resorted to evil.

However, a one-sided view of the civil war has been embedded in the collective consciousness of the West, a view that was created by circles favorable to the Republicans. In large measure, it was due to the fact that many influential intellectuals,

SPANISH SEMINARIAN crucified during the war—painting by Jean Martin.

BRONZE BUST of Gen. Francisco Franco.

VALLEY OF THE FALLEN

On the orders of Gen. Francisco Franco, a mausoleum was established in the Valle de los Caídos (Valley of the Fallen) on November 20, 1958, for victims of the Spanish Civil War. It is located in Cuelgamuros Valley, in the Sierra de Guadarrama mountains, about thirty miles northwest of Madrid. A natural-architectural complex was erected there called the National Monument of the Holy Cross. The complex includes a Benedictine abbey and the Basilica of the Holy Cross of the Valley of the Fallen, which was hewn out of a granite ridge as a sanctuary of national reconciliation. The basilica impresses one by its size; its central nave is six stories tall; its length is 860 feet. Above it towers the world's largest cross, made of stone and measuring about 499 feet.

Gen. Franco made the decision to build the complex on April 1, 1940, the first anniversary of the end of the civil war. He commissioned the work to two architects from the Basque and socialist camps that were hostile to him. Forty thousand urns, containing the ashes of both Nationalists and Republicans killed on all fronts of the war, were deposited in the crypts of the basilica to symbolize the reconciliation of Spaniards after the end of the conflict.

There are two separate tombs in the basilica. In one of them is José Antonio Primo de Rivera, the founder and leader of the national syndicalist Falange Española. The Republicans arrested him several days before the outbreak of the civil war and murdered him in a prison in Alicante on November 20, 1936. In the other was Gen. Franco, who died on November 20, 1975. However, on October 24, 2019, Pedro Sanchez's socialist government had his remains exhumed and transported to a cemetery in El Pardo, near Madrid.

MAUSOLEUM in the Valley of the Fallen, viewed from the Benedictine abbey.

CENTRAL NAVE, Basilica of the Holy Cross, hewn out of a granite ridge (top right).

CRYPT OF RECONCILIATION, containing the ashes of 40,000 Spaniards who fell during the civil war (lower right).

BATTLE OF BELCHITE, 1937—soldiers of the International Brigades on a Soviet T-26 tank.

writers, and artists had found themselves on that side and used their talents to support the Popular Front, including Ernest Hemingway, John Dos Passos, Sinclair Lewis, Edmund Wilson, Aldous Huxley, Lillian Hellman, W.H. Auden, Samuel Beckett, André Malraux, Romain Rolland, Henri Barbusse, André Gide, Louis Aragon, Pablo Picasso, George Orwell, and many more. It was they who became the most effective advocates of the Spanish revolutionaries.

ON THE SPANISH FRONT Joris Ivens, a Dutch documentary filmmaker; Ernest Hemingway, an American writer; and Ludwig Renn, a German writer.

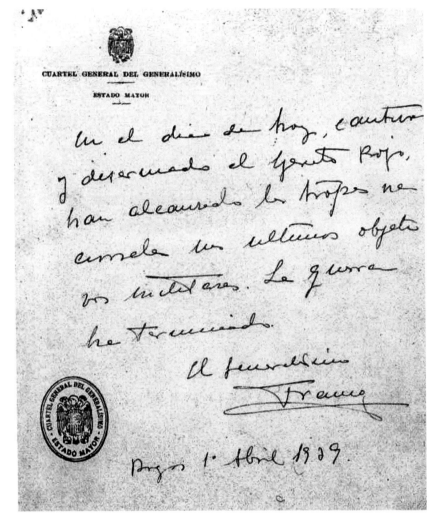

MEMORANDUM
from Franco's supreme headquarters about the end of the civil war, April 1, 1939.

VICTORY MONUMENT
in Toledo honoring the defenders of the alcazar.

Discussions as to the losses suffered during the war by both parties continue to this day. The best-documented work on this issue was published in 1977 by Ramón Salas Larrazábal, a Spanish historian. According to his calculations, 72,344 leftists were victims of executions and pogroms, while the right wing lost 32,021 lives. In addition, after the end of the conflict, death sentences were passed for war crimes. In the years 1939–1950, out of the planned 50,000 executions, 22,642 were carried out. More than half were commuted to prison terms (mainly life imprisonment, later shortened to six or eight years).

Many details pertaining to the victims of that war have not been clarified to this day. Fr. Vicente Cárcel Ortí has been working for years in the Vatican Secret Archives seeking information to bear witness to the truth, a task to which he has devoted his life.

313

The Silence
of Pius XII

CHAPTER 9

The Silence of Pius XII

The Holy See, the Third Reich, and the Holocaust.

The Vatican Secret Archives do not declassify files on people until seventy years after their death. In 1964, however, Pope Paul VI decided to declassify the files on Pope Pius XII, despite the fact that he had only been deceased for six years. Why the exception?

Vatican City

ITALY

PIUS XII SPEAKS to the inhabitants of Rome after it was bombed by Allied air forces on July 19, 1943.

February 20, 1963, marked the first performance of *The Deputy,* a play under the direction of Erwin Piscator, a declared Communist, at the left-wing Freie Volksbühne (People's Independent Theater) in West Berlin.

The play was written by a thirty-two-year-old German, Rolf Hochhuth, a hitherto unknown playwright. That same day, the Rowohlt Verlag publishing house (Hamburg) published the full text of the play. There was a significant difference between the book version and the theater version: the former was 222 pages, the latter ninety pages. Piscator must have made drastic cuts, because otherwise, the stage version would have lasted eight hours. Yet he took care not to omit

that which was of most interest to the public—Pope Pius XII's alleged indifference to the genocide of the Jews.

Significantly less attention was paid to other fictional themes in the play, which depicts Pius XII as cold, ruthless, and calculating. For example, he justifies the bombing of cities. Why? Because he had allegedly received a large amount of money from American Jesuits—the proceeds from the sale of shares in a munitions factory that produced aerial bombs. Reviewers did not take this literary fantasy seriously, but it was otherwise when it came to Hochhuth's fictitious assertions about Pope Pius XII's silence regarding the Holocaust, which the pontiff allegedly ignored because he needed Hitler for his own political machinations. That is what the play's Pius XII tells the character Fr. Riccardo, a young Jesuit who encourages him to defend the Jews. The priest, disappointed by the attitude of the Vicar of Christ, even considers murdering him, but he eventually ends up in Auschwitz. In one of the monologues, Riccardo compares himself to Judas, stating that the Iscariot's sacrifice was greater than Christ's, as he condemned himself to eternal damnation. After the

POPE PIUS XII,
head of the Church from 1939 to 1958.

ST. MAXIMILIAN KOLBE,
Polish martyr, victim of the Nazis.

premiere, Hochhuth said that the figure of Fr. Riccardo was modelled on Maximilian Kolbe, to whom he had dedicated his play.

It did not occur to any of the critics to take the juxtaposition of the Franciscan martyr and the fictional blasphemer seriously. Yet Pius XII's alleged indifference regarding the Holocaust was accepted with total credulity. Hochhuth's public statements undoubtedly had a bearing on this. He claimed that during

STATUE OF PIUS XII, St. Peter's Basilica, Rome.

CUPOLA, St. Peter's Basilica, Rome.

a three-month stay in Rome in 1959, he met eyewitnesses who informed him of Pius XII's cold attitude during the war.

We now know who these eyewitnesses were. One was a German, Fr. Bruno Wüstenberg, who then worked in the Secretariat of State (Holy See). He had a grudge against Pius XII, as the pope had hindered him in his career due to his alleged homosexual tendencies. The ascetic pope was also offended by Fr. Wüstenberg's worldly lifestyle— the priest was well known for racing along the streets of Rome in a red Porsche. Fr. Wüstenberg did not advance in his career until Paul VI's pontificate, when he became an archbishop and apostolic pro-nuncio to Japan.

The other eyewitness was an Austrian inhabitant of Rome since 1923, Bishop Alois Hudal, rector of the Collegio Teutonico di Santa Maria dell'Anima, the main center for Rome's German-speaking community. Bishop Hudal was an advocate of National Socialism (Nazism) and a Third Reich intelligence agent. After the war, he organized the escape of such war criminals as Adolf Eichmann, Josef Mengele, and Klaus Barbie to South America. Hudal could not

POPE PAUL VI
collaborated
as a cardinal with
Pius XII in the
Secretariat of State.

**CARD. EUGENIO
PACELLI** during
a visit to the Italian
government's
headquarters in Rome.

stand Pius XII because of his intransigent attitude towards Nazism and so decided to take revenge.

The Deputy became a media event. The theatrical fiction began to take on a life of its own. Accusations against Pius XII—of his insensitivity to the tragedy of the Jews, and even of collaboration with the Third Reich—began to appear ever more frequently. This prompted Pope Paul VI to declassify (in 1964) World War II—era documents for a group of historians. Pius XII's files were technically classified until 2028, but Paul VI did not want to risk *The Deputy* version of the past gaining traction on the basis of a playwright's poetic license rather than on historical data.

Hence four Jesuit historians were able to familiarize themselves with Pius XII's files, which were housed in the Vatican Secret Archives: a Frenchman, Pierre Blet; an Italian, Angelo Martini; a German, Burkhart Schneider; and an American, Robert A. Graham. Their findings were published between 1965 and 1981, as a series of twelve volumes of files that contained 7,664 pages of documents on Vatican policies during World War II. In 1983, John Paul II allowed unlimited access to

the archives to a German Jesuit, Fr. Peter Gumpel, who was a re-
lator in Pius XII's beatification process.

We met him in a building that belongs to the General Curia of the
Society of Jesus in Rome. Fr. Gumpel, born in Hanover in 1923, spent
only thirteen years in Germany. His family was involved in anti-
Nazi activities (his grandfather was murdered, and his mother ended
up in prison), so he had to leave his homeland. He went to school in
France, Holland, Spain, and Italy, and then joined the Jesuit order in
Amsterdam. He has lived in Rome since 1947, lecturing in theology
and philosophy at the Pontifical Gregorian University. He worked
for many years as an assistant to the postulator of the Jesuits' General Assembly, participating in the beatification and canonization

**FR. PETER
GUMPEL**
and his positio:
6 volumes
on Pius XII,
over 3,000 pages,
prepared for
the Congregation
for the Causes
of Saints.

processes of 147 Jesuits, including Pius XII's beatification process,
which Paul VI initiated in 1965.

Though Fr. Gumpel is ninety-six years of age, he is mentally alert
and has an excellent memory. He spoke of the great shock he had
when he first saw the documents concerning Pius XII in the Vatican Secret Archives—dozens of chests containing sixteen million
documents that have not been catalogued. Nobody had sorted out the
documents, since their scheduled declassification (2028) was in the
distant future. Only two archivists were employed to copy all the
documents and draw up indexes according to names, dioceses, and
subjects. Seeing this state of affairs, Fr. Gumpel appreciated just how

✛

much the four historians had done, who, over a period of sixteen years, published twelve volumes of files.

The extensive archival search revealed a completely different picture of Pius XII than the one depicted in Hochhuth's *The Deputy.* Nevertheless, Pius XII's fictitious, shameful attitude regarding the Holocaust began to be believed widely. British journalist John Cornwell reaffirmed that belief when he depicted Pius XII as an anti-Semite and an advocate of Nazism in his book *Hitler's Pope* (1999). Garry Wills' *Papal Sin: Structures of Deceit* (2000) was along the same lines. Two years later, Constantin Costa-Gavras' film *Amen* used motifs from *The Deputy,* while Daniel Jonah Goldhagen's *A Moral*

HITLER'S POPE,
John Cornwell's book criticizing Pius XII.

A MORAL RECKONING,
Daniel Jonah Goldhagen's well-known book on the Church and the Holocaust.

A ONE-DAY CONCLAVE elected Card. Pacelli as pope.

Reckoning: The Role of the Catholic Church in the Holocaust and Its Unfulfilled Duty of Repair (2002) was also in the same vein.

The above-mentioned authors consolidated the image of an antihero wearing a papal tiara, though this was not based on Vatican documents, not even those published from 1965 to 1981. There was even a permanent exhibition at the Yad Vashem Institute in Jerusalem, where a photograph of Pius XII stood alongside photos of German Nazi criminals, accompanied by a plaque alleging that Pius XII did nothing to save Jews during World War II. In 2007, there was an

international scandal when Archbishop Antonio Franco, the apostolic nuncio to Israel, refused to visit Yad Vashem.

In 2003, John Paul II decided also to declassify documents pertaining to Vatican-German relations during Pius XI's pontificate (February 12, 1922, to February 10, 1939). It was a period when Eugenio Pacelli (the future Pius XII) occupied highly responsible positions, first as a nuncio in Munich and Berlin and then as the Holy See's secretary of state; hence he had a great influence on papal policies regarding the Weimar Republic and the Third Reich.

Among the declassified documents was a letter from Edith Stein, a German philosopher and soon-to-be Carmelite of Jewish descent, to Pius XI. The letter was written two months after the Nazi Party's election victory. Fr. Raphael Wazer, abbot of the Benedictine abbey in Beuron, conveyed the letter to Cardinal Eugenio Pacelli, then

YAD VASHEM, World Holocaust Remembrance Center, Jerusalem.

ADOLF HITLER, chancellor of Germany, surrounded by his ministers on January 30, 1933.

323

EUGENIO PACELLI
as a 20-year-old seminarian.

FILIPPO PACELLI,
Pius XII's father,
a well-known
Roman lawyer.

FRANCESCO PACELLI,
Pius XII's older brother,
the father of four
children.

L'OSSERVATORE ROMANO,
a daily paper founded by Marcantonio
Pacelli; issue of May 15, 1891, including
Leo XIII's *Rerum Novarum*.

THE BLACK NOBILITY

Pius XII (Eugenio Pacelli, 1876–1958)
was a descendant of the Black Nobility,
which had been at the service of popes for
generations. His grandfather, Marcantonio
Pacelli (1804–1890), was a long-standing
official of the Papal States and held, among
other posts, the office of secretary to the
minister of foreign affairs. He became
famous for founding the Holy See's paper
L'Osservatore Romano in 1861.

Filippo Pacelli (1837–1916), the father of
the future pope, also worked for the Vatican, mainly as a lawyer. He was an attor-
ney for the Roman Rota and a member of
the Canon Law Codification Commission.
His brother, Ernest Pacelli, was a financial
adviser to three popes and the founder
and president of the Banco di Roma. Of
Pius XII's siblings, Francesco Pacelli (1872–
1935) turned out to be the best known.
He was Pius XI's lawyer and one of the
negotiators of the Lateran Treaty in 1929.

Als ein Kind des jüdischen Volkes, das durch Gottes Gnade seit elf Jahren ein Kind der katholischen Kirche ist, wage ich es, vor dem Vater der Christenheit auszusprechen, was Millionen von Deutschen bedrückt.

Seit Wochen sehen wir in Deutschland Taten geschehen, die jeder Gerechtigkeit und Menschlichkeit - von Nächstenliebe gar nicht zu reden - Hohn sprechen. Jahre hindurch haben die nationalsozialistischen Führer den Judenhass gepredigt. Nachdem sie jetzt die Regierungsgewalt in ihre Hände gebracht und ihre Anhängerschaft - darunter nachweislich verbrecherische Elemente - bewaffnet hatten, ist diese Saat des Hasses aufgegangen. Dass Ausschreitungen vorgekommen sind, wurde noch vor kurzem von der Regierung zugegeben. In welchem Umfang, davon können wir uns kein Bild machen, weil die öffentliche Meinung geknebelt ist. Aber nach dem zu urteilen, was mir durch persönliche Beziehungen bekannt geworden ist, handelt es sich keineswegs um vereinzelte Ausnahmefälle. Unter dem Druck der Auslandsstimmen ist die Regierung zu "milderen" Methoden übergegangen. Sie hat die Parole ausgegeben, es solle "keinem Juden ein Haar gekrümmt werden". Aber sie treibt durch ihre Boykotterklärung - dadurch, dass sie den Menschen wirtschaftliche Existenz, bürgerliche Ehre und ihr Vaterland nimmt - viele zur Verzweiflung; es sind mir in der letzten Woche durch private Nachrichten 5 Fälle von Selbstmord infolge dieser Anfeindungen bekannt geworden. Ich bin überzeugt, dass es sich um eine allgemeine Erscheinung handelt, die noch viele Opfer fordern wird. Man mag bedauern, dass die Unglücklichen nicht mehr inneren Halt haben, um ihr Schicksal zu tragen. Aber die Verantwortung fällt doch zum grossen Teil auf die, die sie so weit brachten. Und sie fällt auch auf die, die dazu schweigen.

16

EDITH STEIN'S LETTER
to Pius XI, 1933, first page.

EDITH STEIN
took the religious name Teresa Benedicta of the Cross.

secretary of state. According to Pacelli's notes, he read the letter to Pope Pius XI on April 20, 1933.

Edith Stein began her letter thus: "Holy Father, as a child of the Jewish people who, by the grace of God, for the past eleven years has also been a child of the Catholic Church, I dare to speak to the Father of Christianity about that which oppresses millions of Germans." She goes on to describe the repressions suffered by the Jews at the hands of the National Socialists, abuses that "mock any sense of justice and humanity, not to mention love of neighbor". From today's perspective, these persecutions, compared to the genocide that was to follow, do not make such a shocking impression. But they were a severe trauma for the Jewish convert. She was shocked by the aggressive propaganda that stirred up hatred and stripped people of their dignity, brutally suppressing any criticism or opposition and, through boycott measures, undermining people's livelihood, which drove many to suicide. "I am convinced", she wrote, "that this is a general condition which will claim many more victims."

According to her, anyone who remained silent in such a situation was complicit in lawlessness. Hence she appealed to the pope:

Everything that happened and continues to happen on a daily basis originates with a government that calls itself 'Christian'. For weeks not only Jews but also thousands of faithful

RACIAL CLASSIFICATION of the population of Germany according to the Nuremberg Laws.

GERMAN RACIST POSTER warning against overly close contact with people of "lower races".

Catholics in Germany, and, I believe, all over the world, have been waiting and hoping for the Church of Christ to raise her voice to put a stop to this abuse of Christ's name.

Ending her letter, Edith Stein referred to theological arguments, pointing out that National Socialism was not only contrary to Christianity, but also might turn against it explicitly in the future:

Is not this idolization of race and governmental power which is being pounded into the public consciousness by the radio open heresy? Is not the effort to destroy Jewish blood an abuse of the holiest humanity of our Savior, of the most blessed Virgin and the apostles? Is not all this diametrically opposed to the conduct of our Lord and Savior, who, even on the Cross, still prayed for his persecutors? And is this not a black mark on the record of this Holy Year, which was intended to be a year of peace and reconciliation? We all, who are faithful children of the Church, and who see the conditions in Germany with open eyes, fear the worst for the reputation of the Church if the silence continues any longer. We are convinced that this silence will not be able in the long run to purchase peace with the present German government. For the time being, the fight against Catholicism will be conducted quietly and less brutally than against Jewry, but no less

END OF STEIN'S LETTER to Pius XI, signed "Dr. Edith Stein".

17

PROPAGANDA POSTERS of the National Socialist German Workers' Party (NSDAP).

NSDAP MEMBERS, claiming to be true Christians, agitating in front of a church.

systematically. Before long, no Catholic will be able to hold office in Germany unless he dedicates himself uncondition-ally to the new course of action. At the feet of your Holiness, requesting your apostolic blessing, Dr. Edith Stein.[1]

Edith Stein had no doubts as to the Holy See's stance regarding the persecution of Jews. Two years earlier, on March 25, 1928, the Holy Office issued a decree that strongly condemned anti-Semitism. In August 1923, just after the elections that made the Nazi Party the strongest party in the Reichstag, winning 37.3 percent of the votes, there was a German bishops' conference in Fulda that condemned National Socialism as a heresy and declared that any Catholic who became a member of the Nazi Party would be automatically excom-municated.

But things changed. Adolf Hitler became chancellor of Germany on January 30, 1933. On March 5, early elections were called, which saw the Nazis winning 43.9 percent of the votes. On March 24, the Centre Party, which represented German Catholics, voted for the Enabling Act, which granted dictatorial powers to Hitler's govern-ment, while the German bishops withdrew their earlier declaration

327

on March 28, rescinding excommunications but continuing to maintain their reservations about Nazi ideology.

In both cases (the decisions of the German episcopate and the Centre Party), the deciding factor was a fear of Communism, which was winning over more and more followers in Germany. To many people, National Socialism was the only force capable of overcoming Communism. It was a time when Hitler had not yet committed any crimes, whereas Communism had already perpetrated mass genocide, created a system of forced labor, and carried out bloody, systematic political and religious persecutions. When Hitler was taking over power, there was a famine in Ukraine caused by the Soviet regime, and millions starved to death. None of the bishops and politicians at the time imagined that similar things would come about in

ADOLF HITLER was an orator capable of persuading practically the whole German population to follow him.

a nation of *Kulturträger*: poets, philosophers, and composers. A government report of March 23, 1933, written in a conciliatory tone, persuaded many Catholics that the Nazis would do harm.

For years, some maintained that the decisions of the Centre Party and the German episcopate were coerced by the Holy See in order to allow a concordat to be signed with the Third Reich, and that Cardinal Eugenio Pacelli thus allowed the Nazi Party to form a dictatorship. But the declassified documents clearly show that it was a sovereign

decision of the Germans, the politicians and the bishops alike, and that Rome did not exert any pressure on them. Historians such as Thomas Brechenmacher, Michael Feldkamp, and Hubert Wolf confirm this conclusion on the basis of Vatican documents.

Sir Ivone Kirkpatrick, then chargé d'affaires at the Vatican, recalled that during his meetings with Pacelli, the cardinal did not hide his loathing for National Socialism, condemned the persecution of Jews, and was very pessimistic with regard to Hitler, unlike many German Catholics who hoped that the Führer's views would evolve for the better. He saw the concordat with the Germans merely as a legal safeguard for the Church in view of the Nazi Party's ever more aggressive policies.

The concordat negotiations lasted from April to July 1933. At that time, Rome received reports virtually every day as to the brutal anti-Catholic excesses perpetrated by the Nazis. Hence a concordat

SIGNING OF THE CONCORDAT between the Holy See and the Third Reich; Card. Pacelli, secretary of state, is seated in the center.

ARCHBISHOP CESARE ORSENIGO, apostolic nuncio to Germany, at an official meeting on January 12, 1939, with Chancellor Adolf Hitler and Foreign Minister Joachim von Ribbentrop.

EUGENIO PACELLI during World War I with German Army staff, on a peace mission from Benedict XV to Kaiser Wilhelm II.

IVONE KIRKPATRICK, British diplomat in Rome from 1930 to 1933.

HEINRICH BASSERMANN, influential Lutheran theologian in 19th-century Germany.

seemed to be the only way to attain a legal guarantee of security. It was signed in the Vatican on July 20 and permitted Catholic schools and religious, cultural, and charity organizations, but it prohibited the Church from taking part in political and trade union activities.

Ivone Kirkpatrick sent a report to London on August 19, 1933, mentioning a discussion with Cardinal Pacelli, who told him that he had signed the concordat because he had "a gun at his head". He was given a week to make a decision, which came down to a choice between an arrangement on conditions dictated by Hitler or the elimination of the Church in the Third Reich. The fate of twenty million German Catholics was at stake; they would be left without any legal protection. The Centre Party faced a similar dilemma, deciding on July 5 to self-dissolve rather than be completely subordinated to the Nazis—an option that was not available to the Church.

Cardinal Pacelli knew his history. He was well aware that Catholicism had been strongly combated by the authorities in 19th-century Prussia and in the Second Reich. Taking part in the struggle were not only Nationalist forces who accused the Church of disloyalty to the German state, but also Protestant and liberal forces. The Reformation had led to the subordination of spiritual authorities to kings and princes. Since the times of Hegel, the conviction that the Prussian state embodied the highest supernatural ideal had become widespread; the state was due absolute obedience

Heinrich Bassermann, who taught theology at the University of Heidelberg, wrote in 1847:

> We Protestants differ from 11th-century popes in how we understand the state. To us, the state is not a mere dwelling place for godless and power-hungry people. To us, it is in itself a moral and divine order. And even the highest moral order that ever existed on earth. Hence the state must subordinate every other community to itself, akin to links in a chain.

Hence it is not surprising that Bassermann thought that the Church should be subordinate to the state. "For the state", he wrote,

"emcompasses the fullness of moral and spiritual goods, blessings and obligations, and so bears within itself a divine design." [2]

A map of Germany depicting the areas that supported the Nazi Party in the 1932 and 1933 elections, shows that the Nazis had higher levels of support in areas dominated by Protestants than in those that were mostly Catholic. The constant propagation of the principle that the state was superior to the Church bore fruit.

Liberals were another force that combated Catholicism, first in Prussia, then in the united Germany. Under the influence of the Enlightenment, Catholicism, to them, was obscurantism and superstition, to be combated by all possible means. They appealed to the philosophy of Kant, from whom they derived the conviction that man does not discover moral laws but creates them himself. Hence man determines what is good and what is evil—not God, as the Catholics maintained. Since man creates norms, principles, and rules, everything depends on man's "I", while in the collective context "I" becomes "we", which is expressed in the state. During Nazi times, the state was racist, as the chief Nazi ideologist, Alfred Rosenberg, made clear, putting forward his peculiar variant of Kantianism: "The law is what Aryans deem it to be. Lawlessness is that which they condemn." Liberals were for strengthening the state, since they thought that this

OTTO VON BISMARCK, "Iron Chancellor".

CHESS GAME between Bismarck and Pius IX—1875 caricature.

Zwischen Berlin und Rom.

Der letzte Zug war mir allerdings unangenehm; aber die Partie ist deßhalb noch nicht verloren. Ich habe noch einen sehr schönen Zug in petto!

Das wird auch der letzte sein, und dann sind Sie in wenigen Zügen matt — — wenigstens für Deutschland.

Modus vivendi.

BISMARCK AND LEO XIII in their "modus vivendi"—1878 caricature.

was the only way their ideals could be realized. In that context, Catholicism, with its dogmatic teaching, absolute ethics, and propagation of the inseparable link between morality and politics, was very strongly attacked.

That anti-Catholic alliance of nationalists, Protestants, and liberals turned the Church into a public enemy beginning in the mid-19th century, first in Prussia, then in the united Germany, where Catholics were treated like second-class citizens, the greatest threat to German culture, freedom, and customs. It was a time when the modern identity of the German nation was being formed, based on a belief in the state's superior, almost absolute role. The Church's presence was an obstacle in the construction of this monolithic structure, a presence that undermined loyalty to the state.

The height of the conflict came in the 1870s. After the unification of Germany and the proclamation of the German Empire in 1871, Chancellor Otto von Bismarck launched a de-Catholicization policy (*Kulturkampf*). Bismarck was afraid that Catholics, who constituted 36 percent of the German population after the incorporation of Bavaria, would be an element that threatened the unity of the nation, as well as being disloyal, since they were obedient to the pope in Rome. Hence diplomatic relations were broken off with the Holy See, and a series of anti-Church laws were passed. Jesuit activities were banned, as were the activities of other orders, except those that cared for the sick. Emperor William I was in favor of the new law: "The obscurantism that emanates from religious orders, their secret machinations, the servility of their members, seems to make them especially dangerous, and even loathsome."

Further laws ordered the government to take control of the Church school system and appropriate to itself the sole right to form, appoint,

and dismiss religious. High-ranking government officials who were professed Catholics were dismissed en masse. Another law provided for the imprisonment of priests who, by the spoken or written word, "threatened public order"; several bishops were arrested and imprisoned on that basis. Twenty-five percent of the parishes in Prussia were deprived of a priest.

Mieczysław Ledóchowski—archbishop of Gniezno and Poznań, and primate of Poland from 1866 to 1886—became a symbol of resistance to Berlin's policies at that time. Initially, he adopted a conciliatory stance towards the Prussian authorities. But he resisted when anti-Catholic legislation began to be introduced. He was arrested in 1874 and imprisoned in Ostrów Wielkopolski. One year later, Pope Pius IX elevated him to the cardinalate. Since German law prohibited

ARCHBISHOP MIECZYSŁAW LEDÓCHOWSKI, the best-known prisoner of conscience in the Second Reich.

POPE LEO XIII said that the *Kulturkampf* destroyed the Church and the German state, benefitting no one.

CARD. PACELLI as the Vatican secretary of state.

the imprisonment of cardinals, he was released, went to Rome, and became one of Pope Leo XIII's closest coworkers and prefect of the Sacred Congregation for the Propagation of the Faith. De-Catholicization did not end until 1887, and it came about largely due to the resistance of German Catholics, who established the Centre Party, which effectively fought for its own interests in parliament.

Cardinal Pacelli was aware that the essence of de-Catholicization, a cultural, political, and social declaration of war against the Church,

333

CARD. MICHAEL VON FAULHABER, metropolitan of Munich, coauthor of the encyclical *Mit Brennender Sorge.*

KONRAD VON PREYSING, bishop of Eichstätt, later Berlin, elevated to the cardinalate in 1946.

PROCESSION (right) including Card. Clemens August von Galen, ordinary of the diocese of Münster.

was a deification of the state. It turned out that the state usurped prerogatives that were of a divine nature—omnipotence, infallibility—and so demanded absolute obedience from its citizens, making theocratic claims and maintaining the right to bind people's consciences. Many Germans were brought up in that spirit (obedience to authority and not to one's conscience or to unchanging moral norms), wherein the state replaced God and was their primary reference point in life.

Archbishop Pacelli was well aware of this, as he had been an apostolic nuncio in Munich (1917–1920) and in Berlin (1920–1930). Nazareno Padellaro, his biographer, analyzed forty-two speeches that

Archbishop Pacelli made in Germany at that time. It turned out that he criticized National Socialism in as many as forty of the speeches. While in Munich, he observed the beginnings of the Nazi movement and did not have any illusions about it. He never met Hitler and never sought to meet him. In 1933, he was aware that another de-Catholicization policy had been launched. Understanding Edith Stein's fears, he replied to her letter in an official manner.

On June 11, 1933, the German bishops condemned anti-Semitism in a pastoral letter, declaring that it was an injustice which "burdened Christian consciences". Cardinal Michael von Faulhaber of Munich, Bishop Clemens August Graf von Galen of Münster, and Konrad von Preysing, bishop of Eichstätt and later of Berlin, publicly protested against Nazi policies.

On September 1, 1933, at the initiative of the Vatican, an article entitled "The Pope Condemns Anti-Semitism" appeared in the *Jewish Chronicle* and was reprinted by newspapers throughout the world. The article maintained that Pius XI, on hearing of the German repressions against the Jews, "publicly expressed his disapproval", stating that "the persecutions were a testimony to the civilizational poverty of that great nation". He added that Jesus, Mary, and the apostles were Jews and that the Bible was of

POPE PIUS XI
officially condemned Communism and National Socialism.

EUGENIO PACELLI,
apostolic nuncio to Bavaria (1922).

Hebrew origin. He also stated that Aryans had no right to exalt themselves above Semites. A year later, the Holy Office included Alfred Rosenberg's *The Myth of the Twentieth Century* (the most important work of the Nazi Party's chief theorist) in the *List of Prohibited Books.*

On April 28, 1935, Cardinal Pacelli gave a homily to 350,000 pilgrims in Lourdes wherein he condemned National Socialists: "Their

FRANKLIN DELANO ROOSEVELT
had a meeting with Card. Pacelli in 1936.

335

PIUS XI
while working in his Vatican apartment.

MIT BRENNENDER SORGE,
Pius XI's 1937 encyclical, condemned National Socialism.

philosophy is based on assumptions totally contrary to the Christian faith, and the Church will never be on good terms with the Nazis, at any price." His homily echoed around the world, with its visions of the struggle against "the hellish dragon", the "madness of the demon", and the "powers of darkness".

The details of his discussions with the U.S. President Franklin Delano Roosevelt, in November 1936, during his visit to America, are unknown to the public. Cardinal Pacelli then urged the American leader to form an international coalition against National Socialism, foreseeing—which then seemed impossible—Hitler's alliance with Stalin. His proposition, however, was ignored by the White House.

On March 21, 1937, Pius XI's encyclical *Mit Brennender Sorge* was read in all the Catholic churches in Germany; its main author was Cardinal Pacelli. The encyclical had been smuggled into Germany, secretly printed, and distributed to parishes throughout the country. The public reading of the encyclical was like a bolt out of the blue to the Nazis. In the encyclical, Pius XI admitted that he had signed a concordat with the Third Reich after much hesitation, solely out of concern for the religious freedom of Catholics; but the Nazis did not adhere to the terms of the agreement. The pope condemned the aggressive neopagan ideology of the Nazis, the deification of race, nation, and state, seeing it as irreconcilable with the teaching of the

Church, and he called upon German Catholics to resist it. He referred to Hitler (not mentioning his name) as a "mad prophet".

The encyclical infuriated Hitler. From July 20, 1933, to March 21, 1937, the Vatican sent fifty-five diplomatic notes to Berlin, protesting against violations of the concordat. However, it was not until the proclamation of *Mit brennender Sorge* that the Church suffered a wave of intense, systematic repressions. Those involved in printing the encyclical were imprisoned, and twelve printing houses were seized by the government. Crucifixes were removed from schools; praying and singing carols were prohibited. There commenced mass arrests and simulated show trials of religious who were falsely accused of sexual and financial abuse. Priests ended up in concentration camps; 333 German priests were sent to the one at Dachau.

Despite all this, Pius XI did not intend to cease criticizing Nazism. On April 13, 1938, he published an instruction specifying eight

BENITO MUSSOLINI, Italian dictator who introduced racial laws in 1938.

JEWISH SHOPS were boycotted by German Nazi militants throughout the Third Reich.

"absurd dogmas" and "terrible theories" of racism. He addressed it to the academic world, summoning it to combat racial theories which were "sold and disseminated as science, but which corrupted minds and undercut the roots of true religion". In July, he gave four lectures for students at the Gregorian University, condemning aggressive nationalism and racism.

PIUS XI'S SPEECH, broadcast by Vatican Radio.

Papal addresses, however, did not stop Benito Mussolini from introducing legislation modelled on the racist Nuremberg Laws, which treated Jews as second-class citizens. It came into force on September 5, 1938. The next day, during an audience with pilgrims from Belgium, the pope said that "anti-Semitism is a hateful movement, and we Christians must have nothing to do with it." He added a line that was later frequently quoted: "Spiritually we are all Semites."

The Holy See urged the Italian government to annul racist laws, but Mussolini remained inflexible. After Kristallnacht, a pogrom against Jews in Germany on November 9, 1938, the papacy began a campaign to help the persecuted. About two thousand Jews left Germany, mainly converts to Catholicism or spouses of Catholics.

DEATH OF PIUS XI, February 10, 1939.

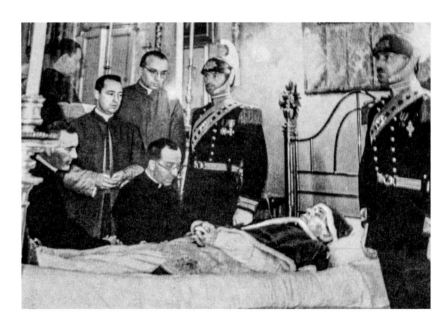

MOLOTOV-RIBBENTROP PACT paved the way for World War II.

HITLER reviewing a parade, October 5, 1939, Warsaw.

SUMMA PONTIFICATUS, Pius XII's encyclical, Polish edition.

The Italian authorities tightened up racial legislation. On November 17, 1938, they banned mixed marriages between Jews and Aryans or non-Aryan Italians. Already existing ones were declared invalid. This was unacceptable to the Church, as it meant that racist law was placed above the sacrament of marriage. Pope Pius XI decided to respond. Despite being eighty years of age, and seriously ill, he began work on another encyclical that was to condemn racism. He also planned to deliver an address on February 11, 1939, aimed at the Fascist government in Italy and the Nazi government in Germany, but he died a day earlier. On March 2, 1939, Cardinal Eugenio Pacelli became Pope Pius XII.

Black clouds were looming over Europe. On August 23, 1939, the Third Reich and the Soviet Union signed a secret pact pertaining to the division of spheres of influence in Europe. On September 1, Germany invaded Poland. They were quickly followed by the Russians, who forced their way into the country on September 17.

World War II had begun. On hearing of this, the pope started work on an encyclical, *Summa Pontificatus*, which was issued on October 20, condemning false teaching and new errors. Though it was framed in religious language, not political, it was no secret that it criticized two totalitarianisms, which were allied with each other: National Socialism and Communism. Pius XII also spoke up for Poland, which "for its fidelity to the Church, for its services in the defense of Christian civilization, written in indelible characters in the annals of history, has a right to the generous and brotherly sympathy of the whole world". In the Third Reich, the encyclical was universally seen as anti-Nazi, and its circulation was prohibited. The German Ministry of Foreign Affairs sent a protest note to the Vatican.

EXORCISM OF HITLER

Fr. Peter Gumpel relates that during the beatification process he discovered that Pius XII frequently carried out long-distance exorcisms on Hitler. This was confirmed under oath by several of Pius XII's close associates, including Fr. Robert Leiber, his personal secretary, and his secretary, Sr. Pascalina Lehnert.
During the exorcisms, Pius XII recited the *Apage Satana* (Greek for "Begone, Satan") from the Roman Ritual while kneeling in his chapel or looking out the window of his apartment. He had no doubt that Hitler was possessed by the devil.

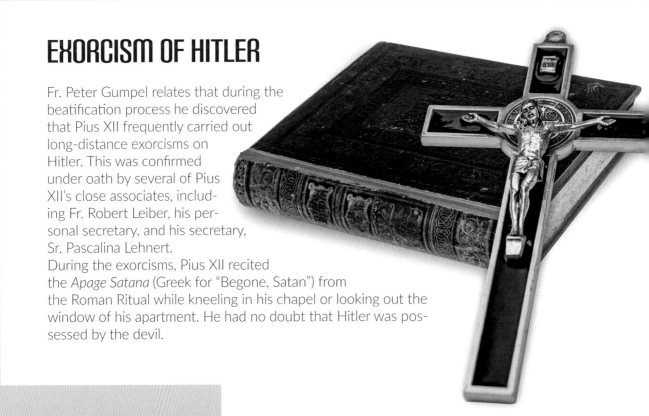

Pius XII repeatedly condemned crime, terror, and totalitarianism, spoke up for defenseless victims, and appealed for respect for the rights of minorities. Yet critics accuse him of being too general and allusive, claiming that he did not unambiguously indicate the perpetrators. However, Pius XII knew that such directness would mean the severance of the concordat with the Germans and an open persecution of Catholics—which Third Reich archives confirm: Hitler was prepared to terminate the concordat if the Church reacted more critically. In February 1940, all the German bishops and vicar generals were summoned to Berlin, where they were informed that any criticism of the government at a time of war would be seen as treason, punishable by death. At that time, harassment and repression intensified against the Church in Germany: property was confiscated, church services were banned, and newspapers were censored.

Marek Jan Chodakiewicz, a Polish-American historian, points out that people in countries where censorship, unjust use of force, and terror are daily occurrences develop a vocabulary that is relatively safe for communicating with one another. Chodakiewicz writes that Eugenio Pacelli "preferred quiet diplomacy and making statements full of allusions". For example, the pope publicly condemned the Third Reich's infringement of Belgium's neutrality by sending the Belgians his "fatherly greetings and blessings" and expressing his hope that "Belgium's complete independence and liberty would be restored." To many people in the free world, the message did not appear to express condemnation, but those living under ruthless totalitarian regimes immediately understood Pius XII's intentions. In Italy, enraged Fascists attacked those who sold the Vatican's *L'Osservatore Romano* and burned copies of the newspaper

POPE PIUS XII
giving a solemn blessing.

JEWS HUMILIATED
by Germans publicly cutting off their beards.

341
✛

WARSAW GHETTO UPRISING, 1943, German soldiers.

CHURCH OF ST. AUGUSTINE, located within the Warsaw ghetto, was one of the few buildings left standing in the Jewish district.

containing the pope's words. The Belgians, however, expressed their gratitude to Pius XII. On another well-known occasion, during his Christmas message in 1942, he prayed for the "hundreds of thousands who, through no fault of their own, and at times just because of their nationality or race, were destined to be exterminated". Although one might now say that it was an inadequate and incomprehensible condemnation of the Holocaust, the German security forces immediately perceived Pius XII's intentions. They said that the pope had "accused the German nation of treating Jews unjustly" and called them "war criminals". Jewish leaders, on the other hand, thanked the pope for the message."

Contemporary critics reproach Pius XII for being indifferent to the Holocaust, as he did not publicly defend the Jews even once. Yet accounts of people who had the opportunity of conversing with him during the war show that he suffered and even shed tears on hearing of the crimes committed against Jews. One of those accounts is from Fr. Pirro Scavizzi, who in May 1942, as an army chaplain to a Knights of Malta hospital train, found himself in German-occupied territory in Eastern Europe. He was the first to inform the pope of the mass executions of Jews. In October, he had an audience with the pope, who said:

Tell everyone, everyone you can, that the Pope is in anguish for them and with them! Say that many times he has thought of hurling excommunications at Nazism, of denouncing the bestiality of the extermination of the Jews to the civilized world. Serious threats of reprisal have come to our ears, not against our person, but against our unhappy sons who are now under Nazi domination. The liveliest recommendations have reached us through various channels that the Holy See should not take a drastic stand.

After many tears and many prayers, I came to the conclusion that a protest from me would not only not help anyone, but would arouse the most ferocious anger against the Jews and multiply acts of cruelty because they are undefended. Perhaps my solemn protest would win me some praise from the civilized world, but would bring down on the poor Jews an even more implacable persecution than the one they are already enduring.[3]

The historians who studied the documents in the Vatican Secret Archives are convinced that Pius XII was right in thinking that outspoken criticism would enrage the Nazis and provoke them to retaliate, which is what they did in German-occupied Holland when the Dutch bishops publicly protested the Nazi persecution of the Jews.

Fr. Peter Gumpel relates that he was in Utrecht Cathedral on July 26, 1942, when Archbishop Johannes de Jong's pastoral letter was read to the congregation, as it was in every Catholic church in Holland. The document condemned the deportations of Dutch Jews (the Dutch hierarchy were not then aware of the fate of those who

FR. PETER GUMPEL
lived in the Netherlands during World War II.

BL. TITUS BRANDSMA,
a Dutch Carmelite, murdered by the Germans in Dachau in 1942.

ROSA AND EDITH STEIN,
two sisters, both murdered by the Germans in the Auschwitz extermination camp.

were deported, other than that they were transported to the East). Initially, the deportations excluded Catholics of Jewish descent, but after the pastoral letter, the Germans deported them too in retaliation. It was then that the Carmelite Edith Stein (whom Pope John Paul II declared a saint of Europe on October 1, 1999) was arrested in the convent in Echt and transported to Auschwitz, where she perished in a gas chamber. Thus one protesting voice cost the lives of several thousand people.

**ARCHBISHOP
ADAM SAPIEHA,**
known as the
"Constant Prince",
metropolitan of
Krakow during
World War II,
elevated to the
cardinalate in 1946.

**GEN. PIETRO
BADOGLIO**
during the war
campaign
in Ethiopia.

Fr. Gumpel also relates that during the beatification process, as many as four witnesses have confirmed that Pius XII planned to publish a very critical document condemning the persecution of the Jews, which he burnt upon hearing what happened in Holland. On two occasions, the pope mentioned his deliberate restraint in order to prevent a greater evil—in his letter to Bishop Konrad von Preysing on April 30, 1943, and in his address to the College of Cardinals on June 2, 1943.

Pius XII was also very restrained in condemning the murder of Poles, as the Polish bishops had urged, stating that opposition would spark even greater repressions. On August 14, 1942, Archbishop Adam Sapieha of Krakow personally burned Pius XII's pastoral letter that was to be read in Polish Catholic churches, as it would have brought about an escalation of terror against defenseless civilians.

But silence did not mean inactivity. Instead of public condemnations, the pope chose cabinet diplomacy and discreet help. There are catalogues of documents in the Vatican Secret Archives that testify to the Church's systematic aid for Jews in Europe on the instructions of Pius XII. Aryan papers—that is, false baptism

certificates—were issued to Jews, and fugitives from ghettos were given shelter in Church buildings; for example, children were sheltered in orphanages run by nuns. False passports were issued, and people were smuggled abroad.

Pius XII's attitude was particularly evident over the nine months (between September 10, 1943, and June 4, 1944) when Rome was occupied by the Germans. After Mussolini was overthrown by his closest collaborators, a new government took

THE CHURCH IN POLAND

Attacked by the Germans and the Soviets in September 1939, Poland was the first victim of World War II. During the war and occupation, Poland lost almost six million inhabitants, including three million citizens of Jewish descent. Interestingly, it was the only country under German occupation that did not collaborate with the Nazis in any way.

The Catholic Church suffered particularly great losses at the hands of the invaders. The Germans murdered about 25 percent of the Polish clergy: five bishops, 1,863 diocesan priests, 580 monks, 63 seminarians, and 289 nuns (as a comparison, the Soviets killed 270 priests, an incomparably smaller number). At the Dachau concentration camp alone, 939 priests perished.

Despite extremely unfavorable circumstances, the Church actively helped with saving Jews. The example came from the hierarchs. Historians have proved that of the fifteen bishops who were at liberty, as many as fourteen actively helped fugitives from ghettos, the sole exception being a German bishop, Carl Maria Splett. Many religious lost their

GERMAN TROOPS
entering Poland on September 1, 1939.

CREMATION FURNACES
at the Nazi concentration camp
in Dachau, Germany.

lives for aiding Jews. Killed in Poland, for example, were Fr. Teodor Popczyk from Częstochowa, Fr. Romuald Świrkowski from Vilnius, and Fr. Adam Sztark from Słonim, as well as Sr. Ewa Noiszewska and Sr. Marta Wołowska.

KARL WOLFF,
German war criminal.
Hitler ordered him
to kidnap Pius XII,
but he delayed,
and the kidnapping
did not take place.

**GEN. WŁADYSŁAW
ANDERS,**
commander of
the Polish II Corps,
gives Pius XII
an abbot's staff
found in the ruins
of the monastery
at Monte Cassino,
during an audience
in January 1945.

power, led by Gen. Pietro Badoglio, who announced a cease-fire
between the Italians and the Allies. In response, the Wehrmacht
occupied most of Italy, including Rome. The Germans immediately began to round up Jews, sending them to extermination
camps.

Hence Pius XII issued an instruction to help the Jews.
About five thousand were hidden in 155 monasteries and convents in Rome, and over three thousand in Castel Gandolfo,
the pope's summer residence. Others went into hiding in, for
example, the Pontifical Gregorian University and the Pontifical Biblical Institute. The chief rabbi in Rome, Israel Zolli,
was saved by hiding in the papal apartments at the Vatican. Papal officials conducted negotiations with high-level German
dignitaries like Ernst von Weizsäcker, Albrecht von Kessel,

and Karl Wolff in order to save specific prisoners. Thanks to
Pius XII, about 80 percent of Roman Jews were saved. So it is
not surprising that the Jews placed a commemorative plaque
on a wall of the Museum of the Liberation in Rome (formerly
the SS headquarters in Rome) thanking the pope for his help
during the war.

Jewish diplomat and historian Pinchas Lapide claims that, as
his research in Israeli archives revealed, Pius XII contributed to
the rescue of between 847,000 and 882,000 Jews. The following,
among others, expressed their gratitude to Pius XII for his stance
during the Holocaust: Chaim Weizmann, Israel's first president;
Prime Minister Mosze Szaret; Yitzhak Herzog, Israel's chief

GOLDA MEIR,
Israeli prime
minister from
1969 to 1974.

POPE RECEIVING SOLDIERS of the Royal 22nd Regiment of Canada after the liberation of Rome in 1944.

GEN. IVAN AGAYANTS, of the KGB, led the disinformation campaign maligning the memory of Pius XII.

ION PACEPA, head of the Romanian secret police, fled to the West in 1978.

347

rabbi; Leon Kubowitzky, secretary general of the World Jewish Congress; Raffaele Cantoni, president of the Union of Italian Jewish Communities; and Joseph Lichten, a representative of the Anti-Defamation League during Vatican II. Reading wartime editions of the *Palestine Post* would be enough to convince one of the great esteem Pius XII enjoyed at that time among the Jewish population.

After Pope Pius XII's death, Charles Malik, president of the United Nations General Assembly, Dwight D. Eisenhower, president of the United States, and René Coty, president of France, spoke of Pius XII's work for peace and democracy. Golda Meir, the Israeli minister of foreign affairs, later prime minister, said:

> During the ten years of Nazi terror, when our nation was suffering a terrible martyrdom, the pope condemned the perpetrators. Our times are richer thanks to the pope expounding on great moral truths above the clamor of the ongoing conflict.[5]

Several dozen years later, all those positive appraisals became irrelevant in the face of the narrative initiated by Rolf Hochhuth. That was perhaps due to the support of Communists, along with their sympathizers and agents throughout the world, for his version. According to Gen. Ion Mihai Pacepa, head of the Romanian secret police, who defected to the West in 1978, the defamation of Pius XII was begun by the Soviets because his intransigent anti-Communism made him one of Moscow's greatest enemies. Hence Ivan Agayants,

BENEDICT XVI during a visit to a Roman synagogue in 2010. He was the third pope, after Peter and John Paul II, to cross the threshold of a synagogue.

head of the KGB, undertook "Operation Seat 12" to undermine Pius XII's authority.

In 2009, Benedict XVI signed a decree commending Pius XII's heroic virtues and so opened the way to his beatification. But many Jewish centers threatened to cease Christian-Jewish dialogue, and Benedict XVI's planned visit to a synagogue in Rome came into question. Although this visit eventually took place in January 2010, the hosts constantly emphasized their discontent about the pope's decree.

Something, however, had started to change, as certain Jewish historians began to defend Pius XII, such as Michael Tagliacozzo, Livia Rothkirchen of the Yad Vashem Institute, and Jenő Lévai, author of *Hungarian Jewry and the Papacy: Pope Pius XII Did Not Remain Silent*. According to these advocates, the Jews ought to be grateful to Pius XII rather than reproaching him. David Dalin also praised Pius XII for his stance during the war and requested a "Righteous among the Nations" medal for him. Similarly, Martin Gilbert demanded that the Yad Vashem Institute exhibition remove the disgraceful information about Pius XII's alleged indifference to the Holocaust; the information was eventually removed.

Pope Francis' intention to make available (March 4, 2020) all the documents in the Vatican Secret Archives pertaining to Pius XII will be another step toward a fuller understanding of the matter.

PAVING THE WAY

Gary Krupp, a Jewish activist from the United States, was convinced that Pius XII was an enemy of his people and a collaborator with the German Nazis. However, when he began to go deeper into history, he came to a completely different conclusion. He now has no doubt that the pope was Hitler's enemy and that he contributed to the rescue of about one million Jews from all over Europe.

Unable to abide the unjust accusations against Pius XII, Krupp founded the Pave the Way Foundation, which documents and disseminates knowledge about Pius XII's real stance regarding the Jews during World War II. Since 2006, the foundation has published over seventy-six thousand pages of source materials, as well as interviews with eyewitnesses who confirm the Holy See's involvement in rescuing Jews. According to Krupp, nobody deserves the gratitude of the Jews more than Pius XII, yet nobody is treated with greater ingratitude than this pope. Yet Krupp hopes that this will change and that eventually the truth will come to light.

GARY KRUPP during a meeting with Pope Francis, who decided to make all the Vatican Secret Archives' documentation on Pius XII available to researchers starting March 4, 2020.

ENDNOTES:

CHAPTER I:
1. *OSTIARIUS* – a function in the ancient Christian Church, later the first level of minor orders (until Vatican II). The ostiarius' (porter's) duty was to open and close the church door, check who entered, and ring the bell at the start of the service.
2. GIOVANNI BATTISTA DE ROSSI, *De origine historia indicibus scrinii et bibliothecae Sedis Apostolicae*, vol. 1, (Rome: Ex Typographeo Vaticano, 1886), 39-45.

CHAPTER II:
1. HEINRICH GRAETZ, *History of the Jews*, vol. 4, trans. James K. Gutheim (Philadelphia: Jewish Publication Society of America, 1894), 46.
2. BARBARA FRALE, "The Chinon Chart. Papal Absolution to the Last Templar Master Jacques de Molay", *Journal of Medieval History* 30, no. 2 (2004): 109-134.

CHAPTER III:
1. INNOCENT III, *De contemptu mundi, sive de miseria humanae conditionis* (Bonn, Germany: Eduardum Weber, 1855), 24-25, 126.
2. See **ANNA FREMANTLE**, *The Papal Encyclicals in Their Historical Context* (New York: Omega-Fremantle, 1963), 70.
3. OLIVER J. THATCHER and Edgar Holmes McNeal, ed., *A Source Book for Mediaeval History* (New York: Charles Scribner's Sons, 1905), 517.
4. AUGUST C. KREY, ed., *The First Crusade: The Accounts of Eyewitnesses and Participants* (Princeton, NJ: Princeton University Press, 1921), 35.
5. *TRANSLATIONS AND REPRINTS FROM THE ORIGINAL SOURCES OF EUROPEAN HISTORY*, vol. 1/2 (Philadelphia: University of Pennsylvania Press, [1897?]), 7.
6. IBID., 8
7. ALFRED J. ANDREA, ed., *Contemporary Sources for the Fourth Crusade*, (Boston: Brill, 2000), 166.

CHAPTER IV:
1. RINO CAMMILLERI, *La vera storia dell'Inquisizione*, (Milan: Edizioni Piemme, 2001).
2. NORMAN P. TANNER, ed., *Decrees of the Ecumenical Councils* (London: Sheed & Ward, 1990), 1:224.
3. BRONISŁAW GEREMEK, "Eksces koncepcji prawniczej u historyka (w sprawie inkwizycji)", *Tygodnik Powszechny*, January 14, 1997: 4; GUSTAW HERLING-GRUDZIŃSKI, "Dziennik pisany nocą", *Rzeczpospolita*, March 15-16, 1997: 2.
4. NORMAN COHN, *The Pursuit of the Millennium* (Oxford: Oxford University Press, 1970).
5. The AUTO-DA-FÉ (Portuguese for "act of faith") was a solemn ceremony during which an Inquisition verdict was delivered, typically clearing the innocent of all charges or drawing a public confession from heretics, who recited the Creed. Those heretics who persisted in their errors were handed over to the secular powers for sentencing. All the persons on trial formed a procession, wearing penitential clothing and carrying candles in their hands. Autos-da-fé mainly took place in Portugal and Spain, where they took the form of a celebration, drawing a crowd of people from the neighborhood. The aim of the rite was reconciliation with the Church through a renunciation of heresy.
6. ANDREA DEL COL, *L'Inquisizione in Italia. Dal XII al XXI secolo* (Milan: Mondadori, 2006).
7. BRIAN B. LEVACK, *The Witch-Hunt in Early Modern Europe* (London: Longman, 1987).
8. FRANCO CARDINI AND MARINA MONTESANO, *La lunga storia dell'Inquisizione. Luci e ombre della "leggenda nera"* (Rome: Città Nuova, 2005).
9. MARINA MONTESSANO, *Caccia alle streghe* (Rome: Salerno Editrice, 2012).

CHAPTER V:
1. MARIA LUISA AMBROSINI, *The Secret Archives of the Vatican*, (New York: Barnes & Noble Books, 1969) 227
2. POPE PAUL III, encyclical letter *Sublimis Deus*, (June 2, 1537), translated in Francis Augustus MacNutt, *Bartholomew de Las Casas: His Life, His Apostolate, and His Writings* (Cleveland, OH: Arthur H. Clark Co., 1909), 427-31.
3. JACEK SALIJ OP, "Kościół starożytny w obronie niewolników", *W drodze*, December 009: pp. 139-140.
4. *WITNESS: WRITINGS OF BARTOLOMÉ DE LAS CASAS*, ed. and trans. George Sanderlin (Maryknoll, NY: Orbis Books, 1992), 66-67.
5. GERÓNIMO DE MENDIETA, *Historia Eclesiastica Indiana*, (Mexico: Antigua Libreria, Portal de Agostino, No. 3, 1870), 312.
6. JOAQUÍN GARCÍA ICAZBALCETA, *Don Fray Juan de Zumárraga*, (Mexico: Antigua Libreria de Andrade Morales, 1881), 49.
7. IBID., 57.
8. MENDIETA, 276.

CHAPTER VI:
1. JOHN PAUL II, Commemoration of the Birth of Albert Einstein (November 10, 1979), in *Discourses of the Popes from Pius XI to John Paul II to the Pontifical Academy of Sciences*, ed. Paul Haffner (Vatican City: Pontificia Academia Scientarium, 1986), 151-56, 153.
2. VITTORIO MESSORI, *Emporio cattolico. Uno sguardo diverso su storia e attualità* (Milan: Sugarco, 1996).
3. MAURICE A. FINOCCHIARO ed. and trans., *The Galileo Affair: A Documentary History* (Berkeley, CA: University of California Press, 1989), 146.
4. JOHN PAUL II, Address to the Participants in the Plenary Session of the Pontifical Academy of Sciences (October 31, 1992).

CHAPTER VII:
1. REYNALD SECHER, *Vendée, du génocide au mémoricide* (Paris: Cerf, 2011), 90.
2. MONIKA MILEWSKA, *Ocet i łzy. Terror Wielkiej Rewolucji Francuskiej jako doświadczenie traumatyczne* (Gdańsk: Słowo/Obraz Terytoria, 2001), 8.
3. PAWEŁ JASIENICA, *Rozważania o wojnie domowej*, (Kraków: Wydawnictwo Literackie, 1985), 11.

CHAPTER VIII:
1. MANUEL DE IRUJO, *Un vasco en el ministerio de justicia*, vol. 2, *La cuestion religiosa* (Buenos Aires: Editorial Vasca Ekin, 1978), 125-26.

CHAPTER IX:
1. EDITH STEIN, "Der Brief an Papst Pius XI.", *Stimmen der Zeit*, 221, no. 3 (2003): 147-50 (translated by Josephine Koeppel et al., archived at https://web.archive.org/web/20110514223613/https://www.baltimorecarmel. org/saints/Stein/letter%20to%20pope.htm).
2. GRZEGORZ KUCHARCZYK, *Kulturkampf. Walka Berlina z katolicyzmem (1846-1918)* (Warsaw: Fronda, 2009), 87.
3. CARLO FALCONI, *The Silence of Pius XII*, trans. Bernard Wall (Boston: Little, Brown & Co., 1970), 238.
4. MICHAEL HESEMANN, *Der Papst, der Hitler trotzte. Die Wahrheit über Pius XII* (Augsburg: Sankt-Ulrich Verlag, 2008), 6.
5. HESEMANN, 6.

SELECTED BIBLIOGRAPHY:

AMBROSINI, MARIA LUISA. *The Secret Archives of the Vatican*. With Mary Willis. Boston: Little, Brown & Co., 1969.

BASZKIEWICZ, JAN *Historia Francji*, Wrocław: Zakład Narodowy im. Ossolińskich, 1978.

BASZKIEWICZ, JAN *Nowy człowiek, nowy naród, nowy świat. Mitologia i rzeczywistość rewolucji francuskiej*. Warsaw: Państwowy Instytut Wydawniczy, 1993.

BIAŁY, LESZEK. *Dzieje inkwizycji hiszpańskiej*. Warsaw: Ksiazka i Wiedza, 1989.

BLET, PIERRE. *Pie XII et la Seconde Guerre mondiale d'après les archives du Vatican*. Paris: Perrin, 2005.

BRATKOWSKI, STEFAN. *Wiosna Europy. Mnisi, królowie i wizjonerzy*. Warsaw: Iskry, 1997.

CAMMILLERI, RINO. *La vera storia dell'Inquisizione*. Casale Monferrato: Piemme, 2006.

CARDINI, FRANCO, AND MARINA MONTESANO. *La lunga storia dell'Inquisizione. Luci e ombre della «leggenda nera»*. Roma: Città Nuova, 2005.

CARDINI, FRANCO. *La tradizione templare. Miti Segreti Misteri*. Florence: Vallecchi, 2007.

CARDINI, FRANCO. *Le crociate in Terrasanta nel Medioevo*. Rimini: Il Cerchio, 2003.

CARDINI, FRANCO. *Processi alla Chiesa. Mistificazione e apologia*. Casale Monferrato: Piemme, 1994.

CARROLL, WARREN H. *The Guillotine and the Cross*. Front Royal, VA: Christendom Press, 1991.

CARROLL, WARREN H. *History of Christendom*. 6 vols. Front Royal, VA: Christendom Press, 1985-2013.

CHÁVEZ, EDUARDO. *Our Lady of Guadalupe and Saint Juan Diego: The Historical Evidence*. Lanham, MD: Rowman & Littlefield, 2006.

CHODAKIEWICZ, MAREK JAN. *Zagrabiona pamięć. Wojna w Hiszpanii 1936-39*. Warsaw: Fronda, 2010.

CISEK, ANDRZEJ MARCELI. *Kłamstwo Bastylii*. Warsaw: Fronda, 2012.

COHN, NORMAN. *The Pursuit of the Millenium. Revolutionary Millenarians and Mystical Anarchists of the Middle Ages*. Rev. ed. Oxford: Oxford University Press, 1970.

EISENBACH, ARTUR. *Hitlerowska polityka zagłady Żydów*. Warsaw: Ksiażka i Wiedza, 1961.

FRALE, BARBARA *Il papato e il processo ai Templari. L'inedita assoluzione di Chinon alla luce della diplomatica pontificia*. Roma: Viella, 2003.

FRALE, BARBARA. *The Templars: The Secret History Revealed*. Translated by Gregory Conti. New York: Arcade Publishing, 2011.

GAXOTTE, PIERRE. *La Révolution Française*. Paris: Tallandier, 2014.

GONZATO, ALESSANDRA, ed. *Lux in Arcana: The Vatican Secret Archives Reveals [sic] Itself*. Paris: Tallandier, 2014.

GRAETZ, HEINRICH. *History of the Jews*. 6 vols. Translated by James K. Gutheim. Philadelphia: American Jewish Publication Society, 1893-1894.

HESEMANN, MICHAEL. *Der Papst und der Holocaust. Pius XII. und die geheimen Akten im Vatikan*. Stuttgart: LangenMüller, 2018.

JASIENICA, PAWEŁ. *Rozważania o wojnie domowej*. Warsaw: Prószyński i S-ka, 1985.

KONIK, ROMAN. *W obronie Świętej Inkwizycji*. Wrocław: Wektory, 2004.

KUCHARCZYK, GRZEGORZ. *Kulturkampf. Walka Berlina z katolicyzmem (1846-1918)*. Warsaw: Fronda, 2009.

LAS CASAS DE, BARTOLOMÉ. *A Short Account of the Destruction of the Indies*. Translated by Nigel Griffin. New York: Penguin, 1992.

LIS, KRZYSZTOF, ed. *Pius XII a Polska 1939-1945*. Warsaw: Wydawnictwo Sióstr Loretanek, 2013.

MELVILLE, MARION. *La vie des Templiers*. Paris: Gallimard, 1974.

MESSORI, VITTORIO. *Emporio cattolico. Uno sguardo diverso sulla storia e l'attualità*. Milan: Sugarco, 2006.

MILEWSKA, MONIKA. *Ocet i łzy*. Gdańsk: Słowo/Obraz Terytoria, 2018.

MOA, PIO. *Los mitos de la Guerra Civil*. Madrid: La Esfera de los Libros, 2014.

ORTÍ, VICENTE CÁRCEL. *Historia de la Iglesia en la España contemporánea*. Madrid: Palabra, 2002.

ORTÍ, VICENTE CÁRCEL. *La persecutión religiosa en España durante la segunda republica (1931-1936)*. Madrid: Rialp, 1990.

RUNCIMAN, STEVEN. *A History of the Crusades*. 3 vols. Cambridge: Cambridge University Press, 1988.

SECHER, REYNALD. *A French Genocide: The Vendée*. Translated by George Holoch. South Bend, IN: University of Notre Dame Press, 2003.

SKIBIŃSKI, PAWEŁ. *Między tronem a ołtarzem. Państwo i Kościół w Hiszpanii w latach 1931-1953*. Warsaw: Wydawnictwo Neriton, 2013.

SZYMAŃSKI, KONRAD. *Wyzwolenie Grobu Chrystusa w Jerozolimy. 900 lecie; 14 lipca 1099-14 lipca 1999*. Poznań: Gazeta Handlowa, 1999.

VIGLIONE, MASSIMO. *"...Rizzate el gonfalone della santissima croce". L'idea di crociata in Santa Caterina da Siena*. Pisa: ETS, 2007.

WARSZAWSKI, JÓZEF. *Akcja antypapieska w Polsce podczas II wojny światowej*. London: Nakładem Katolickiego Ośrodka Wydawniczego "Veritas", 1965.

WOLF, HUBERT. *Papst und Teufel. Die Archive des Vatikan und das Dritte Reich*. Munich: C.H. Beck, 2008.

ŻYCIŃSKI, JÓZEF, ed. *Sprawa Galileusza*. Kraków: Znak, 1991.

✠ ACKNOWLEDGMENTS

The authors and the editor wish to thank the following for their help
in the realization of this book:

Card. Kazimierz Nycz – Metropolitan of Warsaw
Bishop Sergio Pagano – Prefect, Vatican Apostolic Archives
Fr. Paweł Ptasznik – Prelate, Vatican Secretariat of State
Fr. Luis Manuel Cuña Ramos – Director, Propaganda Fide Historical Archives
Xavier de Moulins – Director, Logis de la Chabotterie
Włodzimierz Rędzioch – Contributor, *Inside the Vatican*

Rino Cammilleri, Fr. Vicente Cárcel Ortí, Prof. Franco Cardini, Dr. Barbara Frale,
Fr. Peter Gumpel, S.J., Pío Moa, Dr. Reynald Secher, Massimo Viglione

Marek Adamski, Elżbieta and Stanisław Białaszek, Fr. Matteo Campagnano,
Francoise de Chabot-Darcy, Anusia and Alain de Charette de la Contrie,
Chiara Ejbich, Ewelina Ejbich, Beatriz Gonzáles and José Luis Garcĺa Chagoyán,
Łukasz Grützmacher, Angelika Korszyńska-Górny, Anna and Janusz Kotański,
Ernest Kowalczyk, Anna Kurdziel, Fr. Robert Leżohupski, O.F.M. Conv.,
Grégoire Moreau, Jolanta and Jacek Mycielski, Fr. Jan O'Dogherty, Jose Luis
Orella, Prof. Wojciech Roszkowski, Fr. Łukasz Skawiński, Dr. Paweł Skibiński,
Julita and Patrick Moussette, Zbigniew Stadnicki, Fr. Roman Szpakowski,
Fr. Jarosław Szymczak, Fr. Jerzy Witek, Kasia and Gaetan de Thieulloy,
Sławomir Wawer

Polish edition *Tajne Archiwum Watykańskie*
Published 2020 by Rosikon Press, Warsaw, Poland

Text 2020 © by **Grzegorz Górny**
Photographs © 2020 by **Janusz Rosikoń**

Graphic design **Kryspin Waliszewski**

Collaboration DTP **Honorata Kozon**

Illustrations **Piotr Karczewski**

Collaboration **Jan Kasprzycki-Rosikoń**

English translation **Stan Kacsprzak**

Unless otherwise indicated, all Scripture quotations are taken from the Revised Standard Version of the Bible—Second Catholic Edition (Ignatius Edition) copyright © 2006 National Council of the Churches of Christ in the United States of America.

© 2020 by Ignatius Press, San Francisco, and Rosikon Press, Warsaw

ISBN 978-1-62164-318-0

Library of Congress Control Number 2019949915